# PHILO'S PERCEPTION OF WOMEN

Program in Judaic Studies
Brown University
BROWN JUDAIC STUDIES
Edited by
Jacob Neusner, Ernest S. Frerichs, William Scott Green,
Wendell S. Dietrich, Calvin Goldscheider, David Hirsch, Alan Zuckerman

**Project Editors (Projects)**

David Blumenthal, Emory University (Approaches to Medieval Judaism)
Ernest S. Frerichs, Brown University (Dissertations and Monographs)
Lenn Evan Goodman, University of Hawaii (Studies in Medieval Judaism)
William Scott Green, University of Rochester (Approaches to Ancient Judaism)
Norbert Samuelson, Temple University (Jewish Philosophy)
Jonathan Z. Smith, University of Chicago (Studia Philonica)

Number 209
PHILO'S PERCEPTION OF WOMEN

by
Dorothy Sly

# PHILO'S PERCEPTION OF WOMEN

by

Dorothy Sly

Scholars Press
Atlanta, Georgia

PHILO'S PERCEPTION OF WOMEN

© 1990

Brown Univeristy

Library of Congress Cataloging-in-Publication Data

Sly, Dorothy
    Philo's perception of women / by Dorothy Sly.
    p. cm. -- (Brown Judaic studies ; no. 209)
    Originally presented as the author's thesis (doctoral--McMaster University).
    Includes bibliographical references (p. ) and index.
    ISBN 1-55540-500-2 (alk. paper)
    1. Philo of Alexandria--Views on women. 2. Women in the Bible.
3. Women--Biblical teaching. 4. Bible. O.T.--Criticism,
interpretation, etc., Jewish. I. Title. II. Series.
B689.Z7S57 1990
305.4'092--dc20                                                      90-8786

ISBN 978-1-93067-598-8 (pbk. : alk. paper)

Printed on acid-free paper.

# PREFACE

By interpreting the Scripture of the Jews in terms of the Platonic tradition of his day Philo of Alexandria made a profound contribution to the religious consciousness of the West. His depiction of the journey of the soul became a model of the internalization of religion. It was a great accomplishment.

The present study is not intended to detract from Philo's deserved reputation. Rather it aims to increase our understanding of his world of thought. It rises from the observation that Philo's writing is based on an unquestioned assumption of female inferiority. Today, when women's place in the history of thought draws increasing attention, it is natural that we should try to make sense of that assumption.

This work appeared in its original form as a doctoral dissertation at McMaster University. I should like to acknowledge the support of the members of my doctoral committee. Professor Alan Mendelson directed my studies on Philo and gave meticulous care to my manuscript. I am honoured that mine will be a sister volume to his work on Philo's Jewish Identity. Professor Ed Sanders returned over and over from his position as Dean Ireland's Professor at Oxford in order to see his last McMaster students through their work. His musings initiated the project and continued to give it momentum to the end. Professor George Paul of the Classics Department of McMaster gave me many a bibliographical lead, and was unstintingly generous with his time and advice. I thank them all most heartily.

For assistance in the preparation of camera-ready copy I thank David Brown and his colleagues of Wilfrid Laurier University.

Like many women of my generation, I have led a compartmentalized life. Twenty years of homemaking and teaching elapsed between my undergrad and graduate studies. All the disruptions of my return to university, including a move of 1200 miles, were encouraged and supported by my husband, Douglas, and our family: Gordon and his wife Janine, Gregory, Monty, Kenneth, and Marnie. This book is for them.

# CONTENTS

INTRODUCTION .............................. 1

TRADITIONAL VIEWS OF WOMEN ............... 11

THE STATE OF SCHOLARSHIP .................. 43

PHILO'S LANGUAGE .......................... 59

WOMAN AND VIRGIN ......................... 71

BIBLICAL WOMEN (I): EVE ................... 91

BIBLICAL WOMEN (II): THE OTHERS ........... 111

BIBLICAL VIRGINS (I) ...................... 131

BIBLICAL VIRGINS (II): SARAH AND REBECCA ..... 145

BIBLICAL VIRGINS (III): LEAH (RACHEL), DINAH, TAMAR, AND HANNAH .................. 161

WOMEN OF PHILO'S WORLD ................... 179

SUMMARY AND CONCLUSIONS .................. 215

APPENDIX A ................................ 225

ABBREVIATIONS AND BIBLIOGRAPHY ............ 227

INDEX ..................................... 243

# CHAPTER ONE

# INTRODUCTION

*Philo: the Man and His Work*

Philo Judaeus was an Alexandrian philosopher of the first half of the first century C.E., best known for having consciously created a link between Jewish scripture and Greek philosophy.[1]

Cultural Background

His personal background prepared him admirably for this task. On the Greek side, we can tell from the description of his own education in *Cong.*74-80 that he had experienced the traditional *paideia*. Further, his occasional references to the gymnasium and the theatre show that he was intimately acquainted with the Greek cultural institutions of the city.[2] On the Jewish side, we know that he was prominent within the large Jewish community of Alexandria,

---

[1] Samuel Sandmel, *Philo of Alexandria* (New York: Oxford University Press, 1979), 3-16; David Winston, *Philo of Alexandria: The Contemplative Life, The Giants, and Selections* (New York: Paulist Press, 1981), 1-37; Émile Bréhier, *Les idées philosophiques et religieuses de Philon d'Alexandrie*, 3rd ed. (Paris, 1950), i-iv.

[2] In his article,"The Orthodoxy of the Jews in Hellenistic Egypt," *Jewish Social Studies* 22 (1960), 215-237, Louis H. Feldman addresses the question whether observant Jews like Philo participated in activities which were held under pagan auspices. He concludes (*pace* Wolfson) that they did, indeed, do so, although such action constituted a deviation from orthodoxy.
    Abraham Terian, *Philonis Alexandrini De Animalibus* (Chico, California: Scholars Press, 1981), p.56, suggests a propensity on Philo's part to appropriate experiences from literature. He gives no explicit evidence, however, that Philo's visits to the gymnasium and the theatre were of this nature.

for he was chosen to go on their behalf as head of a delegation to the Emperor Gaius in the year 40 C.E.[3]

His fascination with philosophy enhanced, but did not overshadow, his zeal to give honour and service to the god of his fathers:

> Now philosophy teaches us the control of the belly and the parts below it, and control also of the tongue. Such powers of control are said to be desirable in themselves, but they will assume a grander and loftier aspect if practised for the honour and service of God (*Cong*.80).

His writing reveals that he felt torn between the increasing claims of civic responsibility to the Jewish community, and his own predilection for the contemplative life. As he says in *Spec*.3.1-6,

> There was a time when I had leisure for philosophy and for the contemplation of the universe and its contents . . . . But . . . envy . . . plunged me in the ocean of civil cares, in which I am swept away, unable even to raise my head above the water . . . . And if unexpectedly I obtain a spell of fine weather and a calm from civil turmoils, I get me wings and ride the waves and almost tread the lower air, wafted by the breezes of knowledge which often urges me to come to spend my days with her, a truant as it were from merciless

---

[3] Philo describes the mission in *De Legationem ad Gaium*. For dates and sequence of events consult E. Mary Smallwood, *Philonis Alexandrini Legatio ad Gaium* (Leiden: Brill, 1970).

There is some question as to how large the Jewish population of Alexandria was. Philo claims that the Jews in all of Egypt numbered a million (*Flac*.43). This is probably an inflated figure. S. W. Baron (s.v."population", *Encyclopedia Judaica*, vol.xiii, p.171) says that estimates of the total population of Alexandria range from 500,000 to 1,000,000, of which 40% might have been Jewish. That would set the Jewish population of Alexandria somewhere from 200,000 to 400,000. Jean Juster, *Les Juifs dans l'empire Romain*, (New York: Burt Franklin, 1914), vol.1, p.209, sets the figure higher, calling Philo's estimate hardly exaggerated. But Naphtali Lewis, in *Life in Egypt under Roman Rule* (Oxford: Clarendon Press, 1983) 26-9, uses Diodorus Siculus' figure of 300,000 free inhabitants in the time of Augustus as the basis for limiting the total population of Alexandria to one-half million. His figure would, then, concur with the lower figure in Baron's estimate, i.e. 200,000 Jews.

Introduction                                                        3

masters in the shape not only of men but of affairs, which pour in upon me like a torrent from different sides.⁴

## Philo's Writing

When Philo was able to free himself from specific duties, he devoted his time wholeheartedly to developing the inner life and writing Scriptural exegesis. He expressed his thought in the form and language of Greek philosophy, using the method of allegory. This enabled him to draw timeless truths from beneath the surface of Scriptural texts, and to claim that Moses' words had anticipated the best teachings of the Greek philosophers.⁵

The sheer volume of extant Philonic material affords a broad scope for comprehensive examination of this one man's thought. He is our best-known figure from Diaspora Judaism. Over forty of his treatises have survived, most in the original Greek, but a few only in an Armenian translation.⁶ In the form most accessible to English

---

⁴ Cf. *Provid*.2.115, in Abraham Terian, *De Animalibus*, p. 34: "I always have time to philosophize, to which field of knowledge I have devoted my life; however, many and diverse yet delightful duties that would not be fair to neglect summon me."

⁵ An example occurs in *Heres* 214, where Philo says that the principle behind the theory of opposites, which the Greeks attribute to Heraclitus, was actually discovered by Moses.

⁶ *Quaestiones et Solutiones in Genesin*, books 1-4, *Quaestiones et Solutiones in Exodum*, books 1-2, *De Providentia* and *De Animalibus* are extant only in Armenian. Aucher published them with a Latin translation (Venice, 1822-26). The Loeb English edition (Philo I-IX, translated by F. H. Colson and G. H. Whitaker, Supplement I-II, translated by R. Marcus, Loeb Classical Library {Cambridge, Mass.: Harvard University Press, 1929-1962}), and cited hereafter as *PLCL*, includes *QG* and *QE* (as its supplementary volumes) and the Greek fragments of *Provid*. preserved in Eusebius. It omits the parts of *Provid*. found only in Armenian, as well as the entire treatise *Anim*. An English translation of the latter, by Abraham Terian, was published in 1981 (see n.2).

readers his work is found in the Loeb Classical Library.[7] Recent French and German translations are also available.[8]

## Philo's Innovation

One of the Philonic features that has captured scholarly attention is the interiorization of religion, the interpretation of scripture in terms of the progress of the individual towards salvation. Traditionally, Jews had believed that membership in the covenant community was salvific in itself, provided the members sincerely intended to obey the law. Philo's insistence on the observance of the law indicates that he is unwilling to forego that understanding of religion.[9] But a new element is discernible in his writings, viz., the

---

[7] The Loeb edition is based on the *Editio Major* by Cohn and Wendland (Berlin, 1896-1930), which today is the standard Greek text of Philo.

[8] The French edition of Philo, *Les oeuvres de Philon d'Alexandrie* (Paris: Cerf, 1973), cited hereafter as *OPA*, includes a full translation of *Provid*.1 and 2, from Aucher's Latin, but none of *Anim*.
  The German edition, *Philon von Alexandria: Die Werke in Deutscher Übersetzung*, (Berlin, 1964), cited hereafter as *PA*, has a translation of the same material.
  For further details on texts and editions, see Louis H. Feldman, *Scholarship on Philo and Josephus 1937-1962*, Studies in Judaica (New York: Yeshiva University), pp.2f.; Terian, *De Animalibus*, pp.3-5; Winston, *Philo*, p.302, n.14; Sandmel, *Philo*, "Appendix."

[9] E. P. Sanders argues that in Philo as in all the Judaism of the period, except 4 Ezra, the covenant remains a principal soteriological category ("The Covenant as a Soteriological Category and the Nature of Salvation in Palestinian and Hellenistic Judaism," *Jews, Greeks and Christians*, ed. Robert Hamerton-Kelly and Robin Scroggs, Leiden: E.J. Brill, 1976, 11-44). Such an interpretation can be taken from *Spec*.4.180f.: ". . . the orphan-like desolate state of his people is always an object of pity and compassion to the Ruler of the Universe whose portion it is, because it has been set apart out of the whole human race as a kind of first fruits to the Maker and Father. And the cause of this was the precious signs of righteousness and virtue shown by the founders of the race, signs which survive like imperishable plants, bearing fruit that never decays for their descendants, fruit salutary and profitable in every way, even though these descendants themselves be sinners, so long as the sins be curable and not altogether unto death."

attempt of the individual to make a spiritual journey towards God.[10] The yearning for such a journey can be seen as a mystical quest.[11] Samuel Sandmel captures the way this new understanding colours one's interpretation of Scripture:

> Philo sees in Scripture the experience of every man. In its literal sense it deals with ancient times, events and personalities; allegory, however, makes Scripture the record of the unfolding experience of the reader. Every perceptive man can see in the experience of the patriarchs reflections in himself of the use and development of his innate capacities. By following their example, he can come to perfection, that is, he can live on the level of pure mind, unencumbered by the body. Indeed he can live on the level of the divine mind, the Logos.[12]

This personal appropriation is a development of an old theme. Through rites and festivals, it had long been a feature of Jewish religious practice for the people periodically to relive the corporate experience of their ancestors; thus each generation appropriated the sojourn in Egypt and the Exodus experience (see, for

---

[10] "La vie spirituelle de Philon est une intériorisation de la religion juive . . . . . Il est le premier représentant d'un type nouveau d'homme religieux." Marguerite Harl, *Quis Rerum Divinarum Heres Sit* (*OPA*, vol.15, p.153).
  Sanders, "Covenant," adds to his earlier conclusions (see above, n.9), "It has become apparent in our discussion of Philo that the 'nomism' part of 'covenantal nomism' was for him [Philo] a lesser level of religious experience and activity and that there was an individual religious quest which people already in the covenant should undertake" (p.42).

[11] Goodenough, *An Introduction to Philo Judaeus* (New Haven: Yale University Press, 1940), supporting his understanding of Philo as a mystic, says: "But when, driven by an inner sense of lack, insufficiency, we cry out for a divinity or higher reality who or which will come into us, take away our dross, unite ourselves to himself or itself, then we are mystics" (p.27). Winston, *Philo*, concludes the fourteen-page section of his "Introduction," entitled "Philo's Mysticism," with these words: " . . . Philo was at least a 'mystical theorist' (if not a 'practicing mystic') in the very core of his being and . . . his philosophical writings cannot be adequately understood if this signal fact is in any way obscured" (p.35).

[12] Samuel Sandmel, *Philo's Place in Judaism*, Augmented Edition (New York: KTAV Publishing House, 1971), pp.100f.

example, Deut.26:5-9). Now, in addition to this, Philo takes unto himself personally, in a spiritual sense, the task of resisting the failures of each of the less noble Biblical figures, and emulating the acts of the greater ones:

> Therefore, my soul, if thou feelest any yearning to inherit the good things of God, leave not only thy land, that is thy body, thy kinsfolk, that is the senses, thy father's house, that is speech, but be a fugitive from thyself also and issue forth from thyself (*Heres* 69).

> . . . let us say that the soul of each of us has, as it were, several kinds of man in itself in accordance with the various incidences of similar things. It is as if Esau were in me, an oak inflexible, unbending and hairy, and a type alien to the thoughts of virtue, and confused in his impulses, and yielding to irrational and inscrutable impulses. In me is also Jacob, smooth and not rough. In me are both an old man and a youth, both a ruler and a non-ruler, both a holy person and a profane one (*QG* 4.206).[13]

The reader of Philo's works finds that, overarching the particular purposes of specific treatises, there is an exhortation for other men to undertake the same journey of the soul as he has done. This journey, or mystical quest, has rightly captured the attention of Philonic scholars.

### *The Present Task*

In the course of reading Philo's work it has become increasingly apparent to me that, just as the Biblical figures to be emulated

---

[13] Cf. Harl, *Heres*, p.142-150, and R. M. Grant, *The Letter and the Spirit* (London: SPCK, 1957), p.36.
 Possible exceptions to complete identification are Moses and Isaac, who remain beyond the reach of the ordinary man, though their actions are to be emulated. In *Sac*.5-8, Philo distinguishes these two from "those who learn by hearing and instruction." See also Alan Mendelson, *Secular Education in Philo of Alexandria* (New York: KTAV, 1982), pp.51-55.

are men, so too the individual for whom he proposes the journey of the soul is exclusively the male adult. It is a moot point whether scholars such as Sandmel have recognized this. They certainly have not declared it openly, and the ambiguity of the English word "man" has veiled the issue.[14]

Equally apparent to me is Philo's eagerness to write about women. He has much to say about both the person, "woman," and the abstract concept, "the female."

The task which I have undertaken in the present work, then, is two-fold: to distinguish and separate the material in which Philo is speaking exclusively of men, and to retain for study that which pertains solely to women. The intention is to develop a clear understanding of how Philo perceived women. But that entails a clarification of the term "perception."

In the course of the history of thought the term perception has conveyed a variety of meanings.

"In strict philosophical language," according to the Oxford English Dictionary, perception should be distinguished from imagination, judgement or inference, as simply "the action of the mind by which it refers its sensations to an external object as their cause."[15] This is a very limited definition, and one not at all suitable for my purpose. I am not attempting to photograph the women Philo encountered (an impossible task), but rather to see the role he accorded them within his overall world view. I consider Philo's mind as not merely a receiver, but also a type of filter and processor. The way he depicts women in his writing is determined

---

[14] The same consideration applies to the French *l'homme*, which is used in *OPA* to translate both *anthrōpos* and *anēr*. Although *PA* generally translates these Greek words as *Mensch* and *Mann* respectively, the problem is still not eliminated, because, as I shall demonstrate in chapter 4, Philo generally meant "male adult" by both terms. A reader of German who interpreted *Mensch* in a translation of Philo as always meaning "man or woman" would be misunderstanding Philo.

[15] *The Compact Edition of the Oxford English Dictionary*, 1971 ed., s.v. "perception."

by the way he "sees" them, and that in turn is coloured by his *Weltanschauung*.

Such an understanding of the term "perception" is conveyed in a subsequent definition in the same Oxford Dictionary article: "Perception . . . is a transaction between the outer powers that operate on the mind through the senses and the inner powers of the mind itself, which impose their own form on the things submitted to it."[16] This is the way in which I am using the term in this study. In this sense, perception entails interpretation as well as reception.

In order to be done well, then, the task outlined above must be widened. It requires a sympathetic understanding of the overall way Philo viewed the world, and within that, determination of the role he accorded to women.

*Value of the Study*

What is the importance of knowing how Philo viewed women? To some degree the answer depends on the extent to which one believes Philo reflected contemporary Jewish thought.[17] If he is at all representative, then his writing gives a picture of the options offered to women within certain sections of Alexandrian Judaism.

---

[16] Ibid.; attributed to Raleigh (*Wordsworth*, 1903).

[17] Scholarly opinions vary widely. S. W. Baron believed that he represented the Alexandrian community. "No matter . . . what his private life and predilections may have been, Philo became a true spokesman of the most typical currents in Egyptian-Jewish Hellenism." *A Social and Religious History of the Jews*, Second Edition, Revised and Enlarged, (New York and London: Columbia University Press, 1952) vol.1, p.201.
   Harry Wolfson went even farther than Baron. In his two volume work, *Philo* (Cambridge, Mass.: Harvard University Press, 1947), he presented Philo as representative of mainstream Jewish thought. His belief that Philo typified a homogeneous entity called "Native Judaism" was challenged, however, by Alan Mendelson in "A Reappraisal of Wolfson's Method," *Studia Philonica* 3 (1974-5), pp. 11-26. It was also called into question by Sandmel in *Philo's Place*. He called Philo's a "marginal, aberrative version of Judaism" (p.211). While demonstrating that Wolfson erred in viewing all Judaism as the same, Mendelson and Sandmel did not venture opinions about the size of Philo's following in his own community.

Introduction                                            9

Unfortunately, however, at the present stage of scholarship we do not have sufficient material to make a definitive claim. Nevertheless, even if we adopt a more cautious approach to his importance in his own day, the fact remains that Philo was treasured and preserved in the Christian church, and it is probable that his attitudes to women were influential there:

> Philo's writings were preserved and transmitted by Christians, not by Jews. His legacy of writings was lost to Jews (who have preserved from that age only materials in Hebrew or Aramaic and none at all in Greek). Certainly at various stages in the early Christian centuries there were those who thought Philo was worth preserving. In his own time, were his followers a large group, or a small one--indeed, no more than a coterie of fellow intellectuals? We simply do not know.[18]

Perhaps most important, in undertaking this task, I shall be engaging in the never-ending scholarly task of questioning the presuppositions of earlier work. In this way I may add to the overall understanding of Philo, the man and his work. And within a larger context, I hope to contribute to the growing field of women's studies in religion.[19]

---

[18] Sandmel, *Philo*, p.14. For Philo's influence on early Christian and Neoplatonic writers see Harl, *Heres*, p.153.

[19] "The majority of studies on women in the religions of Greco-Roman antiquity have their origins in the contemporary feminist movement, which has forced the reconsideration both of theological and historical issues in the study of religion." Ross S. Kraemer, "Women in the Religions of the Greco-Roman World," *Religious Studies Review*, April, 1983, p. 127 ; ". . . all in all, there has been very little careful scholarly consideration of women in the varieties of Judaism in late antiquity, a situation which is less a function of the state of the sources than of the concerns of most modern scholars." Ibid., p.131. This article, with its extensive bibliography, traces the growth of feminist studies in religion from the early seventies, when it met with skepticism on the part of established scholars, to 1983, when, according to Kraemer, it had become "not only a legitimate subject of inquiry, but one which offers scholars the opportunity for a substantial reassessment of the study of religion as a whole" (p.133).
    See also the call for historians of religion to alter their approach to old materials, in Rita Gross, "Androcentrism and Androgyny in the Methodology of History of Religions," 7-22 in *Beyond Androcentrism*, ed. by Rita Gross (Missoula: Scholars Press, 1977).

*Method*

Throughout the work I shall attempt to see women through Philo's eyes. In order to do so I shall place his observations within an overall understanding of his view of life. At the same time, because I am writing from the perspective of the present age, I shall draw attention to presuppositions which differ from our own.

I shall pay particular attention to instances where Philo diverges from the Scripture which he is professing to transmit.

The work will be presented in the following order. The chapter following this introduction will be an overview of earlier attitudes towards women on which Philo might have drawn. Next, I shall set the topic in the context of Philonic scholarship. Following that I shall devote a chapter to demonstrating that women were virtually excluded from Philo's material on "man." In the next chapter, I shall examine the connotations of the two Greek words Philo used most frequently to designate women, *gynaikes* and *parthenoi*. Two extensive sections on the female figures of the Bible will follow: one on the "women" and the other on the "virgins." After that I shall examine Philo's statements about the women of his day. The final chapter will be comprised of conclusions.

# CHAPTER TWO

# TRADITIONAL VIEWS OF WOMEN

Philo's depiction of women constitutes a major, though unsystematized, topic in his corpus. Although he must be held responsible for his own expressed opinions, it is obvious that they will have been affected by a number of factors: literature, observation, and personal experience. As background to our present topic, then, we need to consider the available information concerning each of these. An important element in our subsequent study will be awareness of where Philo echoes, emphasizes, or repudiates elements in these milieux.[1]

---

[1] In this survey I try to be comprehensive, within a limited space, and to use primary sources wherever possible. Naturally I am drawn to material which leads to a contrast or comparison with Philo.
    For other surveys see Prudence Allen, *The Concept of Woman* (Montreal: Eden Press, 1985); Vern Bullough, *The Subordinate Sex* (Urbana: University of Illinois Press, 1973); Johannes Leipoldt, *Die Frau in der antiken Welt und im Urchristentum* (Berlin: Union Verlag, 1953), Sarah Pomeroy, *Goddesses, Whores, Wives and Slaves* (New York: Schocken Books, 1975), and *Women in Hellenistic Egypt* (New York: Schocken Books, 1984).
    A useful compendium of textual source material in translation is Mary R. Lefkowitz and Maureen B. Fant, *Women's Life in Greece and Rome* (London: Duckworth, 1982).

## Perception of Women in Literature

### Women in the Bible

*The Pentateuch*

Philo's primary source in literature is unquestionably the Bible, specifically the Septuagint translation of the Pentateuch. He is familiar with the Prophets and the Writings, again in the Septuagint version, but his references to them are far fewer. The Pentateuch, on the other hand, is deeply ingrained in his thought, and is the direct basis of much of his commentary. Philo believes in the timeless value of Moses' words; he never questions Scripture or intimates that he is adapting it to his own period (although certain discrepancies can be noted).[2] He believes, too, that his picture of women as they are and ought to be is drawn primarily from the Pentateuch.

In the Pentateuch we find the story of Israel's formative years, beginning with the creation of the world. The text is generally androcentric, stemming from a society which is thoroughly patriarchal. Man is the key figure, and woman is secondary. The following are observations on the sections to which Philo most frequently refers.

The two creation narratives in Genesis present woman in two different ways.[3] The first features the humanity she shares with man (Gen.1:27). The second casts her in a role derivative from and possibly dangerous to man (2:22; 3:6). Like the temptation story which follows, this creation narrative leads into an aetiological

---

[2] *Mos.*2.14: "But Moses is alone in this, that his laws, firm, unshaken, immovable, stamped, as it were, with the seals of nature herself, remain secure from the day when they were first enacted to now, and we may hope that they will remain for all future ages as though immortal, so long as the sun and moon and the whole heaven and universe exist." Cf. *Hyp.*6.9.

[3] "Judaism was a male-oriented religion with women clearly subordinate. Nevertheless there was considerable ambiguity expressed towards women. The nature of this ambiguity is shown in the conflicting versions of creation" (Bullough, *Subordinate*, pp.40f.).

statement that probably reflects the social reality of its source (Gen.2:24; 3:16-19).

In the large section of Genesis devoted to the stories of the patriarchs, wives are seen as part of the household entourage. The stories centre around the family heads. Thus, we are told that when Abraham left Haran he "took" Sarah (Gen.12:5). Sometimes the women are not even mentioned. For example, Ex.12:37 records that the Hebrews leaving Egypt numbered 600,000 marching men "lᵉbad mittāf (along with those unable to march)," a vague term which in the Septuagint is rendered *plēn tēs aposkeuēs*, "besides the baggage."[4] The recital of faith in Deut.26:5-10 recounts the mighty deeds done for the "fathers" of the race. Throughout the Pentateuch the chosen people is repeatedly referred to as the "sons of Israel."

Women are valued for their ability to bear sons. The Biblical text deplores the barrenness of Sarah, Rebecca, and Rachel. The assumption that pregnancy bestows status leads to tales of rivalry and conflict between pairs of women vying for the same man: Sarah and Hagar, Leah and Rachel.[5]

Yet, almost paradoxically, certain women enter these stories in roles that are crucial to God's plan for Israel. Within the limits I have mentioned, they appear as strong and independent figures. Sarah, for example, takes the initiative in the plan for Hagar to bear Abraham's child in her place. Abraham follows her advice both at this point, and again when she wishes to cast out Hagar and Ishmael (Gen.16:2,6; 21:12). Rebecca's generosity and hospitality encourage Isaac's servant to make himself known to Laban's family (Genesis, chapter 24), and so to choose her as Isaac's bride. When she is his wife, and pregnant with twin sons, she questions God, and receives a direct message about the future of her children (Gen.25:22f.). Subsequently, she forwards the divine plan by thwarting Isaac's intention

---

[4] The RSV translates the noun *aposkeuē* "women and children." Pomeroy (*Egypt*, 100f.) traces its use in Hellenistic Greek culture for "baggage," "family," and even "wife."

[5] Cf. Hannah and Peninnah in 1 Samuel, chapter 1.

to give his blessing to Esau (Gen.27:5-40). Leah manipulates Jacob, in order to become pregnant with a son (Gen.25:23). Even Hagar, the Egyptian slave, receives heavenly visitations (Gen.16:8; 21:17f.).[6] Thus, almost paradoxically, we find embedded in the androcentric text a sympathetic portrayal of strong women.[7]

In the account of the conflict between Israel and Moab, recorded in Numbers, chapters 22-31, the Pentateuch provides yet another portrait of woman. After all other plans have failed, Balak resorts, at Balaam's instigation, to the weapon which almost succeeds in turning the Israelites to apostasy. This is the seductiveness of the Moabite women (31:16). Thus through this story woman takes on the burden of being the potential enemy to God's people, because sexual attraction is the one weapon that can penetrate their armour.

*Biblical Wisdom Books*

Philo used the other books of the Hebrew scriptures far less frequently than the Pentateuch.[8] I find no indication that he drew material about women directly from the Psalms and later Prophets,

---

[6] Cf. Hannah, who prays for a son and vows to dedicate him to God. She does this independently. When her husband finds out, he acquiesces in her decision (1 Sam., chapter 1).

[7] For a full treatment of this theme see "'Mother in Israel': A Familiar Figure Reconsidered," by J. Cheryl Exum, pp.73-85, *Feminist Interpretation of the Bible*, ed. Letty M. Russell (Philadelphia: Westminster Press, 1985), from which the following passage is taken:
> ". . . when the matriarchs appear as actors, they come to life as fully developed personalities, whose struggles and determination are deftly sketched and whose joys and sorrows become real for us. In such stories, they are not appendages of the patriarchs but rather persons in their own right--women participating in a patriarchal culture but sometimes pictured as standing over against it. This is a paradox: though frequently ignored in the larger story of Israel's journey toward the promise, the matriarchs act at the strategic points that move the plot, and thus the promise, in the proper direction towards its fulfillment" (75f.).

[8] See the Scriptural index in *PLCL*, vol.X.

and so I shall pass them over. Sometimes, however, Philo seems to echo the tone of statements found in the Wisdom books. Further, the expression *ta alla* in the following quotation may be a reference to these books; if so, it would suggest that Philo considered Wisdom to be suitable for devotional reading along with the Prophets and the Psalms, which are explicitly named:

> In each house there is a consecrated room which is called the sanctuary or closet and closeted in this they [the Therapeutae] are initiated into the mysteries of the sanctified life. They take nothing into it, either drink or food or any other of the things necessary for the needs of the body, but laws and oracles delivered through the mouth of prophets, and psalms and anything (*ta alla*) which fosters and perfects knowledge and piety (*Cont*.25; see the translator's note, vol.IX, *PLCL*, p.520).

In the Wisdom literature several views of woman are found. The Song of Solomon celebrates her as the object of desire. The book of Ecclesiastes repeats the theme of woman as enemy: it links avoidance of the seductive woman with service to God:

> And I found more bitter than death the woman whose heart is snares and nets, and whose hands are fetters; he who pleases God escapes her, but the sinner is taken by her (7:26).

Proverbs presents two contrasting pictures. On the one hand, it warns against woman's sexual snares (2:16; 5:3-6,20; 6:24-26; 11:22). On the other, it heaps praise on the dutiful wife who tirelessly devotes her energies to her husband's welfare (chapter 31). In chapters 7 to 9 the contrast between the good and bad woman is made explicit: the young man is warned against the lures of the seductive woman and advised to hearken to the words of Wisdom. These chapters probably constitute one of the literary precedents for Philo's presentation of two women in *Sac*.21-45.

In the Wisdom literature there is no trace of the strong and independent woman of the Pentateuch. Its dominant reaction to woman is anxiety.[9]

## Women in Alexandrian Jewish Literature

Although some texts are hard to date, I shall comment on a number which are thought to come from Egypt in the time of Philo, or earlier, and which mention women. A continuation of the trend noted above is apparent.

*Ben Sira*, written in Palestine around 180 B.C.E., was translated into Greek in Egypt around 130 B.C.E. The author expresses strong opinions about women: they exist only in relation to males, and are valued as they contribute to their husbands' pleasure and well-being. Ben Sira's critical comments about women are both harsh and, in one passage referring explicitly to daughters, lewd (26:12). The book is the earliest extant piece of Jewish writing explicitly ascribing the beginning of sin and the resulting death to Eve:

---

[9] Referring to the reported freedom of the women at Elephantine as only an aberration, Leipoldt says (*Die Frau*, p.53):
> "Aber das ist, wenn man aufs Ganze sieht, eine Ausnahme. Schon im Alten Testament wird sichtbar, dass die Frau hier und da in eine immer grössere Unfreiheit gerät. Diese Richtung ist es, die im Leben der Jüdin späterer Zeit sich mehr und mehr durchsetzt."

Bullough (*Subordinate*, pp.41f.), concurs:
> ". . . sex came to be more and more a problem in ancient Israel. In general there seems to have been very little preaching on sex in the pre-exilic period (before the sixth century B.C.). In fact there was little consciousness of sex as a special problem in the pattern of social conduct. After that, however, came a radical change which lasted through the Second Commonwealth and the entry of Rome upon the scene. In this period when much of the scripture was put into written form, there was emphasis upon man as a weak, helpless creature heir to inborn evil tendencies inherited from Adam, his original father. Man's greatest weakness was the lure of sexual pleasures . . . . If a man felt his soul was endangered by sex, women came to be feared and suspected since he was so conscious of the impact they had on him. Asceticism, particularly in sexual matters, became an ideal, and even legitimate sexual pleasures were condemned as sinful."

From a woman sin had its beginning,
and because of her we all die (25:24).¹⁰

Another text from the second century B.C.E., *The Third Sibylline Oracle*, praises the purity of marriage, and castigates sexual aberrations, which the author sees as rampant throughout the Gentile world:

> [The Jews] are mindful of holy wedlock, and they do not engage in impious intercourse with male children, as do Phoenicians, Egyptians, and Romans, spacious Greece and many nations of others, Persians and Galatians and all Asia . . . (594-599).

Along with the other sins of the Gentiles he mentions child exposure:

> Worship the Loving One. Avoid adultery and indiscriminate intercourse with males. Rear your own offspring and do not

---

¹⁰ See Warren C. Trenchard, *Ben Sira's View of Women: A Literary Analysis*, Brown Judaic Studies #38 (Chico, Calif.: Scholars Press, 1982), p.8. In this book Trenchard concludes that Ben Sira's remarks about women "are among the most obscene and negative in ancient literature," and demonstrate that Ben Sira was motivated by a personal bias against women, and "not merely an environmental phenomenon" (p.172). Given the difficulty in determining the place of ancient Jewish writers in relation to their environment, I find the second part of the conclusion, in this otherwise excellent book, questionable.

The attribution of death to Eve recurs in the first century C.E. Greek text of the *Life of Adam and Eve* (called *Apocalypse of Moses*), 14: "Adam said to Eve, 'Why have you wrought destruction among us and brought upon us great wrath, which is death gaining rule over all our race?'" (*The Old Testament Pseudepigrapha*, ed. James H. Charlesworth, New York: Doubleday, 1985, p.277, vol.2, trans. M. D. Johnson). Some scholars have considered this text to be Alexandrian, although Johnson himself believes it is Palestinian (p.252).

*2 Enoch* also attributes death to Eve: "And while he was sleeping, I took from him a rib. And I created for him a wife, so that death might come to him by his wife" (30:17, vol.1, Charlesworth, trans. F. I. Andersen). It is not certain that this text came from Alexandria. "All attempts to locate the intellectual background of 2 Enoch have failed. There must be something very peculiar about a work when one scholar, Charles, concludes that it was written by a hellenized Jew in Alexandria in the first century B.C., while another, J.T. Milik, argues that it was written by a Christian monk in Byzantium in the ninth century A.D." (ibid. p.95).

kill it, for the Immortal is angry at whoever commits these sins (763-766).[11]

*The Testament of Job*, a text dating from the first century B.C.E. or C.E., can be interpreted as denigrating women. It presents the Biblical verse, Job 42:15b, "And their father gave them inheritance rights like their brothers," as meaning that Job's daughters did not actually share in the inheritance but received protective amulets instead (chapters 46-50). R. P. Spittler comments that the passage describing this peculiar gift to the daughters shows "the earlier interest in patience . . . displaced by a concern for ecstatic and perhaps magical participation in the upper world through glossolalia." He also comments that in the author's interest in males shown in 15:4 and in 46:1, "it may be possible to detect . . . rudimentary proto-gnostic interests, such as the process of 'becoming male' as an expression for saving enlightenment."[12] This is interesting for the present study in view of the fact that Philo also equates salvation with becoming male.[13]

*The Wisdom of Solomon*, a text of the first century B.C.E., links sex-related ills with idolatry: child sacrifice, impure marriages, adultery and sex perversion (14:23ff.). It does not, however, make derogatory statements about women. Rather, it personifies Wisdom as a woman, calling her a desirable "bride, companion, kin and friend" (8:16ff).

---

[11] The quotations are from J. J. Collins' translation, in vol.1 of Charlesworth, pp.375 and 379.

[12] The quotations are taken from pp. 836 and 864 (n.46b), respectively, of Charlesworth, vol.1. The translator, R. P. Spittler, raises the possibility that *The Testament of Job* may have come out of the community of the Therapeutae, described by Philo (Charlesworth, vol.1, p.833).
John J. Collins, *Between Athens and Jerusalem* (New York: Crossroads, 1983), says that this work presents womankind as representative of the human state of ignorance (p.222).

[13] See my section on the contribution of Richard Baer to Philonic studies, in chapter 3.

*Third Maccabees*, another text of the first century B.C.E., gives a picture of the restricted lives of young women in Jewish households. According to this text, daughters were expected to be veiled and "enclosed in their chambers"; the author speaks of their "proper modesty"(1:18f.). Brides were kept in the "marriage chamber" away from public view (4:6).

We can detect throughout this Alexandrian Jewish literature a belief that sexual irregularity is a threat to the survival of religion, and that when it occurs woman is somehow at fault. As well, woman is seen as inferior to man; he must control and protect her, and she must serve him.

The virtual equating of virginity with maleness, which is a feature of Philo's writing, can be found in the first century B.C.E. novel *Joseph and Asenath*. It presents a situation in which a foreign woman is rendered acceptable as a bride for the Israelite, Joseph. The procedure involves her repenting, receiving assurance from an angel, and dressing in "a new linen robe . . . and . . . the new twin girdle of . . . virginity"(14:13). Her virginity is mentioned repeatedly in the chapter describing the event (15:2,4,6,7,8,10); in the first instance it appears to be equated with maleness:

> And she went to the man into her first chamber and stood before him. And the man said to her, "Remove the veil from your head, and for what purpose did you do this? For you are a chaste virgin today, and *your head is like that of a young man*."[14]

C. Burchard comments that this verse "may signify that virginity gives a certain equality to the sexes." He refers to 7:7, where Asenath's parents vehemently deny that she is a "strange woman," asserting that she is "our daughter, a virgin hating every man" (n.15b). Although this apparent denial of Asenath's sexuality does not deter the author from proceeding to tell of her fruitful marriage to Joseph,

---

[14] 15:1f., trans. C. Burchard, pp.225f. Charlesworth, vol.2, emphasis mine.

we catch in the earlier part of the story a glimpse of the desirability of virginity and maleness as opposed to womanhood.

## Women in Greek Literature

*Philosophy*

Philo was proud of his Greek education. He appears to have been well-read in the philosophy of the day. Stoic, Platonic, Pythagorean and Aristotelian elements are apparent in his writing.[15] Some philosophers may have been familiar to him through secondary sources--collections, commentaries or popular wisdom. But it is certain that Plato, at least, is one of his primary sources, for he both quotes him and models passages upon readily identifiable sections of the Dialogues. It is clear also that Philo worked directly from Xenophon.[16] Besides this, like all people in the later stages of a tradition, he was heir to a conglomerate of attitudes passed on by way of unquestioned assumptions.

In the following pages I shall scan the portrayals of women in the Greek literature that Philo might have known through his own reading or from secondary and tertiary sources.

## The Pre-Socratics

With the exception of the noble portrayal of some women in the Homeric poems, derogatory statements about womankind can be culled from Greek writers from the earliest times. In both the *Works*

---

[15] "Willy Theiler and, more recently, John Dillon have clearly demonstrated that Philo's philosophical views are Middle Platonist, that is, a highly Stoicized form of Platonism, streaked with Neopythagorean concerns" (Winston, *Philo*, p.3).

[16] Philo was "fully acquainted with the texts at firsthand and in no way restricted to handbooks and secondary digests" (loc. cit.). See my discussion of his paraphrase of Xenophon, in chapter 10.

*and Days* and the *Theogony*, Hesiod (8th or early 7th c. B.C.E.) tells the story of Zeus's creation of Pandora in retaliation for Prometheus' theft of fire: "I shall give them in payment of fire an evil which all shall/ take to their hearts with delight, an evil to love and embrace."[17] All women descend from Pandora. They are a calamity (*Th*.592), liars and thieves (*Op*.78), and evil for men (*Th*.601, *Op*.57). Life without a wife is unthinkable; yet the best of wives is a mixed blessing, and the worst is incurable evil.

> Even so Zeus the Thunderer on High created women
> as an evil for men and conspirers in troublesome works.
> And in exchange for a good he gave a balancing evil.
> Whoever flees from marriage and women's mischievous works,
> being unwilling to wed, comes to baneful old age with
> no one to care for his needs, and though he has plenty to live on
> while he is living, collateral heirs divide his possessions
> when he is dead. As for the man who is fated to marry,
> if he obtains a virtuous wife, one endowed with good sense,
> throughout his life evil and good alternate endlessly.
> But that man who obtains a wife who is thoroughly bad
> lives having deep in his breast a pain which never subsides
> fixed in his innocent heart, and this is an evil incurable.[18]

Writing a little later than Hesiod, Semonides (7th c. B.C.E.) compares woman to a number of animals, most unfavourably, except in the case of the bee.[19]

---

[17] *Works and Days* 57f., taken from *The Poems of Hesiod*, translated with introduction and comments by R. M. Frazer (Norman: University of Oklahoma Press, 1983).

[18] Ibid., *Theogony*, 600-612.

[19] Hugh Lloyd-Jones, in *Females of the Species: Semonides on Women* (London: Noyes, 1975), translates the 115 lines that are extant. He introduces the material by saying in part:
> "Woman's mind was made separately by the god, the poet begins; and he goes on to describe nine disagreeable kinds of women, seven made from animals and two others from earth and sea. Only the tenth kind, made

Zeus has contrived that all these tribes of women are with men and remain with them. Yes, this is the worst plague Zeus has made--women; if they seem to be some use to him who has them, it is to him especially that they prove a plague (95ff.)

Phocylides (late 6th c. B.C.E.) does value a certain type of woman. But it is only for her efficiency, and certainly not for her sexual attractiveness (which is compared to the skittishness of a horse):

The tribes of women originated from these four creatures: one from a bitch, one from a bee, one from a bristled sow, one from a mare with a long mane. The last is graceful, speedy, a runabout, a beauty. The one from the bristled sow is neither bad nor good. The one from the bitch is cross and savage. The one from the bee is a good housekeeper and knows how to work. Pray, dear friend, to get her in delightful marriage.[20]

We observe a pattern established early in the Greek tradition to the effect that woman is at best an efficient help, and at worst a plague on mankind.[21] The nobility of the earliest women in Greek literature--Homer's Helen, Penelope, Andromache--is long forgotten.

---

from a bee, makes a good wife; all the others are portrayed satirically. This occupies the first 93 lines of the poem; and the last 22 consist of general reflections upon women in which they are condemned wholesale, without even an exception in favour of the bee-woman"(p.24).
The quotation from Semonides is taken from this book.
See also E. F. M. Benecke, *Antimachus of Colophon and the Position of Women in Greek Poetry* (Groningen: Bouma's Boekhuis, 1970), p.19.

[20] The quotation is from Lloyd-Jones, *Females*, p.98.

[21] One can understand "mankind" either generically or sex-specifically. Hesiod says that woman was made *anthrōpoisi* (*Th*.570 and 589) and *andrasi* (*Th*.592). See my discussion of these two terms in chapter 4.

The Pythagoreans

The figure of Pythagoras, who flourished in the late sixth century B.C.E., is shadowy. His teachings have to be reconstructed from the writings of others. As a result, there is some uncertainty about their original nature. Pythagoras' influence, however, was long-lasting. Certain doctrines which may have developed along the way were called Pythagorean or, later on, Neopythagorean. The tradition was kept alive and developed through communities in southern Italy and Alexandria.[22]

According to the account written by Aristotle in *Metaphysics* 986a, 22-26, Pythagoras himself developed a table of ten pairs of opposites or contrarieties in which the first item named was superior to the second. It included the pair "male and female." But we need not conclude from this that he completely undervalued women, or viewed them as less human than men. Tempering such evidence of subordination of women is the fact that he had women disciples in his school, including Theano, his wife or daughter. She is known to have actually addressed the question of woman's place.[23] This question also exercised later writers of the school, who wrote under women's names in the period between the third century B.C.E. and the second century C.E. [24] Two extant pieces of Neopythagorean writing stress the domestic role and the support of husband as woman's calling, along with modesty and chastity, and even tolerance of faults in the husband; but they also attribute to her the traditional virtues of wisdom, temperance, justice, courage and good

---

[22] For material on the Neopythagoreans see Pomeroy, *Egypt*, pp. 61ff., Leipoldt, *Die Frau*, p.39, Bullough, *Subordinate*, pp.109ff., and Lefkowitz and Fant, *Women's Life*, pp.104f.

[23] Leipoldt, *Die Frau*, p.39.

[24] Pomeroy, *Egypt*, p.61.

sense.²⁵ Asceticism in matters of sex, as of diet and dress, are features of Neopythagoreanism. Bullough mentions a treatise of the first century B.C.E. in which it is stated that "we have intercourse not for pleasure but for the purpose of procreation."²⁶ There is a notable similarity between some of the Pythagorean and Philonic materials on the matter of sexual restraint for the sake of higher values.²⁷ The difference is that the Pythagorean materials allow women to discipline themselves, whereas Philo advocates control of women by men.

Xenophon

Xenophon was a writer of the late fifth and early fourth centuries, a contemporary of Plato. In his dialogue, *Oeconomicus*, we find the argument that, quite apart from their reproductive functions, men and women differ naturally from one another in character and aptitude. Xenophon has his spokesman Ischomachus tell Socrates how a household ought to be run. He explains that by nature the wife is suited to indoor, and the husband to outdoor, work. Such division of labour follows from the fact that God has given to the wife a greater measure of fear (*tou phobou*), whereas he has given the husband more daring (*tou thrasous*) (VII.22,25). Ischomachus' wife is much younger than her husband (only fourteen years old at

---

²⁵ Holger Theslef, *An Introduction to the Pythagorean Writings of the Hellenistic Period* (Abo, 1961), pp.142-145 = Stob.4.24.10, translated by Flora R. Levin, quoted by Pomeroy, *Egypt*, pp.68-70; Holger Theslef, ed., *The Pythagorean Texts of the Hellenistic Period* (Abo, 1965) pp.151-4, translated in Lefkowitz and Fant, *Women's Life*, pp.104f.

²⁶ Bullough, *Subordinate*, p.109f. Cf. *Jos*.43: "The end we seek in wedlock is not pleasure but the begetting of lawful children."

²⁷ Both Goodenough and Heinemann comment on the similarity in the prescriptions for women's behaviour: E.R.Goodenough, *The Jurisprudence of the Jewish Courts in Egypt* (New Haven: Yale University Press, 1929), p.130; Isaak Heinemann, *Philons Griechische und Jüdische Bildung* (Hildesheim, New York: George Olms, 1973), pp.234f.

the time of marriage), and he takes on the task of domesticating her.[28]

Plato

The nature and amount of Plato's writing are such that it can be read selectively to favour either of two positions: the equality of men and women or the inferiority of women. By a series of questions in the *Meno*, Socrates leads Meno to the conclusion that the virtues for men and women are the same (72c-73c). In the *Timaeus*, however, female incarnation is viewed as inferior to male, and, on the cosmic level, the male is identified with the active source and the female with the passive recipient.[29] In both the *Republic* and the *Laws* we find advocacy of equal education for men and women.

---

[28] In the introduction to his edition of the Greek text, *Xenophontis Oeconomicus* (London: Macmillan, 1885), H. Holden says that Xenophon "insists upon such separation of functions as an ordinance of nature," and adds in a footnote: "Plato on the other hand (Rep.v p.456C, p.466D) maintains that similarity of training and function for both men and women is the real order of nature, and that the opposite practice, which insists on a separation of life and functions between the sexes, is unnatural. Aristotle disputes this reasoning altogether, declaring that Nature prescribes a separation of life and functions between the two sexes . . ."(p.xvii). Prudence Allen, in *Concept* (p.57), draws attention to this treatise of Xenophon, making a similar observation: "Xenophon is the first philosopher [sic] to offer detailed arguments for the separation of virtues for woman and man. Ironically, in Plato's dialogues, Socrates reaches precisely the opposite conclusion, namely that women and men have the same virtues."
 *Oeconomicus* 7-10 is given in translation in Lefkowitz and Fant, *Women's Life*, pp.100-104.

[29] 91a:"According to the probable account, all those creatures generated as men who proved themselves cowardly and spent their lives in wrong-doing were transformed, at their second incarnation, into women." Loeb Classical Library (Cambridge, Mass.: Harvard University Press), hereafter cited as *LCL*.
 50d: "Moreover, it is proper to liken the Recipient to the Mother, the Source to the Father, and what is engendered between these two to the Offspring . . ." *LCL*.

> "We shall have to train the women also, then, in both kinds of skill, and train them for war as well, and treat them in the same way as the men."[30]

> "Let me stress that this law of mine will apply just as much to girls as to boys. The girls must be trained in precisely the same way, and I'd like to make this proposal without any reservations whatsoever."[31]

But in the *Laws* the need for equal opportunity is justified on the grounds that womankind:

> "is inclined to be secretive and crafty, because of its weakness . . . . You see, leaving women to do what they like is not just to lose *half* the battle (as it may seem): a woman's natural potential for virtue is inferior to a man's, so she's proportionately a greater danger, perhaps even twice as great."[32]

On the subject of women, Plato, like Paul, can be read selectively and thus made to say whatever the reader hopes to find. It is likely that Philo found affirmation in Plato for opinions about women that he had already formed.

In his attitude to bodily sex, Plato is less ambiguous. He views the sexual appetite as the result of lower instincts, needing to be dominated by mind. In Book I of *Laws* he condemns homosexual practices as "unnatural crimes of the first rank," which "are committed because men and women cannot control their desire for pleasure."[33] Later, in Book VIII, he decries any sexual activity which is not directed towards procreation:

---

[30] *Plato: the Republic*, trans. by Desmond Lee, 2nd ed., revised (Penguin Books, 1974), p.229, v 452a.

[31] *Plato: The Laws*, trans. by Trevor J. Saunders (Penguin Books, 1970), p.293, vii 804c. Cf. *Timaeus* 18c.

[32] Ibid., p.263, 781a-c.

[33] Ibid., p.61, 636c.

> "this law of ours . . . permits the sexual act only for its natural purpose, procreation, and forbids not only homosexual relations, in which the human race is deliberately murdered, but also the growing of seeds on rocks and stone, where it will never take root and mature into a new individual; and we should also have to keep away from any female 'soil' in which we'd be sorry to have the seed develop . . . . The first point in its favour is that it is a *natural* law."[34]

Plato uses the language of human sexual attraction and reproduction to express his thoughts on spiritual development. Consistent with his valuing of the mind over the body is his enthusiasm for spiritual, rather than bodily, procreation, as expressed by the figure of Socrates in the *Theaetetus*:

> "All this, then, lies within the midwife's province, but her performance falls short of mine . . . . My art of midwifery is in general like theirs; the only difference is that my patients are men, not women, and my concern is not with the body but with the soul that is in travail of birth"(150a-b).[35]

Aristotle

Although Philo seldom calls Aristotle by name (only in *De Aeternitate Mundi* and *Questiones in Genesin*, Book 3), I believe he drew, indirectly at least, on Aristotle's teaching about women. The presuppositions behind his basic allegory appear almost Aristotelian: whereas Aristotle says that mind is to body as man is to woman, Philo says that man allegorically means mind, and woman, sense.

Aristotle believed that although male and female are both rational animals, they are contraries within the same species and

---

[34] Ibid., p.337, viii 838e-839a, emphasis mine.

[35] The full discussion extends from 150a to 151d. Cf. *Symposium* 208e-209d, where Diotima develops the idea of pregnancy in the soul. I discuss Philo's use of the motif of soul-pregnancy in chapter 8.

genus, the female being the privation of the male.[36] He associated soul with male and body with female.[37] In Book 1 of *Politics* he juxtaposed mind and body, male and female, as two pairs in which the superior must always rule:

> And it is clear that the rule of the soul over the body, and of the mind and the rational element over the passionate, is natural and expedient; whereas the equality of the two or the rule of the inferior is always hurtful . . . . Again, the male is by nature superior, and the female inferior; and the one rules, and the other is ruled; this principle, of necessity, extends to all mankind" (1254b, 5-15).[38]

He also attributed less effective rational powers to the woman than to the man.[39] Women are capable of true opinion, not of knowledge. As Prudence Allen has noted,

> [Aristotle] assumed a similarity between the association of the male with soul and the female with body on the one hand, and the association of the male with the higher reasoning capacities and the female with the lower on the other. *This marked the first time in western philosophy that the concept of woman was directly linked with irrational thought.*

---

[36] *Metaphysics* 1055b 18f.: "For every contrariety involves, as one of its terms, a privation." 1058a 29f.: "One might raise the question, why woman does not differ from man in species, female and male being contrary, and their difference being a contrariety" (*The Complete Works of Aristotle, The Revised Oxford Translation*, ed. Jonathan Barnes {Princeton: Princeton University Press, 1984}, hereafter cited as *CWA*, vol.2, p.1667).

[37] *Generation of Animals* 738b 25f., *CWA* vol.1, p.1146: "While the body is from the female, it is the soul that is from the male, for the soul is the substance of a particular body."

[38] *CWA*, vol.2, p.1990.

[39] *Politics* 1260a, 13-15, *CWA* vol. 2, p.1999: "For the slave has no deliberative faculty at all; the woman has, but it is without authority, and the child has, but it is immature."

> Therefore, Aristotle's sex polarity brought about a clear shift on the subject of woman's relation to wisdom.[40]

Since virtue depends on reason, and woman is irrational, she is incapable of virtue in the usual sense. Her virtue lies in obeying man.

> Clearly, then, excellence of character belongs to all of them; but the temperance of a man and of a woman, or the courage and justice of a man and of a woman, are not, as Socrates maintained, the same; the courage of a man is shown in commanding, of a woman in obeying.[41]

Prudence Allen comments on the complete systematization of female subordination in Aristotle:

> . . . the foundation for the sex-polarity theory in ethics followed from the sex polarity in epistemology, which in turn followed from the sex polarity in natural philosophy and metaphysics. Aristotle consistently justifies sex polarity in his entire philosophical corpus.[42]

With Aristotle I end this brief overview of Greek philosophy. It is apparent that from the earliest recorded times, philosophers (with the exception of the Pythagorean women) viewed woman as an anomaly. Gradually they built up a system of thought which rationalized her subordination to the control of man.

---

[40] Allen, *Concept*, p.104, emphasis mine.

[41] *Politics*, 1260a 19-23, in *CWA* vol. 2, p.1999.

[42] Allen, *Concept*, p.111.

## Drama

Philo was primarily a philosopher, but he also was interested in the theatre.[43] In a survey of possible literary influences on his perception of women, we ought not to neglect the playwrights, even though the sheer bulk of the material requires that we rely on secondary sources.

Early Greek literature had extolled the love of man for man, or the sisterly love of woman for man. Love, the passion, had been portrayed as a weakness, and an exclusively female one at that.[44] A change occurred, however, within the Alexandrian school which developed in the Hellenistic period. According to Pomeroy, the playwrights Apollonius and Theocritus presented women as passionate lovers without condemning them for their feelings.[45] Giving specific examples from Theocritus, Pomeroy remarks further that "the employment of the woman's viewpoint is a remarkable and novel feature of some Alexandrian literature."[46] In this period also for the first time drama told of the love of man for woman.

> " . . . in the New Comedy [exemplified by Menander] woman--the woman that can be loved as wife and mother--steps into her true place as object of, and partner in, the intensest and the purest passions of which humanity is capable."[47]

---

[43] *Ebr.*177: " . . . I have often when I chanced to be in the theatre noticed the effect produced by some single tune sung by the actors on the stage or played by the musicians."

[44] Benecke, *Antimachus*, passim.

[45] Pomeroy, *Egypt*, p.79.

[46] Ibid., p.77. See also the article on Greek Love by A. C. Pearson, s.v. "Love" in *The Encyclopedia of Religion and Ethics*, 1915.

[47] Benecke, *Antimachus*, p.163.

On occasion Philo speaks most tenderly of conjugal love, as for example in *Spec*.1.138:

> ... marriages, the first produce of which is a fruit sacred to His service, should be not only blameless but worthy of the highest praise. And reflection on this should lead both husbands and wives to cherish temperance and domesticity and unanimity, and by mutual sympathy shewn in word and deed to make the name of partnership a reality securely founded on truth.

In this regard, he may have been influenced by the theatre of his day.

Alexandrian mime employed the pimp as a stock character. Walter Headlam comments on the pimp, Battaros, of Herodas' Mime II, "The Pandar," that he is "a typical creation of the middle and new comedy," and proceeds to mention nine other writers who present such a person.[48] Along with such characters the mimes featured prostitution and promiscuity. In Herodas' Mime II an old nurse is trying to convince a young woman that once her husband has gone to Egypt he will not return to her:

> "He has forgotten you, and drunk from a new cup. Egypt is the House of Aphrodite. Everything that exists anywhere in the world is in Egypt, money, gymnasia, power, tranquillity, fame, sights, philosophers, gold, young men . . . women, more of them, I swear by the Maiden who is Hades' wife, than the stars which the heaven boasts that it holds, and their looks--like the goddesses who once set out to be judged for their beauty by Paris . . . "[49]

In the fact that prostitution was openly discussed in these productions Philo may have seen a symptom of the general decadence of

---

[48] Walter Headlam, *Herodas* (Cambridge: Cambridge University Press, 1966), xxxviii.

[49] Translated by Lefkowitz in Lefkowitz and Fant, *Women's Life*, p.106.

contemporary society. This may have triggered some of his vitriolic statements about prostitution.

*Women in Society*

Jewish women

From their arrival as settlers in Egypt in the mid-sixth century, the Jews had been allowed to maintain their ancestral ways by a degree of self-government. Under the Romans this pattern continued, with Augustus confirming the privileges they had enjoyed under the Ptolemies, to live under their traditional laws, and to elect their own council of elders.[50] This political independence allowed for a certain amount of separation from the social trends of the Gentile community, but there is too little evidence for a consensus as to the degree of isolation experienced. The same lack of evidence accounts for the largely speculative picture we have of the life of Jewish women.

There may indeed be significance in the silence on some matters. With the exception of life in an ascetic community such as that of the Therapeutae, there appears to have been no respectable position for the single woman within the Jewish community. And statements about the position of married women are drawn from little real evidence. Scholars who write about the equality of women in the Jewish family take for granted the patriarchal system in which every woman is married and the husband is *primus inter pares*.

Regarding the degree of assimilation to Greek ways in Alexandria, Feldman takes a conservative position. He holds that the masses were Hellenized only on the surface and maintained orthodox practice. He finds little evidence for intermarriage, and cites an-

---

[50] Lewis, *Life in Egypt*, p.29.

tisemitism as a factor keeping the Jewish people separate from their neighbours.[51]

In arguing for increased freedom, Baron appeals to evidence of assimilation and to records of the experience of earlier Jewish communities in Egypt. He mentions papyri which "reveal an increase in the rights of Egyptian women which must have affected Jewish practice."[52] He notes also that in the time of Jeremiah women in Egypt appear to have been leaders in the communities and to have instituted worship of the "Queen of Heaven," in open defiance of the prophet, but with the compliance of their husbands (Jeremiah, chapter 44). He considers too the freedom of divorce at Elephantine.

Tcherikover also uses papyrological evidence in arguing for considerable assimilation:

> . . . the family life of Alexandrian Jews, their marriages and divorces, were regulated by Greek contracts in accordance with the principles of Hellenistic law . . . . (W)e are faced with the likelihood that Egyptian Jews lived not according to the precepts of the Bible but according to the principles of Hellenistic common law.[53]

This assimilation indicates to him, however, a loss of freedom. He measures the lives of Alexandrian Jewish women against those of their Palestinian sisters, who "enjoyed a considerable degree of freedom." Tcherikover draws his picture of the latter from the historian Krauss, who lists as maidenly activities the following: going to the well and to the market, appearing before men, working in a shop, engaging in certain businesses and being able to protect one-

---

[51] Feldman, "Orthodoxy," pp.228 and 237.

[52] Baron, *History*, vol.1, p.112. He says,"Both in full freedom of divorce found in the Elephantine colony and in the rejection of divorce by Malachi, the woman's position in Judaism became one of a peer" (ibid., p.114). But cf. Leipoldt, quoted above, n.9.

[53] Victor Tcherikover, *Corpus Papyrorum Judaicarum* (Cambridge, Mass.: Harvard University Press, 1957), vol.1, p.34.

self.[54] Tcherikover's argument turns on the questionable premise, "The Jewish woman . . . was never subordinate . . . ."[55]

Goodenough, on the other hand, defends the position that the rising freedom of gentile women in Egypt rubbed off on their Jewish sisters in the form of greater freedom and equality within the family:

> Within the family the strictest discipline was maintained, though the government of the family was, as in all Egyptian rulership, rather the coordinate reign of the father and mother than the autocracy of the father. Scripture is ignored to allow the mother a place beside the father. . . .[56]

But these judgements are based on scant evidence and have a strongly subjective element. Practically all that can be firmly concluded is that Jewish women had a secure life within the constraints of the traditional family.

The situation of unmarried women is not so clear. It is possible that single Jewish women were forced through economic need to become prostitutes. That there was prostitution in Philo's day is highly likely since it had been rampant in the previous, Hellenistic, period.[57] Heinemann suggests the impossibility of enforcing severe laws against it in a harbour town such as Alexandria.[58] Philo's strong condemnation of prostitution indicates that he saw it as a threat, but we cannot tell from his writing whether it actually existed in the Jewish community.

---

[54] Tcherikover, *Corpus*, vol.1, p.35 and n.91.

[55] Ibid., p.34.

[56] Goodenough, *Jurisprudence*, p.217.

[57] Pomeroy, *Egypt*, p.75: "Alexandria was a cosmopolitan city and there was plenty of prostitution. Procurers and prostitutes appear in the works of Machon and Herodas [3rd c. B.C.E. Alexandrians], and many are found as well in the epigrams." See quotation from Herodas, above.

[58] Heinemann, *Bildung*, p.225.

## Women in Gentile Society

Alexandria was a cosmopolitan city with two discernible classes, quite apart from the Jews. The leading class claimed Greek descent, and despised the lowest, the native Egyptians. Although customs of one group were affected by those of the other, and social climbing by the Hellenized Egyptians tended to blur distinctions, some tendencies in the attitudes of men toward women can be traced to one source or the other.[59]

### Greek women

Since Hellenistic society can be seen as a continuation of Hellenic society, albeit in a different place, it is natural to view the position of Greek-speaking women in Alexandria in the light of the position of earlier women in Athens. That position had been an extremely limited one. Wives and mothers had been banned from male society, while *hetairae* had endured only borderline respectability. The wide differentiation between the sexes in Athens at its height is summed up by Pomeroy: "Rarely has there been a wider discrepancy between the cultural rewards a society had to offer and women's participation in that culture." [60]

Pomeroy's recent book, *Women in Hellenistic Egypt*, covers a period which ended with the death of Cleopatra in 30 B.C.E. Since there is no evidence to suggest a radical change in society in the fifty-odd years that intervened before Philo wrote, we should be able

---

[59] Pomeroy, in the introduction to *Egypt*, indicates that she cannot always distinguish between the two, if they are using the same language, viz., Greek. She says,"My training as a papyrologist has prepared me to work with the Greek papyri, but with only those Demotic documents that have been translated into a modern language. Therefore, this book focuses on Greek women and Hellenized Egyptians" (p.xii).

[60] Pomeroy, *Goddesses*, p.ix.

to rely on Pomeroy's observations for a general understanding of Greek Alexandrian society in Philo's day.

A gradual acceptance of women into society is discernible. In Hellenistic Alexandria women had attained considerable freedom both in the home and in the public sphere. Pomeroy cites a number of factors that may have contributed to the change. Philip of Macedon's marriages to women of foreign and freer ways may have been one.[61] Another could have been the reduction in polarity between the sexes in a non-democratic country where men could not aspire to government.[62] Again, there was the high profile of women rulers in Egypt.[63] Whatever the combination of causes, "respectable women participated in the economy of Ptolemaic Egypt to a greater extent than can be documented for any other Greek society and in ways comparable to the activities of women in later Roman society."[64]

At the same time, there still prevailed certain Greek customs which worked against the high status of women.

Greek law required that an adult woman act with a man as *kyrios* or guardian, although Egyptian law did not. This law existed in Alexandrian society, and there is evidence that it was adopted by

---

[61] Pomeroy, *Egypt*, pp.10-11.

[62] Pomeroy subscribes to the theory that "where there is the greatest assymmetry between the sexes, the male sphere is most endowed with prestige and the female sphere is most devalued" (*Egypt*, xvii). She believes this accounts for the low esteem placed on women in classical Athens.
"The principal reason for the high status of women in Ptolemaic Egypt is the reduction in the polarity between the sexes."(loc. cit.)
" . . . in the economic sphere, as in the political and social realms, there was less distinction between the genders in Ptolemaic Egypt than there was, for example, in Athens or in Greek society in general of an earlier period" (op. cit., p.173).

[63] Ibid., pp.3-40.

[64] Ibid., p.171.

Jewish women, although they too were entitled to live by their own law, which did not require a guardian after the age of twelve.[65]

The Greeks had long maintained the custom of exposing infants, and in all likelihood the majority were female.[66] This custom continued under the Romans, with exposed children that were recovered being reared as slaves.

*Egyptian women*

The Egyptian culture favoured equality of the sexes. Intimacy, rather than reproduction alone, was seen as the purpose of marriage.[67] The Egyptians, like the Jews, did not expose infants.[68] According to Pomeroy, no archaeological evidence of separate women's quarters in houses of Ptolemaic Egypt can be found.[69] This

---

[65] *Spec*.3.67 assumes the need for a guardian: " . . . go to her parents, or, if not, to her brothers or guardians or others who have charge of her . . . ."

[66] Pomeroy attempts to prove the exposure of female babies by referring to records of family members (*Egypt*, p.44): "It is unusual to find more than two daughters in Greek families, or to find a sex ratio that favors daughters over sons." She also quotes the comic poet Posidippus: "Everyone, even a poor man, raises a son; everyone, even a rich man, exposes a daughter" (*Egypt*, p.136). As more evidence she refers to a city law of the Greek city of Ptolemais in Egypt, which calls for a period of purification following certain acts and events, including child exposure (loc. cit.). Another piece of evidence in favour of her conclusion is the letter of Hilarion to his wife (*P.Oxy*.iv.744) which she quotes on p.138: "If by chance you give birth, if it is a boy, let it be; if it is a girl, get rid of it."

The bits of evidence given above do not really meet the criticisms that the data are insufficient. In the article, "Demography and the Exposure of Girls at Athens" (*Phoenix* 35, 316-31), however, Pomeroy attempts to meet such criticism directly. She concedes that there are difficulties presented by the lack of census data and the possibility that girl children were not always carefully counted. Nevertheless, she presents evidence which she believes is sufficient to demonstrate that there was exposure of girl children.

[67] Pomeroy, *Egypt*, p.xviii.

[68] Ibid., p.135.

[69] Ibid., p.134.

indicates, she believes, that women were not confined to certain quarters or carefully guarded (although Philo speaks as though Jewish women were). Indeed, women appear to have enjoyed considerable freedom of movement in Egyptian society. Diodorus Siculus wrote of Egypt that among the common folk the wife ruled the husband, the husbands agreeing in the marriage contracts that in all matters they would obey their wives.[70]

*Roman women*

The Hellenistic Age in Egypt had ended in 30 B.C.E., when Egypt became part of the Roman Empire. Since by this time it was the custom for wives of imperial officials to accompany their husbands on overseas postings, Philo may have known or at least noticed Roman women in Alexandria.[71] Traditionally the Roman woman had no legal rights, but passed from the power of her father to that of her husband. In actuality, her position had changed over the period of the Republic to one of considerable independence. Balsdon says,

> by the last fifty years [of the Republic] . . . her interests lie outside the walls of her home. In politics she is a power in her own right.[72]

The examples that he cites, however, suggest that her public life was usually conducted in conjunction with the career of the men of her family. Balsdon notes also that from the late Republic onward a

---

[70] Cited by Pomeroy, *Egypt*, p.40.

[71] J. P. V. D. Balsdon, *Roman Women* (Westport, Conn.: Greenwood Press, 1962), 59f.

[72] Ibid., p.45.

number of women were highly educated.[73] Child exposure still existed on a scale worthy of note, and, according to Balsdon, some evidence points to the conclusion that baby girls were exposed more often than boys.[74] As in nearly all cultures of the ancient world, sexual fidelity of a husband to his wife was not expected, at least when he was away from home.[75] Again, as in nearly all ancient cultures, female slaves were considered the sexual property of freemen.[76]

Pomeroy, taking a somewhat more conservative view than Balsdon, sums up the position of Roman women as follows:

> In comparison to Athenian women, some Roman women appear to have been fairly liberated, but never did Roman society encourage women to engage in the same activities as men in the same social class.[77]

### Philo's Experience of Women

Very little is known about Philo's personal life. It is assumed that he was married, since he speaks approvingly of the married

---

[73] Ibid., p.56.

[74] Ibid., p.196.

[75] Ibid., p.96. Justinian comments on the *Lex Julia* of Augustus as follows (quoted in Lefkowitz and Fant, *Women's Life*, p.182): "The *lex Julia* declares that wives have no right to bring criminal accusations for adultery against their husbands, even though they may desire to complain of the violation of the marriage vow, for while the law grants this privilege to men it does not concede it to women . . . ."

[76] Paulus, in a third century commentary on Augustus' *Lex Julia*, says: "Fornication committed with female slaves unless they are deteriorated in value or an attempt is made against their mistress through them, is not considered an injury" (quoted in Lefkowitz and Fant, *Women's Life*, p.182). Cf. the implication regarding slaves in *Spec*.3.69: "If anyone . . . turns to rapine and ravishment and treats free women *as though they were servant-maids* . . . he must be brought before the judges" (emphasis mine).

[77] Pomeroy, *Goddesses*, p.ix.

state; in any case, all Jews were expected to take wives. Two factors suggest that he had no children. The first is the complete absence of any mention of his offspring in any source, despite the prominence of his family, both in Alexandria and in Jerusalem.[78] If there had been children, some reference should have survived. The second is his own statement about the man who finds himself wed to a barren wife, a passage which has no Scriptural authority:

> Those who marry maidens in ignorance at the time of their capacity or incapacity for successful motherhood, and later refuse to dismiss them, when prolonged childlessness shews them to be barren, deserve our pardon. Familiarity, that most constraining influence, is too strong for them, and they are unable to rid themselves of the charm of old affection imprinted on their souls by long companionship (*Spec.*3.35).

For knowledge of Philo's personal experience of women we have only this type of implicit evidence.

## *Conclusion*

As one of the leaders in the huge and disparate Jewish community of Alexandria, Philo felt a heavy responsibility for that community's survival. Combining both Hebrew and Greek culture in himself, he was heir to a variety of traditions, most of which cast women into a subordinate role. Yet the subordination was not uniform in nature: in the Pentateuch, for example, it did not always entail inferiority. Nevertheless, it is notable that in each tradition women constituted a "muted" group. They had almost no spokespersons of their own, and tended to be reified by the men who did speak of them.

---

[78] According to Tessa Rajak, *Josephus: The Historian and His Society* (Philadelphia: Fortress Press, 1983), pp.53-5, Agrippa II's sister Berenice married the brother of Tiberius Julius Alexander, who was Philo's nephew.

On the level of social reality, the apparent emancipation of women in Gentile Alexandria coincided with Jewish observation of sexual immorality run rampant. From the literature, we know that in some Jewish men's minds there had existed for some time an association of sexual immorality with apostasy. Since for Philo this was reinforced by Greek teaching of the natural inferiority of women, it is not surprising that the "sexual problem" should weigh heavily on his mind, and that he should see it as a problem created by women.

# CHAPTER THREE

# THE STATE OF SCHOLARSHIP

*Sex Distinctions in Philo*

On the Philosophical Level

Philo's writing is replete with distinctions between male and female. They range over a variety of contexts, extending far beyond straightforward comparisons between men and women. Just as in a musical work the familiar notes of a simple theme may repeatedly catch the attention, so in Philo's writing does the male-female motif. His distinctions between men and women form just one sub-set of the larger body of distinctions based on sex.

*Value judgements*

Philo expresses value judgments by noting significance in the gender of words, by playing on etymological connections, and by attributing masculine and feminine qualities to his philosophical terms. In all instances, masculinity and maleness signify superiority, and femininity and femaleness inferiority. These value judgements pervade his work in such a way that it is impossible to separate the theoretical statements from their application to the human situation. For this reason I take exception to the view that sexual distinctions can be isolated to certain aspects of his thought. Such a view is expressed by Jean Laporte in the introduction to a work in which he devotes part of a chapter, entitled "Woman as Symbol," to Philo.[1]

> . . . woman as symbol . . . is a sign referring to a reality different from the sign itself. For instance, pejoratively, woman could be the symbol of the irrational part of the soul or even of physical and moral weakness. There is no pejorative judgment on women made by the author, who is only making use of a language. The society of the time is responsible for the connection between woman and a negative aspect signified by woman.[2]

Since Philo extends his male-female differentiation in so many directions, Laporte's statement is indefensible.[3] The following survey will demonstrate the point.

Philo sees significance in the gender of Greek words. I can find no precedent for this particular view. Among the Greeks, gender in language appears to have been accepted without question or comment. At a place in his *Rhetoric* where an opportunity to discuss the subject arises, Aristotle says only this:

> A fourth rule is to observe Pythagoras' classification of nouns into masculine, feminine and neuter; for these distinctions also must be correctly given (1407b).

In Plato's *Cratylus*, which is largely concerned with the aptness of words, Socrates argues that names belong to things by nature, not by custom; although he discusses the nature of names at length, he does not mention the significance of gender. The Stoics, moreover, al-

---

[1] Jean Laporte, *The Role of Women in Early Christianity* (New York and Toronto: Edwin Mellen Press, 1982), pp.133f.

[2] Ibid., p.4.

[3] I believe Philo's intertwining of these concepts is a demonstration of the theory of legitimation proposed by Peter L. Berger and Thomas Lückmann, *The Social Construction of Reality* (Anchor Books, 1967), ch.2, part 2. They posit four steps through which expressions used in everyday speech develop into common knowledge (pp.94-96).

though they continued the discussion of the significance of words, do not appear to have directed their attention to gender.[4] On occasion Philo echoes the Stoic theory that language was originally developed by persons of such insight that there was perfect correlation between words and the things they signified, but that as humankind gradually became corrupted, so too did language, with resulting anomalies (*QG* 1:20; *Op*.148, 150). But in the following statements, which indicate that the corruption of language extends to gender, he appears to be improvising.

> . . . joy, the name of which is feminine, while its nature is masculine (*QG* 4:18).

> . . . indeed all the virtues have women's titles [i.e. are feminine nouns], but powers and activities of consummate men (*Fug*.51).

> . . . in the matings within the soul, though virtue seemingly ranks as wife, her natural function is to sow good counsels and excellent words and to inculcate tenets truly profitable to life, while thought (*ho logismos*) though held to take the place of the husband, receives the holy and divine sowings. Perhaps however the statement above is a mistake due to the deceptiveness of the nouns, since in the actual words employed *nous* has the masculine, and *aretē* the feminine form. And if anyone is willing to divest facts of the terms which obscure them and observe them in their nakedness in a clear light he will understand that virtue (*hē aretē*) is male, since it causes movement and affects conditions and suggests noble conceptions, while thought (*ho logismos*) is female, being moved and trained and helped, and in general belonging to

---

[4] See David L. Blank, *Ancient Philosophy and Grammar*, American Classical Studies 10 (Chico, California: Scholars Press, 1982). As background to the main subject of his book, the second century Alexandrian grammarian, Apollonius Dyscolus, Blank discusses the Stoic theory of language but does not raise the question of gender.

A nineteenth century work listed in Blank's bibliography, R. L. Schmidt's *Stoicorum Grammatica* (Halle, 1839), has only one minor reference to gender.

Since modern scholars practically omit the topic, I conclude that they found little reference to it in Stoic literature.

the passive category, which passivity is its sole means of preservation (*Abr*.101f.).

Beneath them all lies the supposition that good things really ought to be signified by masculine nouns.

Another way in which Philo uses language to demonstrate the difference in value between male and female things is to play on the derivation of certain words from the basic terms for "man" and "woman."

From *thēlus*, "female," comes the term *ekthēlunein*, "to make into a woman," which Philo uses to denote the crime of the pederast against his partner (*Spec*.3.39). Although that word may have been chosen for its physical rather than moral aptness, the term *thēludrias*, "a womanish person," in the vice list in *Sac*.32, definitely conveys a judgement of character.

From the noun designating woman, *gynē*, come two derogatory terms referring to homosexual men: *androgynos* (*Spec*.1.325), and *gynaikomorphos* (*Spec*.2.50). As in the case of *ekthēlunein*, it could be argued that the words refer merely to physical matters. With *gynaikeia*, however, Philo intends to convey a moral judgement. *Gynaikeia* is used in the Septuagint as a euphemism for menstruation. Philo extends the meaning of this term to cover the undesirable passions:

> But when God begins to consort with the soul, He makes what before was a woman into a virgin again, for He takes away the degenerate and emasculate passions which unmanned it and plants instead the native growth of unpolluted virtues. Thus He will not talk with Sarah till she has ceased from all that is after the manner of women (*ta gynaikeia panta*), and is ranked once more as a pure virgin (*Cher*.50; cf. *Det*.28; *Spec*.2.54f.; *Ebr*.54-59).

On the other hand, Philo repeatedly plays on the association of *andreia* (courage) with *anēr* (man).[5] Analogous to these terms are the English words "manliness" and "man." *Andreia* is one of the basic virtues for Philo.[6] The most obvious example of his associating the two words is found in this passage from *De Virtutibus*:

> So earnestly and carefully does the law desire to train and exercise the soul to manly courage (*andreia*) that . . . it strictly forbids a man to assume woman's garb, in order that no trace, no merest shadow of the female, should attach to him to spoil his masculinity (*Virt*.18).[7]

In these few examples, we see that Philo uses derivatives of the Greek terms for man and woman not casually, but with the purpose of conveying judgements about character.

I stated at the beginning of this section that Philo attributes masculine and feminine qualities to his philosophical terms. The basic presupposition of his allegory is that mind is masculine and sense-perception feminine.[8]

A variation on his theme of male superiority is the declaration that something or someone he admires is motherless and, therefore, devoid of a feminine element. The Sabbath is "motherless, exempt from female parentage, begotten by the Father alone . . . neither born of a mother nor a mother herself, neither bred from

---

[5] That *anēr* and *andreia* are cognate is understood in the definition of the former in *Thesaurus Graecae Linguae*, 1831-1856, s.v. "*anēr*": "5. *Vir, i.e., Virili animo praeditus, Strenuus, Fortis.*"

[6] See, for example, *Sac*.32, 37; *QG* 4.15, 38. Cf. *LA* 2.97.

[7] The *LXX*, Deut.22:5, on which this passage is based, does not have this reason; it is Philo's addition.

[8] *Op*.165:". . . for in us mind corresponds to man, the senses to woman . . ."; *LA* 3.11:". . . the weak feminine passion of sense-perception . . . the manly reasoning schooled in fortitude . . ."; *LA* 3.202:". . . free and manly reasonings . . ."

corruption nor doomed to suffer corruption" (*Mos*.2.210). Sarah is "declared, too, to be without a mother, and to have inherited her kinship only on the father's side and not on the mother's and thus to have no part in female parentage " (*Ebr*.61; cf. *QG* 4.153, 160).

Activity, completeness, and rationality are masculine, whereas their opposites, passivity, incompleteness and irrationality, are feminine.[9]

> . . . the male is more complete, more dominant than the female, closer akin to causal activity, for the female is incomplete and in subjection and belongs to the category of the passive rather than the active. So too with the two ingredients which constitute our life-principle, the rational and the irrational; the rational which belongs to the mind and reason is of the masculine gender, the irrational, the province of sense, is of the feminine (*Spec*.1.200f; cf.*LA* 2.97).

The soul has female and male offspring; the former are vice and passion, whereas the latter are health of soul and virtues (*Sac*.103).

In borrowing a well-known figure of speech from Plato's *Phaedrus* (253 d,e), Philo adds a sexual distinction: desire is a horse "mean and slavish, up to sly tricks, [that] keeps her nose in the manger and empties it in no time, for she is a female" (*Agr*.73).

Philo appropriates the Pythagorean distinction that odd numbers are male, and even numbers female. The Sabbath, then, although a feminine noun, *hē hebdomē*, is called *andreiotatos arithmos*, "the manliest of numbers" (*Spec*.2.56).

---

[9] Observe the way Plotinus, who also accepts a Platonic psychology, speaks of sense-perception and mind. He rejects the passivity of sense-perception, i.e., the Stoic theory that it consists of impressions (*typoi*) being made upon a passive recipient: ". . . what is seen and what is heard, . . . are not by nature impressions or affections, but activities concerned with that which approaches [the soul]" (*The Enneads*, translated by A. H. Armstrong, Loeb Classical Library, 1966-1984, vol.4, 4.6.2.). The imagery which he employs to show the relation of sense (*aisthesis*) to mind (*nous*) shows difference of rank, but not of sex: "Sense perception is our messenger, but Intellect is our king" (ibid., 5.3.3).

Throughout Philo's work, the reader finds such distinctions given as self-evident. They all must be understood with the presupposition that male is superior to female.

*Creation and production*

For production in both the physical and the spiritual spheres Philo frequently posits the interaction of male and female on the model of human mating. God is always the father. Occasionally Philo suggests that earth is the corresponding mother. Philo says that in the time of creation sweet water was left on the earth

> to prevent it from being entirely dried up, and so becoming unproductive and barren, and enable it like a mother to provide, as for offspring, not one only of the two kinds of nourishment, namely solid food, but both kinds, food and drink. Wherefore the earth had abounding veins like breasts (*Op*.38; cf.43).[10]

Wisdom and Nature are also named as our mother (*Det*.54, 115; *LA* 2.49; *Sac*.98). The Logos is the first-born of God, whose mother is sometimes posited as Wisdom (*Conf*.63).

In one instance, when Philo reveals his most sacred teaching, it is to the effect that God mates with the virtues in the souls of men to produce the offspring happiness (*Cher*.42-48).

Man must choose between his two wives, Pleasure and Toil, out of consideration of the kind of children they will bear him (*Sac*.20).

A mind (*dianoia*) must bear children to God, or be widowed and cast out (*Det*.147). In an autobiographical passage (*Mig*.33-35),

---

[10] ". . . it seems true to say that in Philo's thought there is present the recognition of a female life-principle assisting the supreme God in his work of creation and administration, but also somehow fulfilling the role of mother to all creation. If this concept reveals contradictions that is perhaps because Philo himself was not quite sure what to do with it" (John Dillon, *The Middle Platonists: A Study of Platonism 80 B.C. to A.D. 20*, London: Duckworth, 1977, p.164).

Philo speaks of the need for divine impregnation before his mind can produce thoughts:

> For the offspring of the soul's own travail are for the most part poor abortions, things untimely born; but those which God waters with the snow of heaven come to the birth perfect, complete and peerless (*Mig*.33).

Sexual reproduction thus can be seen as a model on which Philo bases creativity in all spheres.

*Proper functioning of an organism*

Philo expresses the proper functioning of an organic whole as the right relationship between its male and female components, that is, the rule of the masculine over the feminine: "For pre-eminence always pertains to the masculine, and the feminine always comes short of and is lesser than it" (*Fug*.51). The pattern that exists in the family is also suited to the individual and the cosmos:

> . . . by observing the conditions prevailing in your own individual household, the element that is master in it, and that which is in subjection . . . you will gain forthwith a sure knowledge of God and of His works. Your reason will shew you that, as there is mind in you, so is there in the universe, and that as your mind has taken upon itself sovereign control of all that is in you, and brought every part into subjection to itself, so too He, that is endued with lordship over all, guides and controls the universe by the law and right of an absolute sway . . . (*Mig*.185f.).

For an imbalance of the male and female components in the individual, Philo draws a lesson from Adam's heeding Eve's advice:

> Reason is forthwith ensnared and becomes a subject instead of a ruler, a slave instead of a master, an alien instead of a citizen, and a mortal instead of an immortal (*Op*.165).

Proper balance in the individual should follow that of the family:

> There is in the soul a male and female element just as there is in families, the male corresponding to the men, the female to the women. The male soul assigns itself to God alone as the Father and Maker of the Universe and the Cause of all things. The female clings to all that is born and perishes . . . [T]here is no greater impiety than to ascribe to the passive element the power of the active principle (*Spec*.3.178-180).

On the cosmic scale, Wisdom relates to God as woman to man:

> For that which comes after God . . . occupies a second place, and therefore was termed feminine to express its contrast to the Maker of the Universe who is masculine . . . (*Fug.* 51).

## On the Human Level

The examples given above show that Philo's sex distinctions range far beyond statements of differences between men and women. But, as we might expect, they apply here as well. He quotes the following truism from an anonymous poet:

> "Not even a woman so far lacks good sense
> As when the better's there to choose the worse" (*Aet*.41).

In doing so, he is indirectly expressing an opinion generally held by men in the ancient world, viz., that women are inferior beings. But as he moves on from description of women to prescription for their proper behaviour, Philo is speaking as a person particularly concerned with the survival of the Jewish community and its values. Since man is naturally superior to woman (*Spec*.1.201), a man should rule over his wife (*Hyp*.7.3). Man is active and woman passive, as their appropriate behaviour shows (*LA* 2.385; *Spec*.200). Woman's sexuality is a constant threat to the mind and morals of man, even within marriage. Philo says on one occasion that "a wife is a selfish creature, excessively jealous and an adept at beguiling the morals of her husband and seducing him by her continued impostures," and that "she cajoles the sovereign mind" (*Hyp*.11.14). In another place he warns that a man's mind is "trussed and pinioned" by a woman (*Mos*.1.299). The threat that woman poses necessitates strict regulation of her activities:

> A woman, then, should not be a busybody, meddling with matters outside her household concerns, but should seek a life of seclusion. She should not show herself off like a vagrant in the streets before the eyes of other men . . . (*Spec*.3.171)[11]

Only in motherhood does woman take on fulfillment and honour, and command respect equal to that of her husband.[12] But even on that score Philo is subdued.[13]

Although most of his sexual distinctions can be traced to the rich variety of sources on which he drew, Philo is unusual in the extent to which such distinctions are integral to both his philosophy and his practical understanding of life.

---

[11] Goodenough, in *Jurisprudence*, pp.130f., notes a remarkable similarity between these injunctions and statements of the Pythagorean female philosopher Phintys, preserved by Stobaeus.
  Heinemann, in *Bildung*, pp.234f., cites this passage from Goodenough, and adds that this type of restriction on women's movements derives from neither Alexandrian practice nor Biblical example, but from Stoic and Pythagorean philosophy.

[12] *Deus* 13: Hannah's nature "is that of a goodly and happy motherhood." *Decal*.51: Philo speaks of "the duty of honouring parents, each separately and both in common." Cf. *Decal*.107, 119.

[13] Philosophically, he denigrates motherhood (see above, "*Value judgements*."). One example that can be cited is QG 4.160, which says in part: "For the wise and cultivated man comes into being as the portion of the Cause, whereas the wicked man . . . is related to passive matter, which gives birth like a mother."

## Mixing of the Philosophical and the Human

The manner in which Philo moves from theoretical to practical matters and from philosophical to human distinctions works against a clear differentiation between the two. The reader is helped by the fact that the treatises generally called Allegorical tend to have a preponderance of the first use of sexual terminology, i.e. the philosophical, whereas the Exposition and the Miscellaneous Writings have more direct statements about women's behaviour. Moreover, in *Questiones in Genesin* and *Questiones in Exodum*, Philo frequently begins with the literal, human story and moves on to the allegorical explanation, thus making the distinction explicit.[14] But these are only general rules. Within a single treatise Philo frequently handles Biblical material on the two levels adjacently, without a transitional statement. In the following example he interprets the temptation of Eve first in terms of mind and sense within the individual, but then as the cause of woman's situation in life:

> ... in us mind corresponds to man, the senses to woman; and pleasure encounters and holds parlay with the senses first, and through them cheats with her quackeries the sovereign mind itself .... Those who were the first to become slaves to a passion grievous and hard to heal at once had the experience of the wages paid by Pleasure. The woman incurred the violent woes of travail-pangs, and the griefs

---

[14] I am following the custom of dividing the treatises into four groups, as described by Sandmel, *Philo*, chapter 3, "Philo's Writings" (See also Winston, *Philo*, p.6. This division originated in the work of Massebieau and Cohn. See Bréhier, *Les Idées*, p.iii).
"Those treatises on biblical matters that begin with a series of biblical verses, and the content of which is shaped by these verses, are known as the *Allegory of the Law*. Those treatises on biblical matters which lack an opening series of verses and the content of which flows from the title of the particular essay are known as the *Exposition of the Law*" (p.30). The *Miscellaneous Writings* are non-biblical. *Questiones in Genesin* and *Questiones in Exodum* form a fourth category. They overlap the *Allegory* somewhat in being biblical commentary. Sandmel suggests that they may have been written as preliminary notes for treatises.

which come one after another all through the remainder of life (*Op*.165-167).

In the next example he reverses the procedure: from a generalization about women, he draws conclusions about masculine and feminine souls:

> That the rule of custom is followed by women more than men is, I think, quite clearly shown by the words of Rachel, who looks with admiration only on that which is perceived by the senses. For she says to her father, "Be not wroth, sir; I cannot rise before thee, because the custom of women is upon me" (Gen.31:35). So we see that obedience to custom is the special property of women. Indeed, custom is the rule of the weaker and more effeminate soul. For nature is of men, and to follow nature is the mark of a strong and truly masculine reason (*Ebr*.54).

It is evident from these illustrations that Philo does not clearly separate his more theoretical, philosophical, or (to use Laporte's term) symbolic use of sexual terminology from his opinions about sexual differences in humans.

Indeed sometimes Philo seems completely unaware of the shift from one level to another. The following quotation is a commentary on Gen.3:9, "But the Lord God called to Adam and said to him, 'Where art thou?'" In the final words it is difficult to tell whether it is sense-perception, or Eve, or woman in general that is irrational.

> Included then in the call of Adam, the mind, is that of sense-perception, the woman; but God does not call her with a special call; why? because, being irrational, she has no capacity derived from herself to receive reproof (*LA*.3.49f.).

Since Philo's sexual distinctions on the philosophical level are so intertwined with those on the human level, a study of Philo's perception of women will necessarily encompass them both.

## The State of Scholarship

### Recent Scholarship

### Baer's Contribution

Only recently has the question of Philo's sexual distinctions become a subject for extended reflection. Serious discussion began in 1970 with the publication of Richard Baer's monograph, *Philo's Use of the Categories Male and Female*.[15] The book is largely successful in establishing three points.

### Anthropology

First it deals with the place of sexuality in Philo's anthropology. Here Baer concentrates on the treatise *De Opificio Mundi*, for in it Philo interprets the two Genesis accounts of creation. Baer carefully examines Philo's interpretation of Gen.1:26 and 2:7, which he considers the basic texts of Philo's anthropology. He concludes that, in Philo's understanding, the two key verses from Genesis essentially lead to the same view of man, namely that he is a composite creature. In respect of his higher self he is asexual, but in his lower self he is either male or female.[16]

### Soteriology

The second point Baer establishes is the place of sexuality in Philo's soteriology. Sex inhibits salvation. Therefore one must rise above it. Baer coins three expressions for this. The first is to "b-

---

[15] Leiden: E.J.Brill. On pp. 3f. Baer discusses the state of the question up to the time his book was written.

[16] My use of "man", "he", and "his" in this sentence is deliberate. It demonstrates the ambiguity of Baer's wording. As I continue to summarize Baer's position, I shall use these words in the sense that he does. Elsewhere I use the terms only in their exclusive, masculine sense.

ecome one", to rise from multiplicity to oneness. Femaleness, in this instance, represents multiplicity, and maleness unity. Unity is also characteristic of God. This leads to the second expression for salvation, to "become male". Maleness here is not meant in the lower sense of being a counterpart to femaleness, but rather in a suprasexual sense, the sense in which God is male. The third expression is to "become virgin". This is close in meaning to the other two expressions, for it implies controlled, or relinquished, sexuality. It, too, transcends the bodily realm. In salvation one escapes the sexual self which resides in the body.

*Sex function*

For his third point Baer suggests a pattern in Philo's thought which will clear up the existing confusion about the sex roles attributed to (a) God, (b) his powers (*Sophia* {Wisdom}, *Aretē* {Virtue}, and the Logos), and (c) man, in creative activity. In each union, which Philo describes in sexual terms, the superior partner plays the active, male role and the inferior the passive, female role. Thus, in spite of their respective genders, *Sophia* can play the male role in relation to *Anthrōpos* (man), and together they can produce offspring. Baer demonstrates that the sexuality of God's powers, as of the human soul, is functional rather than ontological. This pattern serves to clarify Philo's thought and, at the same time, to cast doubt on the recurrent theory that *Sophia* and *Aretē* are shadows of Mediterranean goddesses, and that Philo deliberately allows the Logos to upstage them.[17]

---

[17] For a recent discussion of this theory see Joan Chambers Engelsman, *The Feminine Dimension of the Divine* (Philadelphia: Westminster Press, 1979). She uses Baer as a source but misinterprets his explanation of the role of Sophia. "It is difficult to say why Sophia was replaced by Logos/Christ. Philo's work indicated the presence of a symbolic misogynism which might have come from a psychocultural need to replace Mother with Father."(p.120) Engelsman's concern is to find evidence of the worship of the divine feminine. The same concern is found in R. Melnick's paper "On the Philonic Conception of the Whole Man," in *Journal for the Study of Judaism* 11 (July, 1980), pp.1-32.

## Baer's Limitations

Baer's title indicates that he intended to limit his work to the concepts of male and female in Philo's philosophy. Because of the intertwining of allegorical and non-allegorical strands in Philo's writing, however, he found it necessary to give some attention to Philo's perception of women.[18] Nevertheless he acknowledges that he has not resolved the apparent tension between Philo's expressed abhorrence of things female and his acceptance of a role for women in God's order:

> In *Vit. Cont.*, in his description of the Therapeutae, Philo shows considerable admiration for the ideal of sexual abstinence and perpetual virginity. But this ideal always more or less remains for him something to be admired from a distance. He was far too much a Jew not to take seriously the divine command to be fruitful and multiply.[19]

Baer makes no attempt to explain the tension or to suggest an overarching principle which would cover both positions.

## Further Scholarship

Nothing substantial has been added to the subject since the publication of Baer's book. An article by Judith Romney Wegner deals directly with Philo's perception of women, but her work is

---

[18] " . . . his [Philo's] depreciation of actual women and of female sense-perception are frequently so closely intertwined that no clear separation between the two can be made" (*Categories*, p.40).
Baer's discussion of women is virtually limited to pages 40 to 44.

[19] Ibid., p.75.

marred by inappropriately emotive language and faulty reasoning.[20] Melnick makes a justifiable criticism of the world-denying aspect of Baer's interpretation, but his attempt to challenge Baer's third conclusion with the conjecture that "there was a long-standing tradition within Judaism of a Female in nature through whom salvation could be sought" is unconvincing.[21] Leonard Swidler and Evelyn and Frank Stagg miss the subtleties of Philo's thought in their search for misogyny.[22] For her book on the concept of woman in philosophy, Sister Prudence Allen has done some independent research on Philo, but largely from one treatise, *Questiones in Genesin*, and her conclusions are limited to a few pages.[23] Unfortunately, she also accepts the dubious findings of Engelsman.[24]

These few short works constitute the recent scholarly work on the topic. There has been no fullscale examination of sexuality, specifically female sexuality, in Philo since Baer opened the subject in 1970. Thus his book remains the foundation for further study.

---

[20] "The Image of Women in Philo", *SBL Seminar Papers* 1982 (California: Scholars Press), pp.551-563. She charges Philo with displaying "a pronounced male chauvinist bias" (p.555) and bases her argument for the irrationality of woman's soul on an uncritical acceptance of Baer's interpretation of *Heres* 138f. (p.552, using Baer, *Categories*, p.19, which is questionable).

[21] I refer to this article in note 17, above. The quotation is from p.7.

[22] Leonard Swidler, *Women in Judaism* (New York: Scarecrow Press, 1976); Swidler's references to Philo are incidental to his main interest, which is women in Palestine and Babylonia.

Evelyn and Frank Stagg, in *Women in the World of Jesus* (Philadelphia: Westminster Press, 1978), discuss Philo on pages 41 to 45. Although they make some insightful comments, they are careless in making the overall judgement that, "Philo's misogyny is so pronounced that his judgment is suspect" (p.38). Philo would not have understood the charge. He uses the word *misogynaioi* only once, and in that instance it signifies men who tire of their wives and try to get rid of them by making false accusations of infidelity (*Spec.*3.79ff.).

[23] *Concept*, pp.189-193.

[24] See note 17, above.

# CHAPTER FOUR

# PHILO'S LANGUAGE

The primary task I have undertaken is to study Philo's statements that specifically pertain to women. In order to determine the parameters of the study, it is necessary to ask whether, or to what degree, he intended to include women in his general statements about the human condition. Can we learn about his understanding of women by reading what he has to say about "man"? Or must we recognize that Philo's generalizations about "man" do not pertain to women at all? I have already stated my conviction that, for the most part, Philo does not consciously include women, and that in this respect he follows both the Jewish and the Greek tradition. In this chapter I intend to demonstrate this by examining some of Philo's language.

This issue appears not to have been raised in the scholarly literature. Perhaps some scholars have considered that the exclusion of women was self-evident. It is possible that others, on the other hand, operated on the tacit assumption that Philo spoke inclusively. Yet the question of language is a timely topic.[1] Interest has developed recently, particularly in North America, in exploring the degree to which masculine terms in language are inclusive. It has drawn attention to the ambiguity of the terms "man", *l'homme* and *Mensch* in modern translations of ancient writers like Philo.[2]

---

[1] See *On the Treatment of the Sexes in Research*, by Margrit Eichler and Jeanne Lapointe (Ottawa: SSHRC, 1985). This booklet summarizes some of the current discussion about the power of language in determining thought about men and women.

[2] *OPA* usually has *l'homme* where the Loeb uses "man." *PA* usually translates *anthrōpos* by *Mensch* and *anēr* by *Mann*.

The problem lies not only in the fact that English (like French) has only one word to translate two Greek words, *anthrōpos* and *anēr*. In German, with its two terms, *Mensch* and *Mann*, one still faces the question whether the more general of the two terms, viz., the first, extends to womankind. Thus, although German is less ambiguous than English or French in this regard, a part of the problem still remains. We need to return to the original texts and try to determine the author's meaning. When we are working with French and English translations, we have the additional task of distinguishing which Greek word for "man" was used in the original.

Since I am working primarily with the Loeb text, I shall address my concern to the problems presented when the text is translated into English.

In the Loeb translation by Colson and Whitaker I find four types of Greek expression rendered in English by "man":
a) *anēr*, when the context does not specify "husband"
b) *anthrōpos*
c) the indefinite pronoun, *tis*, or the relative pronoun, *hostis*.
d) a substantive formed by a combination of the masculine article and an adjective.

We have no way of knowing whether Colson and Whitaker mentally distinguished their use of "man" in (a) from that in (b), (c), and (d). Certainly, in Greek scholarship there has been a tendency to distinguish between *anēr* and *anthrōpos* by using Liddell and Scott's primary definitions: *anēr* means man, opposed to woman, and *anthrōpos* means man, opposed to beast.[3] That is, *anēr* is considered

---

[3] Liddell and Scott, *A Greek-English Lexicon*, 9th edition with supplement (Oxford: Clarendon Press, 1968).

The passages in Hesiod's *Theogony* dealing with the creation of Pandora reveal a masculine meaning for both words. Hesiod prefers *anēr* when speaking of the marriage relationship, but uses *anthrōpos* for mankind before woman was created: he uses the former in 592, "Women, a great plague, make their abodes with mortal men," and in 601, "and evil for men." He uses the latter in 589, "this sheer inescapable snare for men" and 570, "and evil for men." This is an early indication that in the Greek tradition women were considered something other than *anthrōpoi* or *andres*. ( The translations are from Frazer, *The Poems of Hesiod*, and the Greek from the Oxford edition by M.L.West [1978]).

to be sex-specific and *anthrōpos* generic. Masculine pronouns and substantives have generally been assumed to be inclusive. So we might suppose that Colson and Whitaker did make such a distinction in their own minds. But even if this were the case, the problem is really not one of updating their translation with inclusive language for supposedly generic terms, for that would take us no closer to the thought of the original.

The problem is to determine whether Philo was thinking of women as well as of men when he used any of those terms.

Although Philo never states explicitly that he considers women non-persons, his emphasis on the reasoning capacity as the hallmark of *anthrōpos*, and on women's deficiency in that regard, suggests that he certainly did not consider them in the front ranks of *anthrōpoi*. As basic definitions of *anthrōpos*, Philo gives in *Abr*.32 and *Det*.139 "a living creature endowed with reason subject to death" (*to logikon thnēton zōon*) and in *Mut*.119 "the element of the reason" (*to logikon eidos*). He emphasizes, too, that the real *anthrōpos* is the reasoning faculty. "But who else could the man (*anthrōpos*) that is in each of us be save the mind (*nous*)?"[4] " . . . the mind (*nous*) in each of us (*hēmōn*) which in the true and full sense is the man (*anthrōpos*) . . . ."[5] Yet in women it is the unreasoning quality that he stresses. Philo refers in one statement to "sense-perception, the woman" as "unreasoning" (*alogos*), and in another to woman's inability "to reflect greatly" (*LA* 3.50; *QG* 1.46). In one generalization about women he uses the term *oligophrōn*, "endowed with little sense" (*Prob*.117). In another place, citing Julia Augusta as an exception who "excelled all her sex", in that her reasoning had been rendered "manly" (*arrenotheisa*), he remarks that "the judgments of women as a rule are weaker and do not apprehend any mental

---

[4] *Agr*.9; see also *Fug*.71f. and *QG* 4.189.

[5] *Heres* 231; Philo's use of "us" in his generalizations may be in imitation of his master, Plato. In the *Timaeus* 91A Plato's use of it is clearly exclusive of women: " . . . constructing an animate creature of one kind in us men, and of another kind in women."

conception apart from what their senses perceive" (*Legat*.319). These examples would incline the reader to understand that even when he uses the supposedly general term for humanity, *anthrōpos*, Philo is not thinking of women.

Another indication that Philo may not use *anthrōpoi* inclusively is given by his frequent use of the formula "men together with women" (*andres homou kai gynaikes*).[6] The substitution would be, at least, curious if *anthrōpoi* itself had a strongly inclusive connotation.

Yet context plays a role. One can find particular instances where there is no question that Philo is using *anthrōpos* generically.

> Equality too divided the human being into man and woman (*ton anthrōpon eis andra kai gynaika*), two sections unequal indeed in strength, but quite equal as regards what was nature's urgent purpose, the reproduction of themselves in a third person (*Heres* 164).

> Man approaches woman, i.e., the male human approaches the female human (*anēr men gynaiki, anthrōpos d' arrēn anthrōpoi thēleiai*) (*Cher*.43, my translation).

In these two examples Philo uses the conventional distinction between the generic and the specific, i.e. between *anthrōpos* and *anēr*, in order to meet a particular need. Even in the following quotation he may be including women, for the context distinguishes between the children of Eve who live according to flesh and blood--this group would include most women--and the children of Wisdom, who live by the spirit:

> So we have two kinds of men (*anthrōpōn*), one that of those who live by reason, the divine inbreathing, the other of those who live by blood and the pleasure of the flesh. The last is

---

[6] *Spec*.1.144; 2.43; 2.146; 3.48; 3.51; 4.142; 4.218; *Legat*.208; *Mos*.1.134; *Dec*.32; cf. *Prob*.140; *Cont*.80,"*pantes te kai pasai*."
    In chapter eleven, below, I argue that Philo uses this expression as a type of window-dressing. It creates the impression that he includes women in his thought, yet their inclusion is not integrated into the context.

a moulded clod of earth, the other is the faithful impress of the divine image (*Heres* 57).

We see, then, that there is no simple answer to the question whether Philo included women in his generalizations. He is not necessarily consistent in his use of terms. The examples just given show that he does not deny that women are *anthrōpoi*.[7] Yet at the same time we have observed that he does not consciously include women when he is thinking about spheres of interest which in his experience are limited to men.

We can go so far as to conclude that unless Philo is in a situation where he is forced to notice women as people, his tendency is to operate in a male world. For confirmation of this tendency I have looked for instances of the following:
a) uses of *anēr* in ways that are not sex-specific,
b) uses of *anthrōpos*, masculine pronouns, or masculine substantives in sex-specific ways, to designate "male adult,"
c) uses of *anēr* and *anthrōpos* together in the same passage, as though they were synonyms.

If an author uses *anēr* in contexts that are not of themselves specifically male, such a use would indicate that the author thinks of the male adult as the norm for human being. If, on the other hand, he uses *anthrōpos* in statements that pertain only to male adults, then the context would give the same indication. An identical conclusion could be drawn from the use of masculine substantives and pronouns in sex-specific ways. Further, if *anēr* and *anthrōpos* occur in the same passage as synonyms, we would consider that as yet more evidence.[8]

---

[7] It is noteworthy that twice Philo employs the expression *tēn anthrōpon* (*Abr*.94, 247). In each instance it is to designate Sarah, the Biblical woman he most admires. I would interpret it as a compliment to her. She is superior to most women, a real "person." This is particularly evident in the second instance, where Philo says, "Many a story I could relate in praise of this woman."

[8] The same test could be applied to *gynē*, but I cannot recall any instance where *gynē* occurs ambiguously.

We shall begin with *anēr*. In the first two examples Philo uses words related to womanhood to denote persons who have not reached full spiritual development, and *andres* for persons who have. He implies, but does not state explicitly, that the division is between women and inferior men, on the one hand, and superior men, on the other:

> These people . . . recline exceedingly delicately on costly couches and gaily-coloured bedding with which they have provided themselves, aping the luxury of women to whom nature allows an easier mode of life, agreeable to the body of softer stamp which the Creator Artificer has wrought for them. None such is the disciple of the holy Word, but only those who are really men (*andres*), enamoured of moderation, propriety, and self-respect . . . . Such a mode of life . . . is suited to those who are not merely called but really are men (*andrasi*) . . . . [Jacob exemplifies this life, being] at war with every man that is effeminate and emasculated (*ektethēlusmenōi kai androgynōi*) (*Som*.1.122-126).

[People who see good in body and external things, as well as in mind] belong to the softer and luxurious way of life, having been reared up for the greater part of the time from their very cradle in the women's quarter and in the effeminate habits of the women's quarter. Those others are austere of life, reared by men (*andrōn*), themselves too men (*andres*) in spirit, eager for what will do them good rather than for what is pleasant, and taking food suited to an athlete with an eye to strength and vigour, not to pleasure (*Som*.2.9).

In the following passage Philo describes the descent of the soul in terms of *anēr*:

> It is when the mind which has come down from heaven, though it be fast bound in the constraints of the body, nevertheless is not lured by any of them to embrace like some hybrid, man-woman or woman-man (*androgynos ē gynandros*), the pleasant-seeming evils, but holding to its own nature of true manhood (*anēr ontōs*) has the strength to be victor instead of victim in the wrestling-bout (*Heres* 274).

The following nine examples all use *anēr* for the good, self-determining person, the person whose action will make a difference to the welfare of society.

As then in a city good men (*andres*) are the surest warrant of permanence . . . (*Sac*.126).

. . . the virtues are grown-up food, suited for those who are really men (*andrasin hōs alēthōs*) (*Cong*.19).

In my judgement, no good man (*oudeis . . . tōn agathōn andrōn*) is dead, but will live for ever, proof against old age, with a soul immortal in its nature no longer fettered by the restraints of the body (*Jos*.264).

. . . let the idea that gods are many never even reach the ears of the man (*andros*) whose rule of life is to seek for truth (*Dec*.65).

. . . the man (*andros*) who observes the law is constituted thereby a loyal citizen of the world (*Op*.3).

Virtue again produces better conditions in households, city and country, by producing men (*andras*) who are good household managers, statesmanlike and neighbourly (*Mut*.149).

So much for the wealth that is the guardsman of the body, the happy gift of nature, but we must mention also the higher, nobler wealth, which does not belong to all, but to truly noble and divinely gifted men (*andrasi*) (*Virt*.8).

Therefore he held that the wise man's (*sophou*) single day rightly spent is worth a whole life-time. This is what he suggests in another place where he says that such a man (*andra*) will be worthy of blessing both in his goings out and in his comings in . . . (*Praem*.112f.)

Further there have been instances of a household or a city or a country or nations and regions of the earth enjoying great prosperity through a single man (*andros*) giving his mind to nobility of character (*Mig*. 120).

The last example is only one indication that Philo thinks of *andres* as the chief subjects of history. Several others come to mind. Philo says in *Abr*.1 that Genesis tells of how "plants and animals were born . . . and so too men (*andrōn*), some of whom lived a life of virtue, others of vice." In his account of the life of Moses, although he mentions the old men, women and children who accompanied the men out of Egypt, he goes on to say that they were followed by converts who had been attracted by the "divine favour shown to the men" (*to theophiles tōn andrōn*).[9] Earlier in the same treatise he has condemned Greek writers for wasting their talents on other matters "when they should have used their natural gifts to the full on the lessons taught by good men (*tōn agathōn andrōn*) and their lives" (*Mos*.1.3).

By a quotation he takes from Plato's *Theaetetus* (176 c) we are reminded that both in choosing *anēr* to designate a worthwhile person, and in employing the first-person pronoun in an exclusively masculine sense, Philo is following the established convention:[10]

> "In no case and in no way," he says, "is God unrighteous: He is absolute righteousness; and nothing exists more like Him than whoso of us in his turn attains to the greatest possible righteousness. It is by his relation to Him that a man's (*andros*) real attainment is determined, as well as his worthlessness and failure to attain real manhood (*anandria*) . . ." (*Fug*.82).

Both are men, talking to men, about men.

A final quotation will show a use of *anēr* peculiar in that Philo draws his conclusion from the example set by Sarah, a woman. He avoids calling her *gynē*, using *dianoia* instead. She is used here as a role-model not for women, but for men.

---

[9] *Mos*.1.147. Colson translates *andrōn* here as "people." In *PA* the translation is *"der Männer* (d.h. der *Hebräer*)."

[10] For examples of "us men" in Philo and Plato see n.5, above.

And so it was that in the days of old a certain mind (*dianoia*) of rich intelligence, her passions now calmed within her, smiled because joy lay within her and filled her womb . . . joy is not altogether denied to the creature . . . the wise man (*andros sophou*) receives it as the greatest of gifts (*Spec*.2.54f.).

In none of these instances is *anēr* required because of the physical maleness of the persons described. Yet Philo chooses it. This practice is a strong indication that behind his thinking was the presupposition that the subjects of the quest for salvation were men.

These instances of *anēr* where the connotation could support the generic term suggest that Philo equated maleness with self-determining personhood. The reverse situation, the use of the generic form *anthrōpos* in specifically male settings, disregards the female component of the term, and in doing so implies that only men are persons.

Here Philo's dependence on the Septuagint is relevant. The Greek version of the Pentateuch uses *anthrōpos* to translate both the male term '*îš* and the generic '*ādām* in Hebrew.[11] In fact, it is used to translate the former twice as frequently as the latter.[12] I can find at least seventeen instances where *anthrōpos* in the Pentateuch requires a male interpretation, because it refers to specifically male

---

[11] The use of these terms in Hebrew scripture is discussed by Phyllis Bird in "Images of Women in the Old Testament," in *Religion and Sexism*, ed. R. R. Ruether (New York: Simon and Schuster, 1974). She notes that the Pentateuch is generally addressed to men. A vivid example of this is in the Greek version of Ex.32:2f., where an instruction we might expect to be addressed to women is spoken to men: "And Aaron says to them, Take off the golden ear-rings which are in the ears of your wives and daughters, and bring them to me. And all the people (*pas ho laos*) took off the golden ear-rings that were in their [i.e., the women's] ears (*in tois osin autōn*), and brought them to Aaron."

[12] 168 instances, as opposed to 79, according to E. Hatch and H. Redpath, s.v. *anthrōpos*, *Concordance to the Septuagint* (Oxford: Clarendon Press, 1897), vol.1.

functions.[13] Of these Philo quotes six verbatim and makes direct allusions to several others.[14]

The following are some examples. In the second account of the creation, in Genesis 2, the first created person is consistently called by the generic term, either the Greek *ton anthrōpon* (8, 15, 18), or the transliterated Hebrew *adam* (19, 20, 23) and *ton adam* (16, 19, 20, 21, 22, 22). Philo quotes Gen.2:18, "And the Lord God said, It is not good that man (*anthrōpon*) should be alone, let us make for him (*autōi*) a helper corresponding to him (*kat' auton*)." The helper becomes *gynē* (*LA* 2.1).

In reference to mind's "cleaving" to sense-perception (to his way of thinking, the grossest of errors), Philo quotes Gen.2:24, "For this cause shall a man (*anthrōpos*) leave his father and his mother, and shall cleave unto his wife . . . ."[15]

The word *anthrōpos* is used three times in Deut.20:5-7, regarding the man who need not go to war because he has just built a house, or planted a vineyard, or taken a wife.[16] Again, its meaning is exclusively masculine.

One of Philo's oft-used quotations is from Deut.21:15f.,"If a man (*anthrōpōi*) have two wives, one of them beloved and one of them hated, and they shall bear children to him . . . ."[17]

In addition, Gen.20:7 is quoted in *Heres* 258, and Gen.42:11 in *Conf*.41 and 147. The former uses *anthrōpōi* for husband, and the

---

[13] Gen.2:18, 2:24, 20:7, 24:21, 26:11, 38:2, 42:11; Lev.15:16, 20:10, 21:9, 22:12, 22:13; Num.5:15; Deut.20:7,7, 21:15f., 22:30.

[14] See the scriptural index in *PLCL*, vol.X.

[15] *LA* 2.49. *PA* breaks custom here and translates *anthrōpos* as *Mann*, probably because the context so clearly calls for the sex-specific term.

[16] Quoted in *Agr*.148, and alluded to in *Virt*.28.

[17] *LA* 2.48; *Sac*.19-44; *Sob*.21-25; *Heres* 47-49; *Spec*.2.133-139. *PA* again uses the specifically masculine term, *ein Mann*.

latter *anthrōpou* for father--more instances of specifically masculine use of the term.

Besides making these direct quotations from Scripture, Philo uses *anthrōpos* sex-specifically in one of his descriptions of the seven stages of life. Among the "stages of men's (*anthrōpōn*) growth" he lists the "capacity for emitting seed" and "the growing of the beard." He quotes a poem by Solon on "the life of man" (*ton anthrōpinon bion*), regarding growing down on the chin and taking a bride.[18] Finally he quotes Hippocrates: "In man's (*anthrōpou*) life there are seven seasons, which they call ages, little boy, boy, lad, young man, man (*anēr*), elderly man, old man . . . ."[19] Philo appears to be following an unspoken rule taken from the literature in both traditions in which he has been schooled, viz., that it is acceptable to give *anthrōpos* a purely male connotation.[20]

Another version Philo gives us of the seven stages illustrates his use of the masculine substantive as specifically male, rather than generic.

> . . . let every man (*hekastos*) search into his own heart and he will test the truth of this at first hand, with no need of proof from me, especially if he is now advanced in years. This is he who was once a babe, after this a boy, then a lad, then a stripling, then a young man, then a grown man and last an old man (*Jos*.127).

Finally, Philo both accepts and uses *anēr* and *anthrōpos* together as synonyms. This can be seen above in his quotations from Solon and Hippocrates on the seven stages of life, and in the follow-

---

[18] The translators of *PA* render *anthrōpon* as *des Menschen* and *anthrōpinon bion* as *Menschenleben*, but indicate that they have men in mind by rendering "increase of strength" (*pros ischyn epidosis*) as *Steigerung der Manneskraft*.

[19] *Op*.103-105

[20] Cf. *Virt*.36, where *anthrōpos* is "led captive by pleasure, and particularly by the pleasure of intercourse with women."

ing passage where he is talking about religious duties, which were traditionally carried out by men.

> This clearly shews that even the least morsel of incense offered by a man (*andros*) of religion is more precious in the sight of God than thousands of cattle sacrificed by men of little worth (*tis mē sphodra asteios*). And therefore the altar of incense receives special honour, not only in the costliness of its material, its construction and its situation, but by taking every day the earlier place in subserving the thanksgiving which men (*anthrōpōn*) render to God (*Spec*.1.275f.).

*Conclusion*

For want of any secondary literature on the uses of *anēr* and *anthrōpos* in Philo, or in Greek literature in general, I have attempted to supply standards by which to create a convincing answer to the questions raised at the beginning of this chapter. Does Philo consciously include woman in his generalizations about the human condition? And can we learn about his understanding of women by reading what he has to say about "man"? The answer is no.

In presenting this material I have intended not so much to reveal something hitherto unknown, as to emphasize the radical difference between the intellectual world of the ancients and our own, where men and women are encouraged to share equally. In that earlier world, men considered intellectual and spiritual matters to be their domain, and true personhood to belong to them. Women belonged to a totally different sphere, out of sight, and, for the most part, out of mind. The generalizations Philo makes about the human condition are about the persons who have a voice in human affairs, that is, the men. When he does speak about women, he does so deliberately and specifically. What he has to say will be the subject of the remainder of this study.

# CHAPTER FIVE

# WOMAN AND VIRGIN

*Introduction*

Numerous quotations from passages in which Philo uses both the sex-specific and the supposedly generic terms for "man" have provided a cumulative demonstration that in his generalizations about humanity Philo writes from a man's point of view, about men, for men. To find his perception of women it is necessary to look beyond these generalizations.

The terms Philo most frequently uses to designate women, especially the women of the Bible, are *gynē* and *parthenos*, terms usually translated as "woman" and "virgin." In the chapters immediately following this one I shall separate Philo's Biblical women into two main classes according to these terms. It would be useful as a preliminary step, then, to consider exactly how Philo uses the terms.

*Virginity*

I shall begin with summaries of three patterns in Philo which serve to distinguish virginity from womanhood.

Virginity is a state that can be not only lost but also regained.[1] It is associated with freedom from lust and the other passions.[2]

---

[1] In *Praem.*159f., we learn that the woman who has passed child-bearing becomes a virgin again and can bear soul-children.

[2] In *QG* 4.95 we read that the sign of virginity is absence of passion.

Philo frequently associates the passions with menstruation.³ Menstruation, in turn, he associates with womanhood (*Cher*.50). Thus one can conclude that a) virginity and womanhood are mutually exclusive, b) virginity occurs naturally before puberty and after menopause, c) virginity entails freedom from passion, since passion arises at puberty and dies at menopause. That is one pattern that emerges.

According to the second pattern, virginity is lost with the first sexual encounter. It is restored when human sexual relations are abandoned in favour of union with God. Virginity does not preclude motherhood; indeed it enhances it. Women have physical progeny, fathered by men, but virgins give birth to soul-children, fathered by God.⁴ In this pattern one can see that a) virginity is destroyed by intercourse b) virginity is a state preferable to womanhood and c) the function of a female, both virgin and woman, is to bear young, but the virgin bears on a higher level than the woman.

Thirdly, virginity is an escape from bondage to the body.⁵ It is an escape as well from all that womanhood represents. Along with the body, woman represents its animating element, blood.⁶ As the object of physical intercourse, she represents defilement.⁷ And as the

---

³ Philo's association of menstruation and passion is seen in *Det*.28: "In like manner we read, 'Sarah was quit of her experience of what belongs to women'(Gen.18:11); and the passions are by nature feminine, and we must practise the quitting of these for the masculine traits that mark the noble affections." In *Spec*.2.54f. he interprets the same verse (which literally refers to menstruation) as emancipation from lust: ". . . her passions now calmed within her . . . ."

⁴ *Cong*.7: God "opens the womb which yet loses not its virginity."

⁵ This point is made by Baer, *Categories*, pp.51f., with examples from the text.

⁶ *Spec*.4.123: "Blood . . . is the essence of the soul, not of the intelligent and reasonable soul, but of that which operates through the senses, the soul that gives the life which we and the irrational animals possess in common." *Heres* 61: ". . . the blood-soul, by which irrational animals also live, has kinship with the maternal and female line, but has no part in male descent."

⁷ This is not stated directly, but implied by Philo's frequent linking of the terms "virgin" and "undefiled." See examples below.

instrument of generation, she also represents the beginning of corruption. Virginity is removed from all these. Divine intervention, on the allegorical level, rescues all the great mothers of scripture, except Eve, by transforming them into virgins. On the mundane level, asceticism, or time, rescues the Therapeutrides, who are "aged virgins" in whom God has sown "spiritual rays" (*Cont*.68). These women--now virgins--are no longer bound to the body.

How does Philo justify his attributing virginity to certain women that Scripture presents as married? Let us look at the persons he chooses. Hannah and Tamar are virgin mothers Philo mentions briefly. He explicitly calls Hannah a virgin (*Praem*.159) and implies the same of Tamar (*Deus* 136; cf. *Cher*.50, *QG* 4.95). But the ones he discusses at length are the wives of Moses and the patriarchs Abraham, Isaac and Jacob, viz., Zipporah, Sarah, Leah and Rebecca. (Rachel vacillates between virginity and womanhood, and must be dealt with separately.) Sarah is the virgin *par excellence*, for she is done with menstruation, passion, and physical intercourse (the three signs mentioned earlier). With regard to Zipporah, Leah and Rebecca, Philo rests his case on the last of the signs of virginity, release from ordinary marital relations. Philo makes this inference from the fact that Scripture avoids saying that the patriarchs "knew" their wives.[8] The meaning of this deliberate omission, he says, is that God fathered their children. Philo is reluctant to use the term *gynē* when speaking of these women.[9] True, he does not transfer their

---

[8] *Cher*.40: "The persons to whose virtue the lawgiver has testified, such as Abraham, Isaac, Jacob and Moses, and others of the same spirit, are not represented by him as knowing women."

[9] *Cher*.41: "For the helpmeets of these men are called women, but are in reality virtues." Cf. *Post*.78f., where Philo uses the term *symbios* for the admirable partner of the wise man, but *gynē* for the wife of "the low and grovelling Lamech."

In *Cong*.23 Philo does state that it is important to note that Sarah is the real *gynē* of Abraham, but in doing so he is stressing the marital bond implied by the word, not the fact of her womanhood, which he consistently downplays.

See also *Abr*.97 and 247, where Philo calls Sarah *tēn anthrōpon*.

allegorical virginity to the literal stories.¹⁰ Yet he consistently emphasizes the importance of allegorical interpretation, at the expense of the literal.¹¹ Perhaps, then, it is because he regards the matriarchs as qualitatively different, on this important, allegorical level, that Philo makes no explicit suggestion for women to use them as models for their lives.¹² Rather, in speaking of contemporary woman, he dwells on the bodily and social constraints she must endure throughout the years of her womanhood.¹³

*Womanhood*

A careful reading of Philo's remarks on the subject reveals that he saw womanhood as a period of life distinguished by three features: menstruation, intercourse, and child-bearing.

---

¹⁰ *QG* 4.154 and *Mos*.1.28 indicate that he believed Isaac and Moses, respectively, fathered children in the regular way.

¹¹ Even in *Questiones in Genesin*, the most literal of his works, he emphasizes the importance of the allegorical meaning over the literal; see 4.137: "For the inquiry of the theologian is about characters and types and virtues, and not about persons who were created and born." See also the discussion of his interpretation of the Eden story, chapter six, below.

¹² Philo presents the patriarchs as models for men to follow. For example, he says in *Abr*.22f.:"The man of worth . . . spends his days in some lonely farm, finding pleasanter society in those noblest of the whole human race whose bodies time has turned into dust but the flame of their virtues is kept alive by the written records which have survived them in poetry or in prose and serve to promote the growth of goodness in the soul." Moses, in particular, is "a model for those who are willing to copy it" (*Mos*.1.158f.).

Heinemann observes that while Philo in his allegory appears to approve of "manly" women--that is, virgins, whose female sexuality is restrained--in real life he certainly does not. His calling for education "as befits maidens" (*Spec*.2.125) shows his desire to maintain sex polarity (*Bildung*, pp.231f.).

¹³ Commenting on Gen.3.16: ". . . in pain you shall bring forth children, yet your desire shall be for your husband, and he shall rule over you"(RSV), he says,"This experience comes to every woman who lives together with a man. It is (meant) not as a curse but as a necessity."(*QG* 1.49) In *QG* 4.15, the "ways of women" are called "terrible and unbearable sorrow."

The first is apparent from his frequent comments on Gen.18.11: "... it had ceased to be with Sarah after the manner of women" (RSV), in which the Septuagint uses the euphemism for menstruation, *ta gynaikeia*.[14] Exercising his customary interest in etymology, Philo develops the association of *gynaikeia* and *gynē*: at menopause Sarah has returned from womanhood to its opposite, virginity: "He [God] will not talk with Sarah till she has ceased from all that is after the manner of women, and is ranked once more as a pure virgin."[15]  "... some pass from womanhood to virginity, as Sarah did" (*Post*.134). Philo plays on the same association of words in discussing Rachel's statement to her father in Gen.31:35: "Be not wroth, sir; I cannot rise before thee, because the custom of women is upon me." Menstruation is symbolic of all the weaknesses of womanhood:

> So we see that obedience to custom is the special property of women. Indeed, custom is the rule of the weaker and more effeminate soul. For nature is of men, and to follow nature is the mark of a strong and truly masculine nature (*Ebr*.55).

Philo goes on to remark on the moral weakness of the "woman" Rachel, who cannot resist the allure of riches. These comments about womanhood are stimulated by the scriptural reference to Rachel's menstruation. Thus we observe that for Philo menstruation is one of the hallmarks of womanhood.[16]

---

[14] Besides meaning menstruation it is also used to designate women's diseases. "Greek medicine, like our own, did not have a branch to study 'the diseases of men'; maleness was the norm, and women were the deviant forms." Helen King, "Bound to Bleed: Artemis and Greek Women" in *Images of Women in Antiquity*, ed. A. Cameron and A. Kuhrt (Detroit: Wayne State University Press, 1983), p.125.

[15] *Cher*.50. Philo makes the same point, or a similar one, in his eight other comments on the same verse. See the index, in *PLCL* volume X, for their locations.

[16] Indeed, it forms a substratum to his expressed thoughts about women, as I shall demonstrate in the final section of this chapter.

Evidence of the second point, that Philo considered intercourse an essential feature of womanhood, is the statement: "For the union of human beings that is made for the procreation of children, turns virgins into women" (*Cher*.50). Defloration, in marriage, was experienced in Philo's social milieu, indeed in the whole of the ancient world, almost concurrently with menarche, with the result that in the popular perception the two were quite probably regarded interchangeably as the onset of womanhood.[17]

The third sign of womanhood, child-bearing, was the natural outcome of the other two. Philo probably associated *gynē* with *gennan*, to bear: in his translation from the Armenian, Ralph Marcus translates *QG* 1.28 as follows: "And the woman is called the power of giving birth with fecundity," adding in a note that the original

---

[17] Hard facts on marriage age are elusive, but there is general agreement that for girls in the ancient world it was early. Samuel Sandmel, in *Judaism and Christian Beginnings*, says that it was not unusual in ancient Synagogue Judaism (his general term for Judaism outside the temple cult (p.16)) for parents to contract a marriage for their daughter before she reached puberty, and to conclude it as soon as she was physically mature (p.194 and nn.; Sandmel refers to rabbinic literature to support his statements). With reference to Philo's society, (commenting on *Jos*.43) Abel Isaksson says, "we have to bear in mind that the majority of girls were married at the early age of twelve and a half." *Marriage and Ministry in the New Temple* (Lund: 1965), p.40. E. Neufeld, in *Ancient Hebrew Marriage Laws* (London: Longmans, 1944), p.139, says "No minimum age for marriage is laid down in the Old Testament either for boys or girls. From the general circumstances existing in the East in ancient times it can be assumed that children were married at a very early age--even before the age of puberty. But it seems that marriage was usually entered into after puberty."

Hippocrates appears to advocate intercourse before the onset of menstruation. The following quotations are from *On Virgins*, presented in translation in Lefkowitz and Fant, *Women's Life*, pp.95f.: "And virgins who do not take a husband at the appropriate time for marriage experience these visions more frequently, *especially at the time of their first monthly period* . . . . My prescription is that when virgins experience this trouble, they should cohabit with a man as quickly as possible . . . . If they don't do this, either they will succumb *at the onset of puberty*, or a little later . . . (emphasis mine)."

The highest marriage age for girls that I have found is given as sixteen to eighteen in Greco-Roman Egypt (Sarah Pomeroy, *Egypt*, p.107). But this was also in a society in which women enjoyed more freedom than in Jewish, Greek or Roman societies of the ancient world. Since Philo says that the husband takes over from the parents the task of guarding and watching over the maiden (*Spec*.4.178), I would conclude that Jewish girls did not go through a comparable interim period between childhood and marriage.

text (no longer extant) must have had a word-play on *gynē* and *gennan*. These three signs, then, the normal fate of every girl in the Alexandrian Jewish community, constituted womanhood.[18] We may also conclude that concomitant with womanhood was sexual passion, since Philo comments that virginity is freedom from passion (*QG* 4.95), and that at menopause Sarah's passions are finally calmed (*Spec.*2.54f.).

I mentioned earlier that Philo associates defilement and corruption with womanhood. What is the source of this association? Much of Philo's material about women is ostensibly drawn from Scripture. In the book of Leviticus there is a distinction between two types of sexual defilement or uncleanness. The first is cultic, ritual or ceremonial uncleanness, which could be removed by the passage of time and certain ablutions. Intercourse in marriage is of this type (15:18). The second is a violation of law, which incurs human punishment and the wrath of heaven. Adultery belongs here (18:20). Whereas ceremonial uncleanness bars one only from participation in the temple cult, the uncleanness caused by adultery calls for "cutting off," because it is defiance of Torah.[19]

In actual practice, however, the two types of sexual defilement were not so clearly distinguished as this might suggest, even in

---

[18] For the expectation that every girl would marry, see Sandmel, *Beginnings*, p.193. Cf. Helen King, "Bound to Bleed." This article discusses the transition to womanhood in classical Greece, surmising that girls experienced fear at the prospects before them. King reviews the events that marked the transition from virginity to womanhood, viz., menarche, defloration and parturition. Each of these is associated with blood. King bases her thesis on that point and on evidence that a certain form of suicide was common among girls at puberty. She argues that out of fear of bleeding, girls frequently chose suicide by hanging--a "bloodless" death. Her evidence is drawn from *Peri Parthenion*, or *On Virgins*, a 5th or 4th century treatise in the Hippocratic corpus (quoted partially in n.17, above). The author claims that many women choke to death as a result of "visions." The association of blood and womanhood appears to have deep roots. Philo makes it frequently.

[19] Lev.18:29. "Cutting off" is interpreted as divine retribution, "usually in the form of premature death" by G. J. Wenham, *The Book of Leviticus* (Grand Rapids: Eerdmans, 1979) p.285f. It is interpreted as death at the hands of the community, probably by stoning, by A. Noordtzij, *Leviticus*, translated by R. Togtman (Grand Rapids: Zondervan, 1982), p. 156, and J. A. Porter, *Leviticus* (Cambridge: Cambridge University Press,1976).

Biblical times. In separate commentaries on Leviticus, Noordtzij and Porter conclude that some of the laws themselves showed a blending of the two concepts. They suggest, further, the presence of a sexual taboo.[20] Such a taboo had the effect of stigmatizing all sexual activity.

In *Contra Apionem* Josephus speaks of marriage with the clearly apologetic aim of showing that Jews practise self-restraint. He repeats the rule of Lev.15:18 about washing after intercourse, but justifies it with a very Greek piece of reasoning, to the effect that in intercourse soul and body contract defilement or division (2.24.203).[21] This indicates that he thought of marital intercourse as incurring something other than ritual uncleanness. It is a temporary capitulation of the soul-principle to the body-principle.

---

[20] Noordtzij, *Leviticus*, pp.117f.:"The Israelites also regarded uncleanness and sin as being closely related. Because of this, the ritual of cleansing is referred to in Numbers 8:21; 19:12-13, 20; 31:19-20, 23 as 'purification from sin'. . . and in certain cases the bringing of burnt offerings and sin offerings formed part of the ritual of cleansing (Lev.12:6-7; 14:10-20; 15:15)." His publishers add a disclaimer, protesting that Noordtzij is coming too close to attributing the concept of taboo to Scripture.

Porter says, *Leviticus*, pp.82f.: ". . . in Leviticus uncleanness is certainly a concrete and dangerous reality, indicating the presence of something fundamentally wrong, which is why the priestly writers do not draw the clear distinction between ritual impurity and moral sin which comes naturally to us." And on p.119, he says that "the processes of human reproduction are mysterious to early peoples and therefore surrounded by various taboos."

*Encyclopedia Judaica*, s.v. "purity and impurity, ritual": ". . . it seems that any sin is thought of as causing impurity and expressions taken from the purity ritual passages serve figuratively in the Bible as symbols for atonement and repentance. The two terms of atonement and purification tend therefore to merge."

[21] The text of 2.24.203 is obscure. The ms. L reads *psychēs te gar kai sōmatos egginetai molusmos*: "for a defilement of body and soul takes place." But Rengstorf, along with Thackeray, follows Niese (after Eusebius): *psychēs gar echein touto merismon pros allēn choran hypelaben* :"[for the Law] regards this act as involving a partition of the soul [part of it going] into another place"(*LCL*). Thackeray interprets this to mean, "There is transference of part of the soul or life-principle from the father." (vol.1, pp.374f., fn.). Taken either way, the passage indicates a dualism characteristic of Platonism, although it is more sharply expressed in the reconstructed reading. Cf. *Jewish War* 2.154 where Josephus attributes similar dualism to the Essenes: "For it is a fixed belief of theirs that the body is corruptible and its constituent matter impermanent but that the soul is immortal and imperishable" (*LCL*; cf. *Antiquities* 18:18).

As for Alexandrian Judaism, Philo describes a practice that is more stringent than the Scriptural requirement, viz., washing before touching anything after intercourse. The passage is interesting in another way, i.e., in Philo's use of one of his favorite rhetorical devices, moving to the greater from the lesser, that is, in employing the *a fortiori* argument.[22] Here he draws a conclusion about adultery from an implication about the impurity of marital intercourse. The fact that he argues in this way indicates that he sees a point of comparison between the two activities, and I can see no other point but the belief that each activity entails a degree of defilement.[23] The passage reads as follows:

> So careful is the law to provide against the introduction of violent changes in the institution of marriage that a husband and wife, who have intercourse in accordance with the legitimate usages of married life, are not allowed, when they leave their bed, to touch anything until they have made their ablutions and purged themselves with water. This ordinance

---

[22] T. Conley draws attention to this rhetorical device or "dialectical topos" in "Philo's Use of Topoi", pp.171-178, in *Two Treatises of Philo of Alexandria*, edited by John Dillon and David Winston (California: Scholars Press, 1983). He gives as examples *Deus* 26 (the imperturbability of man and of God) and 78 (the brightness of the sun and of God's powers). In order to use such a device, it is necessary for Philo to see a point of comparison between the two things that he names.

[23] Alan Segal, in *Rebecca's Children: Judaism and Christianity in the Roman World* (Cambridge, Mass.: Harvard University Press, 1986), emphasizes that first-century Jews liked to see themselves, and to be seen, as sexually self-restraining: "Because of the sensuality that prevailed among the uneducated pagan classes, a life of chastity and abstinence was viewed by educated Jew and Gentile alike as the sign of a morally serious religion" (p.48). The following quotation is from his chapter on the Pharisaic leadership, but could well pertain to sexual teaching among the Jews in Alexandria: "Insistence on purity was a practical device to enforce endogamy and a symbolic device to oppose contact with Gentiles. Although impurity need not necessarily express immorality, the ambiguity inherent in the concept was often exploited" (p.125).

extends by implication to a prohibition of adultery, or anything which entails an accusation of adultery.[24]

We see, then, that Philo (and his community, if he is interpreting their actions accurately) considered the sexual act to some degree defiling. In his writing, the defilement appears to attach itself permanently to women.[25] Although Philo never makes such a statement directly, his association of words leads to that conclusion. For the remainder of this chapter I shall demonstrate that this is so.

Over and over again, Philo contrasts virginity with defilement, as the following quotations will show. (The emphasis in the quotations is mine.)

> For it is meet that God should hold converse with the truly *virgin* nature, that which is *undefiled* and free from impure touch . . .(*Cher.*50).

> Rebecca was a *virgin* . . . because virtue is essentially free from alloy and false semblance and *defilement* (*Post.*133).

> . . . the glorious beauty, inviolate, *undefiled* and truly *virginal* . . . (*Cong.*124).

> What fair thing, then, could fail when there was present God the Perfecter, with gifts of grace, His *virgin* daughters, whom

---

[24] *Spec.*3.63. Goodenough comments on this statement in *Jurisprudence*, as follows: "Philo says that so strong is the Jewish feeling against intercourse even between man and wife that it requires that both parties rise and wash after a connection (3.63). This seems not to have been strictly required by the rabbinical tradition . . . but . . . it was one of the cardinal laws for Jews in the Diaspora." (p.89), and, "Pure, in the sense of the Jews at the Temple, no Jew in the Diaspora could keep himself; but purity in its religious sense was still one of their dearest aspirations, and when they observed the substitute traditions they had the satisfaction of calling themselves *sphodra katharoi*" (p.144).

[25] Although logic would demand that Philo consider men also defiled in this way, I do not find a parallel association of words in his writing. Perhaps it is because he considers the male the active partner, responsible for his own behaviour, that Philo lays more emphasis on men's self-restraint, and less on defilement, which connotes a certain passivity.

> the Father that begat them rears up uncorrupted and *undefiled* (*Mig*.31)?

> "Bethuel," a name meaning in our speech "Daughter of God"; yea, a true-born and *ever-virgin* daughter, who, by reason alike of her own modesty and of the glory of Him that begot her, hath obtained a nature free from every *defiling* touch (*Fug*.50).

> . . . *undefiled* and *virgin* thoughts. . . (*Som*.2.184).

> But among the virtues some are ever *virgin*, some pass from womanhood to virginity, as Sarah did: for "it ceased to be with her after the manner of women". . . . But the *ever-virgin* is, as he says, absolutely not known by a man. For in reality no mortal has been permitted to *defile* the incorruptible growth . . .(*Post*.134).

These statements all contrast defilement with virginity. Since virginity is the opposite of womanhood, the obvious inference is that Philo associates defilement with woman, i.e. with the sexually active female. This is never, however, stated directly. Philo makes the connection implicitly, not explicitly.

The picture of womanhood as a state of defilement (which Philo paints through word associations such as the ones above) is quite different from the one he paints when he is speaking straightforwardly. For example, when he justifies the subordinate role of women, he uses the argument that the proper role for a wife is one of obedience:

> . . . wives must be in servitude to their husbands, a servitude not imposed by violent ill-treatment but promoting obedience in all things (*Hyp*.7.3).

Or in giving the reason why the Essenes do not take wives, he suggests a practical reason, viz., that the wife will distract her husband and disturb his life:

> . . . no Essene takes a wife, because a wife is a selfish creature, excessively jealous and an adept at beguiling the

morals of her husband and seducing him by her continued impostures (*Hyp*.11.14).[26]

It can be observed, then, that although on the rational level, as these quotations illustrate, Philo puts forth reasonable arguments for the inferior position afforded women, an unarticulated revulsion against womanhood is revealed in his association of words, that is, of "virgin" with "undefiled," especially on the allegorical level.

I shall illustrate the same pattern in Philo's attitude(s) to motherhood. Philo frequently praises motherhood, as in his comments on the commandment to honour one's parents (e.g., *Spec*.2.225; *Deus* 119; *Virt*.130). Occasionally he may include mothers in generalized complaints. But this is done on the rational level; Philo states his opinion and supports it with reasons.[27] On another level, however, we find that motherhood is associated with corruption, and motherlessness is a sign of purity. This type of statement has precedents in Plato's doctrine that birth into the world of becoming entails corruption.

> Birth . . . is accomplished through other things decaying (*phtheiromenōn*) and decay (*phthora*) through fresh births (*LA* 1.7).

> [the Sabbath] was also ever virgin, neither born of a mother nor a mother herself, neither bred from corruption (*phthora*)

---

[26] Isaksson, *Marriage*, (pp.63-65) notes that Josephus and Philo give essentially the same reasons for the Essenes' abstaining from marriage. He goes on to demonstrate that they are wrong--that the Essenes abstain from sexual relations out of desire to be constantly prepared to engage in holy war. This would discount any objection that Philo is merely quoting the Essenes on the point, and make it more likely that he is expressing his own reasoning on the matter.

[27] *Spec*.4.68: "Now the principal cause of such misdeeds is familiarity with falsehood which grows up with the children right from their birth and from the cradle, the work of nurses and mothers and the rest of the company, slaves and free, who belong to the household."

nor doomed to suffer corruption (*phtharsomenē*) (*Mos*.2.210; cf. *Heres* 216).[28]

[Sarah] is declared, too, to be without a mother, and to have inherited her kinship only on the father's side and not on the mother's, and thus to have no part in female parentage . . . . She is not born of that material substance perceptible to our senses, ever in a state of formation and dissolution . . . (*Ebr*.61).[29]

But if children become zealous emulators of maternal depravity, they will draw away from paternal virtue and depart from it through desire of pleasure in a wicked stock, and through contempt and arrogance toward the better they are condemned as guilty of wilful wrongdoing (*QG* 1.92).

. . . the blood-soul, by which irrational animals also live, has kinship with the maternal and female line, but has no part in male descent. Not so it was with Virtue or Sarah, for male descent is the sole claim of her, who is the motherless ruling principle of things, begotten of the father alone (*Heres* 62).

---

[28] Philo uses the same word, *phtheirō*, to mean "defile", "corrupt", and "deflower a virgin".

[29] Although the wording of this passage, as well as of the two preceding ones, is reminiscent of Platonic metaphysics, that does not negate its relevance to motherhood. Plato transferred the concept of human reproduction to the cosmic sphere, as we saw in the survey in chapter two, above.

A general revulsion against motherhood is expressed in the Greek myth of Athena's springing from the head of Zeus, thus avoiding birth, as well as in Pausanias' statement in Plato's *Symposium* that the Heavenly Aphrodite differs from the common Aphrodite by being motherless.

The final example given above is one of many in which Philo juxtaposes the ideas of "female" and "blood."[30] Usually he does not explicitly mention menstruation, although one might surmise that it lies behind this particular association. But on the few occasions he does speak directly about menstruation, Philo shows most clearly and dramatically that his rational thought is undergirded by an unspoken taboo. On the one hand, he suggests practical reasons for the wisdom of the Biblical injunction about a menstruating woman. On the other hand, he chooses menstruation as the symbol of evil. I shall demonstrate these two approaches.

First let us look at the reasoned discussion he applies to the subject of menstruation. The following passage is Philo's commentary on Lev.18:19:

> Whenever the menstrual issue occurs, a man must not touch a woman, but must during that period refrain from intercourse and respect the law of nature. He must also remember the lesson that the generative seeds should not be wasted fruitlessly for the sake of a gross and untimely pleasure. For it is just as if a husbandman should in intoxication or lunacy sow wheat and barley in ponds or mountain-streams instead of in the plains, since the fields should become dry before the seed is laid in them. Now nature also each month purges the womb as if it were a cornfield--a field with mysterious properties, over which, like a good husbandman, he must watch for the right time to arrive. So while the field is still inundated he will keep back the seed, which otherwise will be silently swept away by the stream, as the humidity not only relaxes, but utterly paralyses the seminal nerve-forces, which in nature's laboratory, the womb, mould the living creature and with consummate craftsmanship perfect each part

---

[30] See n.6, above. The association of blood with woman goes back in the Greek tradition at least to Aristotle. Cf. *History of Animals* 521a, 23-27, taken from *CWA*, vol.1, p.827: "Blood in the female differs from that in the male, for, supposing the male and female to be on a par as regards age and health, the blood in the female is thicker and blacker than in the male; and with the female there is less on the surface and more internally. Of all female animals the female in man is the most richly supplied with blood, and of all animals the menstruous discharges are the most copious in woman."

of body and soul. But if the menstruation ceases, he may boldly sow the generative seeds, no longer fearing that what he lays will perish (*Spec*.3.32).

Here we have a carefully executed argument in support of the regulation against intercourse with a menstruating woman. Philo is not so much arguing that it should be observed as demonstrating that it is a reasonable law. There is no suggestion of woman as danger. Philo begins by identifying the prohibition as part of the law of nature. He proceeds by reasoning on the grounds of a) observation, b) literary precedent, and c) analogy.

The basic premise is that the purpose of intercourse is conception. The corollary of this is the principle that a man should not seek self-indulgence in sex, as did Onan.[31] The empirical evidence upon which Philo probably draws is that the menstrual period is the least fertile time in a woman's cycle.[32]

The metaphor of the field is a literary convention which he might well have remembered from Plato. In fact, there is a remarkable resemblance between the first part of the passage and *Laws* viii 838e-839a:

> . . . I said I knew of a way to put into effect this law of ours which permits the sexual act only for its natural purpose, procreation, and forbids not only homosexual relations, in which the human race is deliberately murdered, but also the growing of seeds on rocks and stone, where it will never take root and mature into a new individual . . . . The first point in its favour is that it is a natural law.[33]

---

[31] Cf. *Post*.180f.; *Deus* 16-18.

[32] Throughout his work Philo demonstrates a good knowledge of medical matters. Therefore this type of knowledge would not be unlikely.
Philo may also have gained this information from a medical source. Soranus, a Greek from Ephesus practising in Rome in the first century C.E., wrote that the best time for conception "is when menstruation is ending and abating" (given in translation in Lefkowitz and Fant, *Women's Life*, p.220).

[33] Saunders (trans.), *The Laws*, p.337.

In order to suit the topic at hand, Philo extends the metaphor to one of ponds and streams inundating a field. The stream washes away the seed before it takes root. Then the metaphor of the field changes to something more reminiscent of the "receptacle" of *Timaeus* 49a, namely the laboratory. The reasoning is Philo's own: the seed is rendered impotent by the menstrual flow, and unable to develop into body and soul.

Philo appears to believe that the essential part of the fetus is contributed by the father. Prudence Allen observes that medical knowledge about the process of generation was, at this time, largely based on analogy. She has surveyed the different analogies used by Greek philosophers, noting the relative contributions they accorded male and female. Although the idea of a double-seed had been proposed--roughly balancing the male and female contributions to the fetus--Plato preferred the single-seed theory.[34] In the *Timaeus* he proposed a cosmic male source producing offspring in a female receptacle, and in the *Laws*, as we have seen, male seed sown in a female field. In the passage we are examining Philo appears to be following Plato's lead.

Philo has two more reasoned discussions of menstruation. Here his argument is based on ideas of male and female roles in generation that are reminiscent of Aristotle.[35]

> . . . the matter of the female in the remains of the menstrual fluids produces the fetus. But the male [provides] the skill and the cause. And so, since the male provides the greater

---

[34] Prudence Allen, *Concept*. Empedocles (c.450, B.C.E.) proposed equal contributions, and Hippocrates (contemporary of Plato) had a double-seed theory, the man producing intelligence, and the woman beauty. Also see Bullough, *Subordinate*, pp.62ff.
    The point about medical knowledge being based on analogy is also made by Lefkowitz in *Women's Life*, p.81.

[35] *Generation of Animals*, Book 1, 716a, 5-7, in vol.1, *CWA*, p.1112: "For, as we said above, the male and female principles may be put down first and foremost as origins of generation, the former as containing the efficient cause of generation, the latter the material of it."

and more necessary [part] in the process of generation, it was proper that his pride should be checked by the sign of circumcision, but the material element, being inanimate, does not admit of arrogance.[36]

It is of the nature of nothing earth-born to take form apart from wet substance. This is shown by the depositing of seeds, which either are moist, as those of animals, or do not grow without moisture: such are those of plants. From this it is clear that the wet substance we have mentioned must be a part of the earth which gives birth to all things, just as with women the running of the monthly cleansings; for these too are, so physical scientists tell us, the bodily substance of the fetus.[37]

In these three passages we see Philo's considered theories about woman's part in procreation, and in particular the function of menstruation.

A passage that has been overlooked in the scholarly literature presents a totally different view of menstruation.[38] In *Fug*.177-201, Philo discusses at length one of his favorite motifs, the fountain. From Biblical texts, he produces five "fountains" or "sources," and interprets them allegorically. He arranges them in such a way that the first and fifth correspond, as being of the greatest value; they represent the *logos*, human and divine. Similarly, the second and

---

[36] *QG* 3.47.

[37] *Op*.132.

[38] It was drawn to my attention by an incidental remark in an article by Jacques Cazeaux, "Aspects de l'exégèse Philonienne", *Revue des sciences religieuses* 47 (1973), pp.262-269. Cazeaux's interest is in the intricate structure of the passage *Fug*.177-201. But he remarks in passing that the figure of speech for the evil that man can fall into on his journey to God is provided by the "tabou sexuel" of menstruation.

Cazeaux again uses *Fug*.177-201 to illustrate Philo's pattern of exegesis, in "Philon d'Alexandrie, exégète," pp. 156-226, *Aufstieg und Niedergang der Römischen Welt* (Berlin and New York: de Gruyter, 1984). Menstruation here is "la souillure du Mal" and "l'hypothèse funeste" (pp.159f.).

fourth correspond; they are education and judgement, human sources of good. In the center, standing apart, is the "source" of evil:

> Let us now consider the spring of folly, respecting which the lawgiver has spoken in these terms: "Whosoever shall have slept with a woman in her separation hath unclosed her spring, and she hath unclosed the flow of her blood; let them both be put to death" (Lev.xx:18) . . . . This is the great deluge in which "the cataracts of heaven," that is of the mind, "were opened," "and the fountains of the abyss," that is of sense-perception, "were unclosed" (Gen.vii.11). For only in this way is a deluge brought upon the soul, when as though from heaven, that is the mind, wrong-doings burst upon it as in a cataract; and from sense-perception below, as it were from the earth, passions come welling up . . . . Such are the springs of sinful deeds . . . (*Fug*.188-194).

What a contrast this is to Philo's interpretation of the similar injunction in Lev.18:19, which we read earlier! Here menstruation is the metaphor for the spring of all evil that befalls man: of folly (*aphrosynē*), of injustice and wrongdoing (*adikēmata*) of passions (*ta pathē*) and of sins (*ta hamartēmata*), all welling up from the abyss. In this passage we do not hear Philo the rational natural scientist who spoke in the examples given earlier. The choice of material for this allegory takes us behind and below "the processes of his reasoning" to a level of taboo which must surely be taken into account if we are to understand his perception of women.[39]

In this passage Philo explicitly expresses his revulsion at the "blood" of womanhood. Throughout his work blood is used in association with passion, woman, beasts, and irrationality--all ele-

---

[39] Wolfson advised that "we must try to reconstruct the latent processes of his [Philo's] reasoning, of which his uttered words, we may assume, are only the conclusions" (*Philo*, vol.1, p.106).
  Compare with this passage another, *Conf*.23ff., which interprets the "fountains from the earth" of Gen.7:11 as streams of passion issuing from the body, with the result that "all things burst forth without restraint to supply abundant opportunities to those who were all readiness to take pleasure therein" and nothing in the soul "was left free from disease and corruption."

ments man must escape in the odyssey back to his homeland in God.[40]

*Conclusion*

In this chapter I have argued that a blood taboo lurks beneath the surface of Philo's thought. Womanhood is associated in his mind with blood, evil, defilement and corruption. God may elevate the great women of Scripture by transforming them into virgins. But there is nothing to rescue the ordinary woman. Throughout her child-bearing years, she cannot escape the fate imposed by her body. The odyssey of the soul is denied her, for she is trapped in a foreign land, the land of Egypt, of passion, the land whose river flows with blood. She is incapable of self-control, being driven by passion, and so must be controlled from without.

---

[40] In the essays that introduce her translation of *Quis Rerum Divinarum Heres Sit* in *OPA*, Marguerite Harl speaks of the theme of odyssey: "we see Philo using the language of Greek culture to help us understand an idea deeply embedded in the Biblical text: the mythical theme of the exile and return of the soul to its fatherland is effectively present in Greek literature in the form of the allegorical exegesis of the return of Ulysses to his beloved fatherland." (p.111, my translation).

# CHAPTER SIX

# BIBLICAL WOMEN (I): EVE

*Introduction*

In examining Philo's treatment of the female figures of Scripture one can detect a division into two types: women and virgins. Baer's monograph, *Philo's Use of the Categories Male and Female*, as we saw in chapter three, established that the virgin is the spiritual equivalent of the male; both are virtually asexual beings. There is a sizable number of female figures in Scripture whom Philo treats as virgins, even though at one time or in one mode of interpretation they bore the hallmarks of womanhood. If we are sensitive to Philo's terminology, we can no longer consider them simply "women." Thus they are not included in the subject matter of this chapter and the next.

Philo does deal with several Biblical figures, however, whose womanhood stands unquestioned. Eve is by far the most prominent. Others who receive considerable attention from him are Miriam, Hagar, the wives of Lot and Potiphar, and certain groups of unnamed Hebrew and foreign women. This chapter is devoted to Eve, and chapter seven to the others.

We may expect that Philo's portraits of these women will be derogatory. But it is not our purpose to disclose Philo's "misogynism," or his "negative" view of women. It is, rather, to try to determine and then to understand exactly what he did say about them.[1] Did he paint them all the same or are there differences?

---

[1] Swidler, in *Women in Judaism*, used such terms extensively. Jacob Neusner criticized Swidler, rightly, I believe, on that point: "In the end he can only set up two categories for interpretation, and they produce no interpretation at all. These are, first, 'positive,' and second, 'negative' sayings.... It follows that, for Swidler,

And, if there are, what do they mean? Such an enterprise will require first a detailed examination of what Philo did say, and, only after that, conclusions.

### Woman as Archetype

### Eve

Let us begin with the first woman, Eve. The initial question to be considered is whether Philo sees her as a special case in so far as he regards her as a mythical person. Is she, for this reason, qualitatively different from the later women of Scripture?

In speaking of the Garden of Eden story Philo certainly does not shrink from using the term "myth."

> These words in their literal sense are of the nature of a myth. For how could anyone admit that a woman, or a human being at all, came into existence out of a man's side?[2]

But we ought to take particular note of the qualifying phrase "in their literal sense." Philo always considers the literal facts of the old

---

masses of material have been suitably pigeonholed and utilized by his judgment that some is favorable, some is unfavorable, and, in the balance, the overall effect is negative. What we learn from this judgment, how we may better understand the data he has assembled, and the means by which we may interpret in a richer and fuller way than before the larger constructions out of which the data are drawn are questions he does not answer. He cannot." *A History of the Mishnaic Law of Women* (Leiden: E.J.Brill, 1980), vol.5, pp.246f. Similarly, Rosemary Radford Ruether, while giving an excellent summary of Baer's contribution to the subject, settles for the term "negative" for Philo's picture of womanhood: "Although the negative use of the female as symbol of the carnal is primary, Philo does have a secondary use of the feminine, as the passive receptivity of the soul to divine power. Here the matriarchs symbolize the spiritual or virginal feminine, but only when they have quit sexual relations and procreation and become chaste." *Sexism and God-Talk* (Boston: Beacon Hill Press, 1983), p. 146.

[2] *LA* 2.19.

stories to be much less significant than the allegorical meaning.³ Historicity is something outside his concern. Therefore the literal sense of stories, whether myth or hard fact, matters little; the stories are only vehicles for truth, and not the truth itself. Philo makes the point even more clearly in another reference to the Eden story:

> Told in this way, these things are like prodigies and marvels, one serpent emitting a human voice and using quibbling arguments to an utterly guileless character, and cheating a woman with seductive plausibilities . . . . But when we interpret words by the meanings that lie beneath the surface, all that is mythical is removed out of our way, and the real sense becomes as clear as daylight.⁴

Generally, he makes the distinction that the myths of the Bible differ from those of Greek literature because the former have an underlying meaning, and therefore should not be called *simply* mythical.⁵ This distinction--which underlies his thought without always being made

---

³ "Having adopted the didactic value of Scripture as primary, Philo makes the issue of whether an 'event' in the Bible actually happened, as recorded, secondary." Mendelson, *Education*, p.63.

⁴ *Agr.*97. Philo is no more consistent in his use of terms like myth than we are. He condemns the "mythical fictions of the impious" that attribute bodily functions to God (*Deus* 59). He also condemns the religious rites of the Midianites, by calling them *mythikas* (*Spec.*1.56). He denies that Moses made up "myths" or accepted them from others, and declares that his own teachings are not "myths" of his invention (for Moses, see *Op.*2; for himself, see *Abr.*243, *Som.*1.172, *Mut.*152). Yet he sees the truth of one of the old Greek myths, calling it by that name: "So runs the myth of the men of old. We take the same line . . ."(*Plant.*120).

⁵ For example, in *Conf.*1-14 he raises the objection that the Tower of Babel story is a myth comparable to the myths in Greek culture. But then, rather than refute the charge, he goes on instead to give a deeper meaning: "But we shall take the line of allegorical interpretation."
Philo must have been aware of the practice of treating Homer allegorically, which was begun as early as the sixth century and flourished among the Stoics in Hellenistic times. (See R. M. Grant, *Letter*, pp.1-9.) But he would have considered the truths thus revealed as "human," whereas those derived from Scripture were "divine."
See also Christoph Riedweg, *Mysterienterminologie bei Platon, Philon und Klemens von Alexandrien* (Berlin and New York: de Gruyter, 1987), p.86, n.56.

explicit--leads him to make statements that appear to be contradictory. At one point the Eden story is a myth and at another it certainly is not:

> Now these are no mythical fictions, such as poets and sophists delight in, but modes of making ideas visible, bidding us resort to allegorical interpretation guided in our renderings by what lies beneath the surface (*Op.*157).

Philo's objection is thus a matter of semantics. He would not have Scripture dismissed as "mere" myth. But neither does he consider Adam and Eve historical characters. They are--to render the quotation literally--"types directing us to allegorical interpretation" (*deigmata typōn ep'allegorian parakalounta*) (*Op.*157).

In the matter of interpretation, Philo takes virtually the same approach to the Eden myth as to the later Biblical stories. For example, he dismisses the literal meaning of the story of Hagar and Sarah by saying, ". . . do not suppose that you have here one of the usual accompaniments of women's jealousy. It is not women that are spoken of here . . ." (*Cong.*180).[6] Since Philo's concern is with allegorical meaning and not with distinctions between myth and history, it follows that Eve should not be considered qualitatively different from the other female figures of the Bible solely on the grounds that she is a mythical character.

If, then, Adam and Eve are to be taken no less seriously than the other Biblical figures, what are the "types" they represent? Philo's conscious effort is to transform the main characters of the story, viz., Adam, Eve and the snake, into interacting aspects of the individual. He continues the passage from *Agr.*97 (quoted above) by

---

[6] And in *Conf.*190, reflecting on his interpretation of the story of the Tower of Babel, he says: "This is our explanation, but those who merely follow the outward and obvious think that we have at this point a reference to the origin of the Greek and barbarian languages. I would not censure such persons, for perhaps the truth is with them also. Still I would exhort them not to halt there, but to press on to allegorical interpretations and to recognize that the letter is to the oracle but as the shadow to the substance and that the higher values therein revealed are what really and truly exist."

saying, "Following a probable conjecture one would say that the serpent spoken of is a fit symbol of pleasure . . . . " Pleasure, the serpent, deceives the senses, Eve, and they, in turn, entice the mind, Adam. Thus the drama of Eden is worked out within each individual "man." Primarily, all Philo's allegorical interpretation of the story is a development of that pattern.

But interwoven with it is another set of types. Adam is the prototype of man as husband, Eve the prototype of woman as wife, and the snake ever-present lust which threatens to throw the relationship out of kilter, by causing the husband to listen to his wife's advice.[7]

These two sets of types--one within the individual and the other in the social unit--are analogous to one another. In true Platonic style, Philo envisions a proper order of being within every composite unit, whether it be the universe, the nation, the family or the individual. The order follows the principle of *dikaiosynē*, justice, whereby the strong rules and the weak follows.[8] Just as sense-perception and mind in the individual have their own proper functions based on fixed characteristics, so do woman and man in an inter-personal relationship. The Garden of Eden story provides both sets of *typoi*.

---

[7] Philo considers a man's listening to his wife to be symptomatic of a state of imbalance. In *LA* 3.222-245 he explains at some length that that is what is really meant by Gen.3:17: "Because thou hast listened to the voice of thy wife, and hast eaten of the tree, of which I commanded thee not to eat, cursed is the ground in respect of thy labours." The correct pattern is that the wife should heed the husband. Adam upsets the pattern by listening to Eve. (There is an exception, however. Sarah, a "different woman" [i.e. a virgin] deserves the obedience of her husband.) In society in general, as well as in the marriage relationship, men should rule women. In *Virt*.38, the seduction of the Israelites by the Midianite women is described as a defeat of men by women--a perversion of the natural order, which brought disastrous results.

[8] Philo spells out this principle in *LA* 1.70-72. Using a tripartite division of the individual--into mind, high spirit and passion--he says that justice occurs "When the three parts of the soul are in harmony . . . for it is justice for the better to rule always and everywhere, and for the worse to be ruled; and the reasoning faculty is better, the lustful and the high-spirited the inferior." Cf. *Abr*.74, *Virt*.13, *Som*.2.153f., *LA* 3.84, *Agr*.73.

Occasionally the distinction between the two sets becomes blurred. This is particularly apparent when we find Eve, the person, presented as weak-minded. If Philo were extending his understanding of the composite individual to woman, then Eve, like Adam, would consist of sense-perception ruled by mind. But Philo speaks as though in the woman Eve the mind is no longer in charge:

> It is said that she (Eve), without looking into the suggestion, *prompted by a mind devoid of steadfastness and firm foundation*, gave her consent and ate of the fruit, and gave some of it to her husband . . .(*Op.*156, emphasis mine).

> Included then in the call of Adam, the mind, is that of sense-perception, the woman; but God does not call her with a special call; why? because, *being irrational*, she has no capacity derived from herself to receive reproof (*LA* 3.50, emphasis mine).

His generalizations about the character of women, made in the course of his commentary on the story of Eve, give further indication that Philo does not extend his understanding of the individual to women.[9] Rather, because he associates the weaker qualities with sense-perception and has arbitrarily designated them female, he speaks as though these predominate in each individual woman. Regarding the creation of Eve from Adam's side, he says,

> Inasmuch as the moulding of the male is more perfect than, and double, that of the female, it requires only half the time, namely forty days; whereas *the imperfect woman, who is, so*

---

[9] In *Heres* 138f. and *Agr.*139, where he is speaking of the *logos tomeus* making equal divisions in the creation, Philo equates woman with man as a rational creature. These passages are, in this regard, different in tone from the rest of Philo's writing.

*to speak, a half-section of man,* requires twice as many days, namely eighty.(*QG* 1.25, emphasis mine).[10]

Other indications of his transference of the qualities of sense-perception to all women follow:

> . . . woman is not equal in honour with man (*QG* 1.27).

> . . . woman is more accustomed to be deceived than man . . . . . the judgment of woman is more feminine, and because of softness she easily gives way and is taken in by plausible falsehoods which resemble the truth (*QG* 1.33).

> For the judgements of women (*tōn gynaikōn*) as a rule are weaker and do not apprehend any mental conception (*noēton*) apart from what their senses perceive (*Legat*.319).

> It was the more imperfect and ignoble element, the female, that made a beginning of transgression and lawlessness, while the male made a beginning of reverence and modesty and all good, since he was better and more perfect (*QG* 1.43).

> . . . woman is of a nature to be deceived rather than to reflect greatly, but man is the opposite here (*QG* 1.46).

> For just as the man (*ho anēr*) shows himself in activity and the woman (*hē gynē*) in passivity, so the province of the mind is activity, and that of the perceptive sense passivity, as in woman (*gynaikos tropon, LA* 2.38).

---

[10] The thought that the female embryo takes twice as long as the male to be formed appears in the Mishnah. " . . . a male is fully fashioned after 41 days, but a female only after 81 days" (*Niddah* 3.7).

It was also believed by Aristotle: " . . . within the mother the female takes longer in developing . . ." (*Generation of Animals*, 775a, 11f., in *CWA*, vol.1, p.1199).

This belief may have been related to another ancient one, that a male baby is felt moving in the womb much sooner than a female. Pliny the Elder said in his *Natural History*, "If the child is a male, the mother has a better colour and an easier delivery. There is a movement in the womb on the fortieth day. In the case of the other sex . . . the first movement is on the nineteenth day" (quoted in translation in Lefkowitz and Fant, *Women's Lives*, p.218).

Philo arrives at this understanding of the nature of woman in a manner that is less than logical, in that it is based on unquestioned presuppositions. He accepts as "knowledge" ideas about the passivity, softness, and imperfection of women that had been in circulation since the time of Aristotle, as the following passages show:

> In all genera in which the distinction of male and female is found, nature makes a similar differentiation in the characteristics of the two sexes. This differentiation is the most obvious in the case of human kind . . . . For the female is softer in character . . . woman is more compassionate than man, more easily moved to tears, at the same time is more jealous, more querulous, more apt to scold and strike. She is, furthermore, more prone to despondency and less hopeful than the man, more void of shame, more false of speech, more deceptive . . . . [11]
>
> But the female, as female, is passive, and the male, as male, is active, and the principle of movement comes from him.[12]
>
> . . . females are weaker and colder in nature, and we must look upon the female character as being a sort of natural deficiency.[13]

The "foundation" texts of Philo's anthropology, according to Baer, are Gen.1:27 and 2:7.[14] After a detailed study, Baer concludes that man lives, as it were, in two realms.[15] In the higher realm man,

---

[11] *History of Animals* 608a, 19 - 608b, 12, in *CWA*, vol.1, 948f.

[12] *Generation of Animals* 729b,12-14, in *CWA*, vol.1, p.1132.

[13] *Generation of Animals*, 775a, 14f., in *CWA*, vol.1, p.1199.

[14] Baer, *Categories*, p.22.

[15] Baer does not use inclusive language, and appears unaware of the issue and its ramifications. I use "man" here in the same undiscriminating way that he does.

like God, is asexual.¹⁶ Two of the three terms that Philo would apply to the state of being in this realm, however, have connotations that are sexual (in spite of being used here to denote asexuality): becoming male and becoming virgin.¹⁷ The obvious implication is that for Philo the only truly, inescapably sexual person is *gynē*. Baer does not go so far as to draw this conclusion. He does concede that Philo speaks disparagingly of women, but he does not venture far beyond the philosophical categories into their implications for life. I have set that task for myself; I believe Philo's commentaries on the story of Eve reveal much new material about his anthropology.

The Biblical sources, which Philo takes from the Septuagint, are the story of the creation of Eve in Gen.2:18-25, and the story of the temptation and the expulsion from Eden in Gen.3:1-21. An overall treatment occurs in *Op*.151-179; more detailed commentary on the same material is found in *Legum Allegoriae*, with the creation of Eve in Book 2 and the eating of the fruit in Book 3. A third treatment occurs in *QG* 1.23-53. (In this third commentary, Philo usually prefaces the allegorical material with remarks on the literal story; this gives rise to some of his most damning statements about women.) Apart from these three major blocks, there are brief references and allusions to Eve in several other treatises.¹⁸

The basic premise of Philo's allegory is that man symbolizes mind and woman sense-perception. The fact that he presents this as self-evident raises the possibility that he took it over from some fund of "knowledge." Indeed that is the burden of *Spec*.3.178, where Philo claims to have received his teaching from oracular men (*thespesiōn andrōn*) who

> think that most of the contents of the law-book are outward symbols of hidden truths, expressing in words what has been

---

¹⁶ Baer, *Categories*, chapter 2.

¹⁷ Baer, *Categories*, chapter 3.

¹⁸ *Cher*.40, 43, 53f., 57-65; *Post*.33, 124-126, 170; *Agr*.95-99, 107f.; *Cong*.171; *Gig*.65; *Heres* 52f., 164; *Op*.76; *Sac*.1; *Virt*.199.

left unsaid. This explanation was as follows. There is in the soul a male and female element just as there is in families, the male corresponding to the men, the female to the women . . . (cf. *Abr.*99).[19]

This, in turn, may have been a development of Aristotle's belief that "while the body is from the female, it is the soul that is from the male."[20] John Dillon speculates that it is "a distinctly Pythagoreanizing piece of imagery."[21] Whatever the source, we should not be surprised that Philo did adopt it, given our knowledge of the traditions on which he drew. Anthropologists have observed that the relating of woman to body and nature, and of man to mind and culture, and the concomitant belief in male superiority, have been

---

[19] E. R. Goodenough, in *By Light, Light* (New Haven: Yale University Press, 1935), p.242, says, " . . . the allegories of the events in the lives of the Patriarchs, far from being sporadic as they appear on first reading, are always true to a definite plan from which Philo rarely, if ever, deviates. That plan seems not at all the creation of Philo, but a settled tradition of interpretation which Philo is freely drawing upon, but not inventing."

More recently, Burton Mack writes, "Taken together the evidence is overwhelming that Philo was consciously in an interpretative enterprise in which large numbers of Jewish exegetes were, and had been at work, and which appears to have been the occasion for lively debate and serious position-taking" ("Philo Judaeus and Exegetical Traditions in Alexandria," 227-271, *Aufstieg und Niedergang der Römischen Welt* II 21.1, Berlin and New York: de Gruyter, 1984, p.243).

Cf. Wilfred Knox, *Some Hellenistic Elements in Primitive Christianity* (London: Oxford University Press, 1944), p.34.

[20] *Generation of Animals*, 738b, 25f., *CWA*, vol.1, p.1146.

[21] *The Middle Platonists*, p.175. Dillon bases his suggestion on "an interesting parallel" in the undatable work of 'Callicratidas', *On Happiness in the Home*, preserved in Stobaeus. "Here the *logismos* is compared to the master of the house, *epithymia* to the wife, and *thymos* to the young son, who obeys now one and now the other."

common to all cultures.²² Philo appears to be voicing a universal tendency.

More specifically, since he was a close scholar of Plato, he may have recognized a literary justification for the distinction in a section of the *Timaeus*:

> And within the chest . . . they fastened the mortal kind of soul. And inasmuch as one part thereof is better, and one worse, they built a division within the cavity of the thorax-- as if to fence off two separate chambers, for men and for women--by placing the midriff between them as a screen. That part of the soul, then, which partakes of courage and spirit, since it is a lover of victory, they planted more near to the head, between the midriff and the neck, in order that it might hearken to the reason, and, *in conjunction therewith*, might forcibly subdue the tribe of the desires . . . .²³

The adaptation is not perfect, since here Plato is using a tripartite division of the individual into mind, upper soul and lower soul, a division Philo adopts frequently, but not in his basic allegory.²⁴ It should be noted, however, that Plato aligns the upper soul with the mind (as indicated by the words "in conjunction therewith"); thus Philo could, quite conceivably, reconcile Plato's description to his own more customary bipartite division of the soul.

Philo's dependence upon the *Timaeus* on this point is shown by the close resemblance of *QG* 4.15:

---

[22] Sherry B. Ortner, "Is Female to Male as Nature is to Culture?" in *Woman, Culture and Society*, ed. Michelle Zimbalist Rosaldo and Louise Lamphere (Stanford: Stanford University Press, 1974), pp.67-87, says that women are universally seen as related to nature and men to culture. E. E. Evans-Pritchard, *The Position of Women in Primitive Societies and Other Essays in Social Anthropology* (New York: 1965), p.54f., notes that in all societies "men are always in the ascendancy."

[23] 69E-70A, taken from the Loeb edition, translated by R. G. Bury (emphasis mine).

[24] D. T. Runia, in *Philo of Alexandria and the Timaeus of Plato*, (Leiden: E.J.Brill, 1986), p.309, makes note of the discrepancy.

> The soul has, as it were, a dwelling, partly men's quarters, partly women's quarters. Now for the men there is a place where properly dwell the masculine thoughts (that are) wise, sound, just, prudent, pious, filled with freedom and boldness, and akin to wisdom. And the women's quarters are a place where womanly opinions go about and dwell, being followers of the female sex. And the female sex is irrational and akin to bestial passions, fear, sorrow, pleasure, and desire, from which ensue incurable weaknesses and indescribable diseases.

The first part of this quotation we recognize as Platonic. The detailed description of the female which ensues has no apparent source in the section of the *Timaeus* quoted above; but it does resemble material found in the passages which follow. The lower soul is called, in 70d, "that part of the Soul which is subject to appetites for foods and drinks, and all other wants that are due to the nature of the body . . . ," and in 77b Plato says,

> seated . . . between the midriff and the navel . . . [it] shares not at all in opinion and reasoning and mind but in sensation, pleasant and painful, together with desires . . . it continues wholly passive . . . it is not endowed by its original constitution with a natural capacity for discerning or reflecting upon any of its own experiences.

This is only one instance of Philo's paraphrasing his source.[25] It gives us one other possible justification for his *a priori* statement that male represents mind and that female represents sense, body and passion. Whatever the source may be--philosophical precedent, Alexandrian exegetical practice, or observation of the working of society--

---

[25] Other instances are: a) his adaptation of the story of the temptation of Hercules from Xenophon, in *Sac*.21-45, b) his secret teaching of the meaning of the mystery, in *Cher*.42-48, which has remarkable similarities to Diotima's teaching about the marriage of the soul, in Plato's *Symposium*, c) his deliberate contrasting of the banquet of the Therapeutae with those described by Xenophon and Plato, in *Cont*.57-63.

in his hands the analogy proliferates until his work fairly redounds with sexual distinctions.[26]

Philo sees a basic irony in the story of Eve, based on the derivation of her name from the Hebrew word for "life," and its translation in the Septuagint (Gen.3:20) into *Zōē*: "The man called his wife's name Zoe, because she was the mother of all living." Although her name was "life," she was actually his death.

> . . . Sense, on whose just-fashioned form the earthly mind, called Adam, looked and gave the name of what was his own death to her life.[27]

This play on words with respect to Eve may have been commonplace in Philo's milieu, for the *Life of Adam and Eve*, believed to have come from an Alexandrian Jewish writer early in the Christian Era, also attributes death to Eve.[28] A second passage where Philo links Eve to death is *QG* 1.37: ". . . it was fitting that man should rule over immortality and everything good, but woman over death and everything vile."

These two attributions of death to Eve may have been generated more by the opportunity for a play on words than by Philo's actual thought on the matter. Usually he portrays her in a much more passive position. Eve, sense-perception, is intended to be a helper to Adam, mind, but if he does not exercise sufficient control over her, she will be influenced by his enemy, the passion pleasure, into causing harm to the two of them. The onus is on Adam, for

---

[26] It is interesting that Plotinus, the later interpreter of Plato, apparently saw no such sexual distinctions in the master. There is no indication of them in his work. See ch.3, n.9, above.

[27] *Heres* 52. For Philo's own words on the death of the soul see *LA* 1.105-108.

[28] This work is mentioned in the survey of Alexandrian Jewish literature in chapter two, above. See also n.10, ch.2, where I note that this thought first appears in Ben Sira. This is "the oldest tradition ascribing the first sin and its consequences mainly or exclusively to Eve" (Bruce J. Malina, "Some Observations on the Origin of Sin in Judaism and St. Paul," 18-34 *Catholic Biblical Quarterly* 31, p.24).

Eve is incapable of sound judgment. Adam errs, first in being overly attracted to her, and second in heeding her words. The following paragraphs will show Philo's position in detail.

Philo believed that sense-perception was necessary for the proper functioning of mind. Without it "the Mind was docked of all its powers of sense-perception, thus truly powerless. It was but half the perfect soul . . . a mere unhappy section bereft of its mate. . . ."[29] He transferred this thought to the domestic scene by expressing the necessity for a man to have a woman in his life:

> . . . everything which is without a woman is imperfect and homeless. For to man are entrusted the public affairs of the state; while to a woman the affairs of home are proper. The lack of her is ruin, but her being near at hand constitutes household management (*QG* 1.26).

Though necessary, woman also presents danger, because she is the means whereby evil reaches man. In the events leading up to the expulsion from Eden, Eve acts as she does as a result of her intrinsic nature, and because Adam does not restrain her. At times Philo's words indicate that the evil which accrues to her comes from without; it is somehow indirect:

> . . . sense-perception comes under the head neither of bad nor of good things, but is an intermediate thing common to a wise man and a fool . . . . Reasonably then, since it has no evil nature on its own account, but halts between good and evil, inclining to either side, it is not pronounced guilty till it has owned that it followed evil (*LA* 3.67).

Yet the evil is there. Philo speaks of Eve as the pimp who procures partners for the harlot, pleasure (*Op.*165). She is "the beginning of evil" who led Adam "into a life of vileness," and she "becomes for him the beginning of blameworthy life" (*QG* 1.45; *Op.*151).

---

[29] *Cher.*59; cf.62; *LA* 2.7f.; *Mig.*104f.

The crux of the problem in the Eden story is that the proper order of things is disturbed. Behind Philo's thinking lies the venerable and persistent tradition of the Great Chain of Being. According to that theory:

> Everything except God has some natural superior; everything except unformed matter has some natural inferior. The goodness, happiness, and dignity of every being consists in obeying its natural superior and ruling its natural inferiors.[30]

The theory is traced by Arthur Lovejoy to a fusion of ideas from Plato and Aristotle.[31] In Philo we find a Middle Platonic version, significant (for the present study) in its placing woman one link lower on the chain than man.[32]

Philo expresses this principle by the term "justice". It means that all the elements in the story--God, man, woman, pleasure--have

---

[30] C. S. Lewis, *A Preface to Paradise Lost* (New York: Oxford University Press, 1970--first published 1942), p.75.

[31] *The Great Chain of Being* (Cambridge, Mass.: Harvard University Press, 1936).

[32] Plotinus, living in the third century, presents a NeoPlatonic version of the Chain: "So it goes on from the beginning to the last and lowest, each [generator] remaining behind in its own place, and that which is generated taking another, lower, rank; . . . when it comes to a man (*anthrōpon*), either the movement is wholly in the soul's reasoning part or it comes from Intellect, since the soul has an intellect of its own and a self-originated will to think, or in general to be in motion . . . . It is then like a long life stretched out at length; each part is different from that which comes next in order, but the whole is continuous with itself, but with one part differentiated from another, and the earlier does not perish in the later" (5.2.2).
It is noteworthy that in Plotinus' scheme men and women are ranked together, whereas for Philo man is superior. Since this is evident only from Plotinus' silence about sex differences, I cannot supply a quotation to illustrate it. But the following quotation from Porphyry's *Vita* sheds light on the matter: "There were women, too, who were greatly devoted to him: Gemina, in whose house he lived, and her daughter Gemina, who had the same name as her mother, and Amphiclea, who became the wife of Ariston son of Iamblichus, all of whom had a great devotion to philosophy" (9). The quotations are from Armstrong's translation in the Loeb Classical Library.

their proper places. Philo states the principle in terms of sense-perception and mind as follows:

> Most profitless is it that Mind should listen to Sense-perception, and not Sense-perception to Mind: for it is always right that the superior should rule and the inferior be ruled; and Mind is superior to Sense-perception (*LA* 3.222).

The principle can be extended to include God on the one end and pleasure on the other. God has the most important role, and Mind must acknowledge that leadership. Pleasure is of very slight importance--it "contributes to the permanence of our kind" (*LA* 2.7).

> A created being cannot but make use of pleasure. But the worthless man (*ho phaulos*) will use it as a perfect good, but the man of worth (*ho spoudaios*) regards it as just necessary and serviceable and no more (*LA* 2.17).

Adam's error is that his life loses balance, and he affords to passion, through sense-perception, the honour he owes to God: "he prefers the love of his passions to the love of God" (*LA* 2.51).

Philo thinks the Bible alludes to this loss of balance in Gen.2:24 (as in 3:17), which he interprets as a description of man's fallen state: "For this cause shall a man leave his father and his mother, and shall cleave unto his wife, and the twain shall be one flesh." Herein lies Adam's wrongdoing.

> For the sake of sense-perception the Mind, when it has become her slave, abandons both God the Father of the universe, and God's excellence and wisdom, the Mother of all things, and cleaves to and becomes one with sense-perception and is resolved into sense-perception so that the two become one flesh and one experience . . . . But if Sense the inferior follow Mind the superior, there will be flesh no more, but both of them will be Mind (*LA* 2.49f.).

This pattern of behavior is one that Adam has set for mankind (though Philo's further teaching shows that he did not consider it inevitable, or permanent). It is a distortion of God's intention for man:

> Reason is forthwith ensnared and becomes a subject instead of a ruler, a slave instead of a master, an alien instead of a citizen, and a mortal instead of an immortal (*Op*.165).

In the field of personal relations, Philo draws from Adam's inability to control Eve a lesson for marriage: ". . . he wishes that man should take care of woman as of a very necessary part of him; but woman, in return, should serve him as a whole" (*QG* 1.27). ". . . woman, taking the rank of servant, is shown to be obedient to his life" (*QG* 1.29).

Philo sees significance in the fact that, according to Scripture, Eve was created later than Adam. Some of his comments may reflect the general situation in ancient society, in which the wife was commonly younger than the husband, and thus fell naturally into the role of daughter, rather than partner. Philo says that woman is not equal to man in honour, and also that she is not equal in age but younger, that man should care for woman as a daughter, and that woman should honour man as a father.[33] We noted earlier, on evidence from Samuel Sandmel, that it was customary for girls to marry at puberty or shortly thereafter; for men, on the other hand, Philo recommends the age of forty (though this is far later than the

---

[33] For the youthful age of a bride in the ancient world generally, see the reference to the fourteen-year-old bride in Xenophon (ch.2, above).
   The Philonic reference is to *QG* 1.27. Philo's picture of the Jewish wife resembles woman according to the letter of the Roman law, but certainly not according to the Roman practice of his day: " . . . in the early days of Rome . . . the wife passed out of the authority of her father and owed all but inescapable submission to her husband . . . . Well before the end of the Republic women rebelled against such servitude and, though the original forms of marriage were still recognized in law, they were rare in practice. The 'free marriage' had taken their place" (Balsdon, *Roman Women*, p.179).

average age of eighteen given by Sandmel).[34] In any case, the age difference would account in part for the expectation that the husband would control his wife as a father would his daughter.

According to Philo the whole problem presented by sexual desire does not affect man until woman is created. Then she gives rise to it, unwittingly, and simply by virtue of being woman. Philo sees sexual control as a man's responsibility.[35] Woman's lust, as we have seen, is a feature of her womanhood, which not she, but the men in her life, her father and her husband, must control by controlling her. But man must control his own lust. Adam does not succeed in doing so. A Jewish man, however, need not remain at the Adam stage. He can move on to become a Noah, an Enoch or a Jacob, and possibly even an Abraham.[36] Philo does not appear to offer to women any similar solution to the problem created by their own sexuality. He does not credit, or burden, them with sexual accountability.

In the Biblical story the expulsion is occasioned by the eating of the forbidden fruit. Philo gives the story a second ending: Adam is bitten by the serpent. Eve does not participate in this, except by virtue of lending her name to the creature; Philo calls it

---

[34] I refer to Sandmel's discussion of the subject of marriage age in n.17, ch.5. For the specific ages of 18 and 40 see Sandmel, *Beginnings*, p.193 and *QG* 4.154.

Raphael Loewe, in a tendentious study commissioned for the Church of England, comments, "A number of seeming disabilities of women fall into place when it is appreciated that the law could not presuppose much maturity in the average housewife." *The Position of Women in Judaism* (London, 1966), p.23. He believes that in the centuries around the turn of the era Jewish women married at age 12 and men around 20.

[35] Judaism, he believes, provides a man with the means to deal with the problem. His circumcision is an ever-present symbol of "the excision of excessive and superfluous pleasure, not only of one pleasure but of all the other pleasures signified by one [i.e. sex], and that the most imperious" (*Spec*.1.9).

[36] Mendelson, *Education*, outlines the directions and distances a soul can move, in chapter 4, "Paths to the Heights."

"Eve's serpent."[37] There is little doubt that in both cases Philo sees the "fall" as sexual. The serpent represents pleasure, and the most intense pleasure Philo knows is that experienced by a man in intercourse.[38] In *Op*.152 he states explicitly that sexual desire is the cause: when Adam and Eve see one another, *eros* intervenes, sets up desire, and begets "bodily pleasure, that pleasure for the sake of which men bring on themselves the life of mortality and wretchedness in lieu of that of immortality and bliss." Several other passages imply that it was sexual desire that caused Adam's sin.[39] In the *Timaeus*, which he knew well, Philo may have thought that he recognized a direct reference to the forbidden fruit of Genesis in the statements that "a man's seed grows to abundant volume in his marrow, as it were a tree that is laden beyond measure with fruit," and intercourse is "culling as it were the fruit from trees."[40] There is no doubt then that uncontrolled womanhood is the occasion for the first sin of man.

*Conclusion*

In this chapter I have begun the study of the women of Scripture by discussing the considerable amount of material Philo has written about Eve. I found that she is seen in two ways: as the lower, sense-centred part of Everyman, and as the person Everywoman. In both roles, Eve is the archetypal female.

---

[37] References to "Eve's serpent" occur in *LA* 2.79ff. and *Agr*.95ff. It is contrasted with Moses' serpent, which brings salvation, and Dan, who becomes a serpent destroying the enemy. Eve's serpent brings death.

[38] See the Greek text of *LA* 2.74: "*ginontai de hai sphodrotatai kai suntonoi* (or *suntonōtatai*) *peri tas gynaikas homiliai.*" The Loeb translation blurs the fact that Philo means the pleasure of the male. See also n.35, above.

[39] Baer lists them in *Categories*, n.1, p.38.

[40] 865C and 91C.

As the lower element in Everyman, Eve is sexual passion which causes destruction, even death, if uncontrolled. She is irrationality, which must be overruled by masculine reason. But she is also sense-perception, which, when it functions properly, is essential to the well-being of mind.

As Everywoman, Eve is incapable of self-control. Her inner imbalance, i.e. the predominance of sense over mind, renders her destructive of herself and others. Her place in society is in subordination to her husband. Her function is to contribute to his welfare.

# CHAPTER SEVEN

# BIBLICAL WOMEN (II): THE OTHERS

Chapter six was an introduction to Philo's treatment of Biblical women and a detailed examination of his portrayal of Eve. In this chapter I shall continue that work by studying Philo's presentation of other female figures of Scripture who are not transformed into virgins. I shall arrange them topically.

### Woman as Seductress

Philo retells two Biblical stories in such a way as to present women as Sirens who threaten the integrity of the pious Jew, indeed of society itself.[1] The women are two-dimensional characters who serve as foils for the admirable responses of men. Joseph is confronted by Potiphar's wife, and Phineas faces the seduction of his fellow Jews by the Midianite women. Each man makes the choice that is correct for him: for Joseph, it is flight; for Phineas, fight.

### Potiphar's Wife

There are five passages in which Philo recalls the encounter between Joseph and Potiphar's wife: *Jos.*37-80, *LA* 3.236-241,

---

[1] Although the seductive women are also foreign women, I do not believe their foreignness is the major factor in Philo's mind. It should be noted that Philo is not categorically opposed to foreign women. See his comments about Tamar, Bilhah and Zilpah in *Virt.*220-225. Note also that Philo passes up any opportunity to comment negatively on the foreignness of Moses' wife; in fact, in *LA* 2.66f., he says Moses "deserved praise" for his marriage.

*Mig*.19f., *Som*.2.106, and *Conf*.95. The first is a lengthy retelling of the narrative and the second a discussion of its allegorical meaning. The final three are shorter references.

Although Philo does not always praise Joseph, he consistently does so with respect to this incident. Joseph is self-control (*LA* 3.237). Potiphar's wife epitomizes Egypt, which Philo consistently interprets as the body and passion.[2] Confronting the innocent youth, Joseph, she is "wicked sense" (*LA* 3.243). Philo expresses her destructiveness also by using the imagery of fire. She exemplifies the women who "kindled a fire" against Moab--in this case the consuming, destructive fire of passion (*LA* 3.225). The fire imagery is repeated in *Jos*.41, where she is said to have "fed the fire of lawless lust till it burst into a blaze." Philo also calls Potiphar's wife pleasure, bodily pleasure, lust, desire, unrestrained passion, and a lovesick liar.[3] From such formidable danger, young Joseph does well to run away. Potiphar's wife represents raw, uncontrolled, dangerous womanhood.

## The Midianite Women

The Midianite women of Numbers 25 play major roles in one of Philo's favorite stories, that of Phineas. Philo retells the story three times, and refers to it on several other occasions.[4] Like Potiphar's wife, the Midianite women represent womanhood as sexual danger:

> Joseph, however, being but a youth and lacking strength to contend with the Egyptian body and vanquish pleasure, runs away. But Phinehas the priest, who was zealous with the zeal

---

[2] See the index entry in *PLCL*, vol.X, p.303. She is explicitly named "the Egyptian body" in *LA* 3.241.

[3] *LA* 3.237, 239, *Mig*.19, *Som*.2.106, *Jos*.49, 66, 40, 80.

[4] *Mos*.1.106ff.; *Virt*.34ff.; *Spec*.1.55ff.; *LA* 3.242; *Conf*.55ff.; *Ebr*.73ff.

## Biblical Women (II): The Others

for God, has secured his own safety, not by flight, but by grasping the "spear," i.e. the spirit of zeal, he will not desist before he has "pierced the Midianitish woman," the nature that has been sifted out of the sacred company, "through the womb" (Numb.xxv. 7f.), that she may never be able to cause plant or seed of wickedness to shoot up (*LA* 3.242).

Philo's implication here, that the Midianite women are the seed-bed of wickedness, parallels his calling Potiphar's wife "wicked sense."

"Sifted out of the sacred company" (*tēn ekkekrimenēn theiou chorou*) is, however, an expression we did not meet earlier, and one that raises an interesting issue. It could as accurately be translated "expelled from the sacred chorus," and it makes a double allusion. In the *Phaedrus* 246-7 the makeup of the soul is explained by the image of the winged two-horse chariot. The gods, in their divine chariots drawn by noble steeds, form the celestial chorus that moves harmoniously through the heavens. The human mind drives a mixed team; it may rise or fall, depending on the degree to which it controls the two horses--high spirit and lust. It is possible for mind to join the gods: "He may follow who will and can, for jealousy has no place in the celestial choir (*phthonos exō theiou chorou histatai*)." We know that Philo is impressed by this passage, for he quotes the final clause once verbatim (*Prob*.13), and paraphrases it elsewhere as follows: "But wickedness has been exiled from the divine choir" (*LA* 1.61). In the following passage we find virtually an enlargement of the same idea, but the concluding expression, with its naming of persons barred from the temple, suggests that Philo has in mind the Jewish tradition as well as the Greek:

> In the bad man the true opinion concerning God is hidden in obscurity, for he is full of darkness with no divine radiance in him, whereby to investigate realities. *Such an one is in banishment from the divine company [choir], like the leper and the man with an issue* (*LA* 3.7, emphasis mine).

Couched amid such scriptural allusions, the reference to a choir in this passage must be to the choir led by Moses and Miriam:

> Then sang Moses and the children of Israel this song to God, and spoke, saying, Let us sing to the Lord, for he is very greatly glorified: horse and rider he has thrown into the sea . . . . And Mariam the prophetess, the sister of Aaron, having taken a timbrel in her hand--then there went forth all the women after her with timbrels and dances. And Mariam led them, saying, Let us sing to the Lord, for he has been very greatly glorified: the horse and rider has he cast into the sea (Ex.15:1-21, LXX).

There is a double allusion, then, in Philo's statement that the Midianite women have been expelled from the sacred chorus. According to the imagery of the *Phaedrus*, the horse that represents bodily sense has dragged their chariots down to earth. But according to the Biblical imagery, they have been evicted from Miriam's chorus.

In one of his full accounts of the story, that in volume one of his *Life of Moses*, Philo takes the single phrase "by the counsel of Balaam" in Num.31:16 and blows it into a vivid and lengthy account:[5]

> Knowing that the one way by which the Hebrews could be overthrown was disobedience, he set himself to lead them, through wantonness and licentiousness, to impiety, through a great sin to a still greater, and put before them the bait of pleasure. "You have in your countrywomen, king," he said, "persons of pre-eminent beauty. And there is nothing to which a man more easily falls a captive than woman's comeliness. If, then, you permit the fairest among them to prostitute themselves for hire, they will ensnare (or "hook" {*agkistreusontai*}) the younger of their enemies. But you must instruct them not to allow their wooers to enjoy their charms at once. For coyness titillates, and thereby makes the appetites more active, and inflames the passions. And, when their lust has them in its grip, there is nothing which they will shrink from doing or suffering. Then, when the lover is

---

[5] Josephus also enlarges upon the story, in *Antiquities of the Jews*, Bk. 4, Ch.6. It is likely that it was a very popular Biblical story of the period. New Testament allusions to the story occur in 2 Pet.2:15, Jude 11, and Rev.2:14.

Biblical Women (II): The Others                    115

in this condition, one of those who are arming to take their prey (*thēran*) should say, with a saucy air: 'You must not be permitted to enjoy my favours until you have left the ways of your fathers and become a convert to honouring what I honour. That your conversion is sincere will be clearly proved to me if you are willing to take part in the libations and sacrifices which we offer to idols of stone and wood and the other images.' Then the lover, caught in the meshes of her multiform lures (*sagēneutheis pagais polyeidesi*), her beauty and the enticements of her wheedling talk, will not gainsay her, but, with his reason trussed and pinioned (*exēgkōnismenos*), will subserve her orders to his sorrow, and be enrolled as a slave of passion" (*Mos*.1.295ff.).

In this passage, the Midianite women are active, rather than passive. This in itself is "unnatural," for, as we have already observed, Philo believes that woman is by nature passive. Sexually, the Midianite women are the aggressors. They use hunting tactics: they "ensnare" or "hook" their "prey" in " the meshes" of "multiform lures", "trussing" and "pinioning" them.[6] In other places, Philo suggests that they employ magic.[7] Like unsuspecting fish and fowl or victims of magic, the men are cast in roles of helpless passivity. Again, this state of affairs is a perversion of nature's intention. Clearly, the Midianite women conspire to overthrow the law of nature.

Just as clearly, Philo sees adultery (for that is what he calls their action in *Mos*.1.300) as the prime cause of idolatry, and the sexually aggressive woman as a powerful danger. He is, of course, remaining true to the Septuagint in linking adultery with idolatry:

> . . . the people profaned itself by going a-whoring after the daughters of Moab. And they called them to the sacrifices of

---

[6] Philo frequently uses *agkistreuō*--to catch with a barbed hook--for the actions of seductive females; e.g. Pleasure in *Op*.166 and *Sac*.21 (cf. *Agr*.24 and *Mut*.172).

[7] In *Mos*.1.311 Philo uses the word "bewitched", and in *Spec*.1.56 he accuses them of using "love charms."

their idols; and the people ate of their sacrifices, and worshipped their idols (Num.25:1, *LXX*).

But by his repeated references to the story, and specifically to Phineas' heroism, Philo shows that the link becomes a major motif in his thinking.

It is noteworthy that he treats the story literally as well as allegorically. Thus the Midianite women are not only *typoi* of the lower elements in an individual's soul, but also guides to apostasy. This is made evident by Philo's use of the story in *De Specialibus Legibus* 1, one of the treatises in his Exposition of the Law. Writing for his own community, Philo advocates that

> all who have a zeal for virtue should be permitted to exact the penalties [for apostasy] offhand and with no delay, without bringing the offender before jury or council or any kind of magistrate at all, and give full scope to the feelings which possess them, that hatred of evil and love of God which urges them to inflict punishment without mercy on the impious (*Spec*.1.55).

He proceeds then to retell the story of Phineas, characterizing the slain woman as an "instructor in wickedness." Phineas' action in spearing the one couple spurred on his fellows, who "massacred all their friends and kinsfolk who had taken part in the rites of these idols made by men's hands."[8] When the story is told, with greater detail, in *Mos*.1.305, Philo says that the women "caused the ruin of their paramours, of their bodies through lust, of their souls through impiety." In the third retelling, in *Virt*.34ff., the women are characterized as not having had a taste of sound education (*paideia*)--an

---

[8] The wording of the Septuagint is enigmatic regarding the nature of the plague: Num.25:7-9 reads that Phineas "took a javelin in his hands and went in after the Israelitish man into the chamber, and pierced them both through, both the Israelitish man, and the woman through her womb; and the plague was stayed from the children of Israel. And those that died in the plague were four and twenty thousand." See *PLCL*, vol.6, p.434 (n.) and p.603f.(n.) Philo interprets the plague as being the rash of sexual misdemeanours. *Mos*.1.303f. makes it clear that the 24,000 were killed by the sword.

obvious anachronism, but also clearly descriptive of certain women of Philo's day.⁹ Thus it is evident that Philo sees in the literal meaning of the story a lesson about the danger woman presents to man.

He also emphasizes its allegorical meaning. By his action, Phineas "put a stop to the revolt within himself and turned clean away from his own pleasure . . . ." Thus he "put an end to the intestine war of lusts in the soul" (*Post*.183; cf. *Ebr*.73-75).

Taken allegorically or literally, the Midianite women represent a danger which must be destroyed.¹⁰

*Women in Non-Seductive Roles*

In Philo's picture of Potiphar's wife and the Midianite women, their sexual attractiveness is emphasized. I turn now to women who are seen in non-seductive roles--Lot's wife, Moses' sister Miriam, and the two groups of unnamed Hebrew women.

Lot's Wife

In *Fug*.119-131 Lot's wife is named among those from whom the Joseph-type should flee. But she is not presented as a

---

⁹ *Paideia* designates a Greek ideal which can hardly be applied to an earlier and different culture. (When Philo uses it of Moses he explains that Greek teachers supplied it {*Mos*.1.23}.) Strictly speaking, Philo should not apply it to women of any culture. From the little that he says about the schooling of girls, we know that his ideal of *paideia* for women was not the same as for men. For example, he speaks of "education (*paideia*) as befits maidens," in *Spec*.2.125. See Mendelson, *Education*, p.28.

¹⁰ It is significant that the Midianite *men* could not defeat the Hebrews (*Mos*.1.263: "the power of the Hebrews was invincible in battle") but the *women* could. Thus Philo's account is not *merely* another story of the Hebrews overcoming a foreign threat. The female element is crucial to the story.

seductive woman, as are Potiphar's wife and the Midianite women. Her femaleness is simply a sign of inferiority.

Although she bears no name but his, Lot's wife is not treated by Philo as a component part of her husband, or the cause of his downfall.[11] She is not held responsible for his failures. Rather, she is treated as a *typos* in herself, representing a class of person. But here we encounter the same confusion that occurs with the portrayal of Eve. By virtue of being a woman, Lot's wife is one whose lower qualities overpower her higher ones. Literally, the salt, which in small quantities should give flavour and preservation, takes over her whole being and renders the land "unproductive and unfruitful" (*QG* 4.52). In her being, sense-perception "inclines toward sense-perceptible things" and "changes into an inanimate thing by separating itself from the mind, for the sake of which it was animated" (*QG* 4.52). She has the typically "feminine" characteristics of being enslaved to custom and hostile to truth.[12] Although the Biblical account implies that her fault lies in overt disobedience to God's command (Gen.19:17,26), Philo stresses the imbalance in her being which inevitably leads to her turning back. Elsewhere Philo attributes this type of imbalance to the prototypical woman Eve (*Op*.156, *LA* 3.50--quoted in chapter six).

Since sexual attractiveness does not play a part in the story of Lot's wife, she is represented not as dangerous to man, but as self-destructive. Furthermore, Philo draws from her story a lesson not for women, but for men.

> Those with no desire either to find or to seek grievously impair their faculty of reason, by refusing to train and exer-

---

[11] Lot stands on his own, and gets a mixed treatment: when he goes up into the cave with his two daughters, he is called the "progressive mind [which] becomes still purer" (*QG* 4.55), but he is also Mind that does not acknowledge God, and, consequently, the father of daughters and, through them, of accursed offspring (*QG* 4.55; *Post*.175f.; *Ebr*.164).

[12] *Ebr*.164: "she who was turned into stone, whom we might call 'custom,' if we gave her her right name . . . ."; cf. *Ebr*.74: ". . . custom the woman-like . . . ."

cise it, and though capable of being keen-sighted, become blind. This is the meaning when he says that "Lot's wife turned backwards and became a pillar" (Gen.xix 26) and here he is not inventing a fable but indicating precisely a real fact. For a man (*hos*) who is led by innate and habitual laziness to pay no attention to his teacher neglects what lies in front of him . . . and so he turns into a pillar and becomes like a deaf and lifeless stone . . . (*Fug*.121f.).

Lot's wife is the person who never completely eradicates the desire of pleasure, and is therefore a lost soul, denied repentance:

> For many souls have desired to repent and not been permitted by God to do so, but have gone away backward as though drawn by a change of current. This befell Lot's wife . . .(*LA* 3.213).

We have seen then that Lot's wife typifies both woman and unreasoning man.

Thirdly, she is a tendency within the individual. Just as the Joseph-soul wisely fled from Potiphar's wife, so should he flee from Lot's wife: they both represent "those empty notions which resemble the practices of women rather than men" (*Fug*.128). The difference is that in the case of Potiphar's wife the danger is sexual boldness, whereas with Lot's wife it is a stultified mind.

### Miriam

Of all the Scriptural women whom Philo names, Miriam is the most independent. She is associated only indirectly with a father, and not at all with a husband.

Miriam receives mixed treatment. In a total of seven references to her in Philo's works, three deal with her reprehensible behaviour in rebelling against Moses, and four with her sharing the leadership of the choirs with him. Words used about her range from *ho phaulos* (worthless) to *prophētis* (prophetess).[13]

Numbers 12 is the account of the objections of Miriam and Aaron to Moses' marrying an Ethiopian woman. The Lord's anger is kindled against them, but only Miriam is punished. She is stricken with leprosy.

Where we begin the following quotation, Philo has been deploring the foolish mind, the opposite of prudence, and by way of an illustration takes up the story of Miriam:

> Accordingly Aaron, the sacred word, begs of Moses, the beloved of God, to heal the change in Miriam, that her soul may not be in travail with evils; and so he says, "Let her not become as one dead, as an abortion coming forth from the womb of a mother; consuming half of her flesh" (*LA* 1.76).

Thus Miriam exemplifies the foolish mind (*ho aphrōn nous*). Her error lies in the fact that she speaks out against Moses. In *LA* 2.66f. the incident is used again to illustrate sense-perception's defiance of mind. Miriam, as sense-perception, exemplifies shamelessness.

> Even in the case of Miriam, when she spoke against Moses, it is said, "If her father had but spat in her face, should she not feel shame seven days?" (Num.12:14) For veritably shameless and bold was sense-perception in daring to decry and find fault with Moses for that for which he deserved praise.[14]

---

[13] Thus she is ranked in both the lowest and highest of Philo's three categories of people. See *Gig*.60-63 where some (at least) prophets are called "men of God." Ex.15:20 calls Miriam "prophetess."

[14] Num.12:14 is difficult to understand. Martin Noth interprets it as meaning that Miriam got off lightly with a punishment suitable for a girl's trivial offence against her father--even though she had turned against God's chosen one (*Numbers* {London: SCM Press, 1968}, p.97). Philo appears to interpret in that way. It is her shamelessness that he emphasizes. It is consistent with Philo's other statements about woman speaking boldly to man, or being heeded by man, that he presents Miriam as reprehensible for challenging Moses. Philo does not draw a similar lesson from the fact that Aaron too has criticized Moses' action.

I shall return to Miriam's shame in chapter eleven.

The incident is mentioned for the third time in *LA* 3.103, in a passing reference to "the occasion . . . of the rebellion of Aaron, Speech, and Miriam, Perception . . . ."

In all three references, Miriam's behaviour is reprehensible. As an individual, she is acting like a woman, in the sense of a person whose lower self rules the higher. On the interpersonal level, she is at fault for challenging Moses' authority.

The references to the choirs of Exodus 15 present Miriam in a different light. I have already mentioned Philo's allusion to this choir in his statement that the Midianite women had been expelled from the sacred chorus.[15] One of his fuller references to the story is in *Agr.*80f.:

> The choir of the men shall have Moses for its leader, that is Mind in its perfection, that of women shall be led by Miriam, that is sense-perception made pure and clean . . . . So we find the Song by the seashore sung by all that are men, with no blind understanding but with keenest vision, with Moses as their leader; it is sung also by the women *who in the true sense are the best, having been enrolled as members of Virtue's commonwealth*, with Miriam to start their song (emphasis mine).

The emendation of Scripture, so that only "the best" women may join the chorus, drew a comment from the translator, F. H. Colson:

> . . . there is also an allusion to the opening words, "Then sang Moses and *the sons of Israel*," which, as usual, he interprets as "those who see." The contrast, however, between "all the men" or "all that are men," and "*the best women*" is curious, for in Ex.xv.20 *all* the women sing the song. Perhaps Philo's memory of the passage misled him.[16]

---

[15] Above, in the discussion of the Midianite women.

[16] *PLCL*, vol.3, p.491.

In attributing the distinction among women to a memory loss, Colson has missed a point. Some women are unworthy; from the reference noted earlier, we can identify these as the Midianite women, or at least the types they represent. On the other hand, there must be some real women--not virgins--who are worthy. It appears then, that Philo sees three classes of female persons in the Bible, rather than the two I have presented up to now. "Women" are divided into two subsections: those who sing in the chorus of Miriam, and those who are expelled. Perhaps an examination of Philo's two other references to the choirs will illuminate the matter.

In these references Miriam and her women appear at first glance to be treated as though they are the equals of Moses and the men. It is the harmony of the two choirs that is emphasized:

> . . . they set up two choirs, one of men and one of women, on the beach, and sang hymns of thanksgiving to God. Over these choirs Moses and his sister presided, and led the hymns, the former for the men and the latter for the women (*Mos.*1.180).

> He divides the nation into two choirs, one of men, the other of women, and himself leads the men while he appoints his sister to lead the women, that the two in concert might sing hymns to the Father and Creator in tuneful response, with a blending both of temperaments and melody . . .(*Mos.*2.256).

This is the idyllic picture of the male and female working in harmony as they are intended. But note the subtle distinction in rank between Moses and Miriam in the second quotation. The ruling role of the male element is present but almost imperceptible. Moses "appoints" Miriam.

In the light of these passages I suggest the hypothesis that there is a group of women who are acceptable to Philo. They may appear to exercise independence, like Miriam and her "best" women. But they are operating within a framework prescribed by men, and in their actions they defer to men. They do not step outside the bounds, like the Midianite women. Let me test this hypothesis with respect to two other groups of Biblical women.

## The Hebrew Midwives

Another group of women who earn Philo's admiration consists of the midwives of Exodus 1, who scheme to save the male children from Pharaoh's decree of death. They receive the briefest mention. But they, again, are women Philo praises. They are treated as complete and well-balanced souls, i.e., as independent persons. By "saving the males' lives" they are likened to souls that seek God's hidden mysteries (*LA* 3.3; cf. *LA* 3.243). They are God-fearing souls that

> looking beyond things perceived and the senses which perceive them, inhabit mind and understanding, educated in and associating with matters which form reason's contemplation, even as souls do that are in quest of things out of sight (*Mig*.214f.).

Like the "perfected" Jacob, they earn for themselves "dwelling-places" (*Mig*.214). Here we have a group of women dissociated from sense and linked with mind. Like Miriam and her choir members, these midwives appear to represent for Philo a good and acceptable type of womanhood.

The Hebrew midwives fill a specific role that serves the male population; they save the male babies' lives, thus ensuring the preservation of the sons of Israel. We might say, then, that they too defer to men.

## Women Who Contribute to the Tabernacle

*Mig*.97-105 is Philo's interpretation of the account in Exodus 35 and 38 of the people bringing decorations for the tabernacle.

Philo emphasizes the voluntary action of the women, actually surpassing Scripture on this count, as a comparison of verses will show:

> A) And the men, even every one to whom it seemed good in his heart, brought from the women, even brought seals and ear-rings, and finger-rings, and necklaces, and bracelets, every article of gold. And all (*pantes*) as many as brought ornaments of gold to the Lord, and with whomsoever fine linen was found; and they brought skins dyed blue, and rams' skins dyed red (Ex.35:22f., *LXX*).

> a) Moses gave in charge not to men only but to women also to provide the sacred appointments of the Tabernacle: for it is the women who do all the weavings of blue and scarlet and linen and goat's hair, and they contribute without hesitation their own jewellery, "seals, ear-rings, rings, bracelets, hairclasps," all that was made of gold, exchanging the adornment of their persons for the adornment of piety (*Mig*.97).

> B) He made the brazen laver, and the brazen base of it of the mirrors of the women that fasted, who fasted by the doors of the tabernacle of witness, in the days in which he set it up (Ex.38:26, *LXX*).

> b) Nay, in their abounding enthusiasm, they dedicate their mirrors for the making of the laver, to the end that those who are about to perform sacred rites . . . may be helped to see themselves reflected by recollecting the mirrors out of which the laver was fashioned . . . (*Mig*.98).

After emphasizing the initiative of the women in this way, Philo goes on to describe these women as *astai* and truly *asteiai*--citizen women who are truly noble and refined. Then, after a short digression about unworthy women, he returns in *Mig*.102 to speak of the beauty engendered through the correct interaction of the sense-perceptible and the intellectual. In doing so he uses the model of the high priest's garments. But this is clearly a development in thought arising from the preceding discussion of the interaction of men and women in adorning the tabernacle. Finally, he brings in another illustration, the two-part choir. We have already examined several references to a choir. In this one Philo most clearly subordinates the female role to the male:

> . . . that our whole composite being, like a full choir all in tune, may chant together one harmonious strain rising from varied voices blending one with another; the thoughts of the mind inspiring the keynotes--for the leaders of this choir are the truths perceived by mind alone--while the objects of sense-perception, which resemble the individual members of the choir, chime in with their accordant tuneful notes (*Mig*.104).

In accordance with my hypothesis, we see in this extended passage that good women act with apparent initiative and freedom, indeed more than Scripture affords them, but always in the role prescribed by men, and in a manner that enhances the male activity.

*Woman Absorbed by Man*

Hagar

The story of Hagar's relationship to Abram and Sarah is told and allegorized in both *De Congressu Eruditionis Causa* and *Questiones in Genesin*. Besides these accounts, it is recalled in nine other treatises.[17] Yet, in spite of the wide coverage the story is given,

---

[17] *LA* 3.244; *Cher*.3,6,8; *Sac*.43; *Post*.130,132,137; *Sob*.8; *Fug*.1,5f.,202f.,-211f.; *Mut*.255; *Som*.1.240; *Abr*.247-254.

Hagar's typology can be stated simply.[18] She represents the middle stage of education, the encyclical studies.[19]

An understanding of education in the ancient world will provide necessary background for our appreciation of Philo's choice of Hagar to represent the middle stage.

A fairly fixed type of education was established early and transported, as part of Greek culture, throughout the Mediterranean world. For centuries after the time of Plato there was little change. Thus it is not surprising that Philo's description of the learning process evokes memories of the description in Plato's *Republic*, and his disdain of sophistic education resembles to some degree Plato's differences with Isocrates. Plato had quarrelled with Isocrates over the latter's emphasis on rhetoric at the expense of mathematics and philosophy.[20] In popular education it was Isocrates and the sophists who won out. Philo's yearning to take the best features out of Plato is demonstrated by the fact that, although he lists rhetoric among his subjects, he is constantly warning against its misuse by the sophists. Another point on which Philo resembles Plato is his insistence that education should not be wasted on the young. For Plato the encyclical studies were begun at age twenty, after lower education and two years of military service were completed. The study of philosophy covered the years from thirty to fifty. Philo advocated the beginning

---

[18] Mendelson, *Education*, gives a clear outline (p.67), as well as the history of the figure of speech Philo has adopted here (p.xxiii), mentioning the "ancient maxim attributed to Ariston of Chios, 'Those who neglect philosophy and spend their time on ordinary studies are like the Suitors who desired Penelope but slept with her maids.'" He also gives a detailed account of Philo's recommendations for secular education.

[19] Colson persists in translating *mesē paideia* as "lower education". Marcus, the translator of *QG*, corrects it to "intermediate education."

[20] Cf. H. I. Marrou, *A History of Education in Antiquity*, trans. by George Lamb (London: Sheed and Ward, 1956). On p.224 Marrou says ". . . ultimately, in the eyes of posterity, it was Isocrates who carried the day, not Plato: the culture that arose out of classical education was essentially aesthetic, artistic and literary, not scientific." See also Werner Jaeger, *Paideia: the Ideals of Greek Culture*, translated from the second German edition by Gilbert Highet, in 3 vols. (Oxford, 1939-1944).

of the encyclical studies at seventeen, and graduation to philosophy as late as forty.[21]

Since Philo's understanding of learning is an adaptation of Plato's, let us recall the salient features of the theory of the Divided Line, found in the *Republic*, Book 6, 509c5-d6. Types of thought are to be imagined as set out on a line which is bisected in such a way that the first section deals with knowledge derived from the physical world and the second section with knowledge of the intelligible world. The type of knowledge in the first section is called *doxa*, opinion (but it is broken down into *eikasia*, conjecture, and *pistis*, knowledge of physical objects). *Doxa* deals with the world of becoming, is established through sense-perception, and is subject to error. Turning to the second part of the line, we also find a division in two. First there is *dianoia* and, following that, *noēsis*. The learning that takes place on the first half of the line relies on sense-perception, and lacks certainty. That on the second half weans itself away from reliance on the senses. Plato uses mathematics as the subject which effects the transition, yielding *dianoia*, and preparing the mind for the pure thought of philosophy.[22]

Philo's scheme lacks the fine distinctions of Plato's. Yet it does retain the essential features of a) the progressive nature of learning, that is, the need for the encyclia to precede philosophical studies, b) the dependence of the encyclia on sense-perception, and c) the eventual freeing of the mind from the senses.[23]

Philo fits Abram's concubine, Hagar, and his wife, Sarah, into this scheme, by having Hagar, the woman, represent the en-

---

[21] Mendelson, *Education*, pp.41f.

[22] This interpretation leans heavily on that of Sir David Ross, *Plato's Theory of Ideas* (Oxford: Clarendon Press, 1951), especially p.65.

[23] Mendelson, in *Education*, makes the point that Hagar is not actually abandoned, for the Encyclical studies can lead beyond themselves to awareness of one's own nothingness, and thence to an appreciation of the greatness of God. They also have value in themselves. The distinction between "abandoning" and "growing beyond" is rather fine. It does not affect the point to which I am leading, that Hagar is "used."

cyclia, and Sarah, the virgin, represent philosophy or Wisdom. The choice is dependent on Philo's basic allegory, viz., that woman--in this case, Hagar--represents the senses, which are needed in the encyclia, and that the virgin represents the stage that supersedes the senses.

There is little to add to this basic pattern. For the purposes of the present study, however, it is noteworthy that the allegory presupposes a view of woman as valuable only in service to man, to the extent that her personhood is engulfed in his. In this respect Hagar resembles the virgins of Scripture, who lose their personhood in Philo's allegory, becoming parts of their husbands (see chapter eight).

Hagar's good character does not ameliorate her situation:

> . . . my handmaiden, outwardly a slave, inwardly of free and noble race, tested by me for many years from the day when she was first brought to my house, an Egyptian by birth, but a Hebrew by her rule of life.[24]

She is to be abandoned along with her offspring.

> When all this is come to pass, then will be cast forth those preliminary studies which bear the name of Hagar, and cast forth too will be their son the sophist named Ishmael (*Cher.*8).

Sarah's banishing of Hagar is interpreted allegorically as her demanding that Abram reject Hagar once he has used her, even though he "thinks it hard to reject . . . the education by means of which he was brought into union with virtue"(*LA* 3.145). Philo castigates Hagar's offspring Ishmael as the "female and unvirile" bastard and sophist (*QG* 4.148; *Sob.*8).

---

[24] *Abr.*251. This is actually higher praise than Scripture affords Hagar: "and she had an Egyptian maid whose name was Hagar" (Gen.16:1b). Ginzberg, however, in *Legends of the Jews* (Philadelphia, 1946-7), vol.1, p.237, mentions a tradition that Hagar was the daughter of Pharaoh: "taught and bred by Sarah, she walked in the same path of righteousness as her mistress."

A footnote to the story of Hagar is the fact that Philo attributes shame, "the outward expression of inward modesty," to her: "Hagar's motive for departing is shame" (*Fug.*5). Philo does not spell out the reason Hagar should feel shame. It can hardly be something she has done, for throughout the story she has been passive, not active. The judgment, then, seems harsh, for she has done nothing to warrant shame.[25]

## Conclusions

The purpose of this chapter has been to continue looking at the women of Scripture who are featured in Philo's writing with their womanhood neither denied nor disguised. I have postponed discussion of the women he has renamed virgins.

I have attempted to discover what Philo says about each of these individuals and groups of women, what the similarities and differences are, and how we should interpret his portrayals of these women in the light of his overall philosophy.

In the case of Potiphar's wife, the Midianite women, Lot's wife, the "lower" Miriam, and Hagar, certain elements of the archetypal woman are exaggerated. Only in the "better" Miriam, and in certain groups of Hebrew women, does Philo appear to break his pattern.

Potiphar's wife and the Midianite women represent the sexual aspect of Eve. They are so dangerous that the only appropriate

---

[25] In order to understand this point, one must note the discrepancy between the Hebrew text and the Septuagint. According to the former, Hagar flaunted her pregnancy: " . . . she looked with contempt on her mistress" (Gen.16:4, RSV), and that is Sarah's complaint to Abraham: " . . . she looked on me with contempt" (16:5). But Philo's source reads differently: " . . . and her mistress was dishonoured (*ētimasthē*) before her," and Sarah complained,"I was dishonoured (*ētimasthēn*) before her." Cf. *Cong.*139 and especially 151ff., where Philo interprets Sarah's complaint to mean that Abraham has "turned from" her. At issue is Abraham's attitude, not Hagar's. This understanding of the text harmonizes with Sarah's final statement in Gen.16:5: "God judge between you and me."

In chapter eleven I return to the question of Hagar's shame.

response on the part of some men is to flee. Only the strongest of men, like Phineas, can destroy these women.

Lot's wife and the "lower" Miriam represent the irrational aspect of Eve. Lot's wife is unbalanced and self-destructive. Miriam does not know her place, questioning the judgment of God's elect.

Hagar is woman consumed by man. She serves his purpose, and is absorbed. She is shamed and her offspring is rejected.

The "higher" Miriam, the choristers, the midwives and the women who adorn the tabernacle display neither of Eve's weaknesses, i.e., raw sexuality and irrationality. Nor are they demeaned like Hagar. Thus, at first glance they appear to be atypical of Philo's women. Their behaviour is rational and praiseworthy. They are portrayed as self-determining individuals. Miriam cooperates with Moses in leading the women's section of the choir when he appoints her to do so, and the midwives save the male babies. The Hebrew women under Philo's hand surpass their Scriptural originals by volunteering their goods for the tabernacle. Such persons present almost an ideal picture of womanhood.

But I do not believe that they entirely contradict the view of womanhood that I have attributed to Philo. First, their sexuality is not an issue. Second, they are functioning in roles that support and enhance males. The midwives save the babies so that they may grow into manhood. Miriam may function temporarily as Moses' equal, but he appoints her. The women contribute to the tabernacle which is essentially a men's institution.

Nevertheless, we have seen enough evidence to entertain the possibility that certain women, probably those who fit into the roles established for them in his ideal society, do evoke Philo's approval. This is essentially the hypothesis raised earlier: that "good" women may appear independent but must operate within a framework prescribed by men and in their actions must defer to men.

# CHAPTER EIGHT

# BIBLICAL VIRGINS (I)

*Introduction*

The Biblical women who remain *gynaikes* fall into two classes: unworthy and/or dangerous (Eve, Potiphar's wife, the Midianite women, Lot's wife, and the "lower" Miriam), and noble and supportive (the choristers, the midwives, the women who adorned the tabernacle, the "higher" Miriam, and Hagar). All (except Lot's wife, who simply exemplifies the *phaulos*) are assessed with respect to their relation to men. The ones who seduce, disturb, question, or challenge men fall into the first class. The ones who cooperate with, assist, and enhance men fall into the second.

The purely functional value of woman is underscored in Philo's treatment of Hagar. Transformed allegorically into *paideia*, she is absorbed by Abraham. (Although Abraham is also allegorized--so as to become a prototype of the man seeking God--he retains his personhood.)

This absorption of woman by man is also a leading motif in Philo's treatment of the Biblical women he calls virgins. Just as Hagar is the lower education which man takes unto himself, so Sarah and Leah are the higher learning or wisdom which becomes a part of the wise man. Thus, by turning Biblical women into virgins, Philo shows two apparently contradictory tendencies. He enhances the status of these women by elevating them to virginity, but he negates their personal individuality by having them absorbed by their husbands.

This method of dealing with women enables Philo to do a number of things. He can spare the admirable women of Scripture the ignoble attributes normally associated with womanhood. Furthermore, he can account for the behaviour of respectable women of Scripture who do not fit the model of *asteiai gynaikes* which we encountered in chapter six. Sarah and Rebecca, for example, are pictured in Scripture making decisions and taking independent action, even as married women.

He can also remain true to Scripture. If Philo is to do this, he needs a device for accounting for independent female behaviour within marriage. When he transforms certain wives into something better than women, viz., virgins, then it becomes understandable that their husbands should heed what they say.[1]

Another thing this enables him to do is to present the great heroes of Israel's past as sexually restrained, since their wives are, allegorically at least, virgins. The apologetic aim is frequently apparent in Philo's writing, and whenever possible he emphasizes the moral uprightness of his tradition, that is, the virtue of self-restraint, *sōphrosynē*. In face of the sexual laxity which he has observed in larger society, the aspect of self-control which he stresses is the sexual one.

Finally, he can develop a motif which has precedents in both the Greek and the Jewish tradition, and is understandable even to the pagan mind, that of the *hieros gamos*, the marriage of the souls, and the divine impregnation.

## De Cherubim 42-48

In order to grasp this motif, we can turn to a passage where it appears in concentrated form, *Cher.*42-48. I shall discuss this passage in detail, because I believe it is central to an understanding of Philo.

---

[1] In *Abr.*100f. Philo goes so far as to reverse the sex roles in the marriage of Abraham and Sarah; by doing so he virtually changes Sarah into a man. The reader will recall that Baer established that both "becoming virgin" and "becoming male" denote salvation in Philo.

This is one of numerous passages where Philo uses the language of the mysteries.[2] It is unique in that he both prefaces and concludes the passage with warnings that the message is not to be revealed to the "uninitiated."

> For this is a divine mystery and its lesson is for the initiated who are worthy to receive the holiest secret, even those who in simplicity of heart practise the piety which is true and genuine, free from all tawdry ornament (*Cher*.42).

> These thoughts, ye initiated, whose ears are purified, receive into your souls as holy mysteries indeed and babble not of them to any of the profane (*Cher*.48).

The question why Philo employs the language of the mysteries has exercised the minds of many.[3] It is no longer considered likely that he was influenced simply by his awareness of pagan mystery religion, as suggested by Goodenough.[4] Lilla notes that in Plato, Philo, Plotinus, the Nag Hammadi writings, and Clement of Alexandria, one can detect the literary device of employing mystery language to express key doctrines. He concludes, with respect to

---

[2] See also *LA* 2.57, 3.3, 3.27, 3.219, *Sac*.60, *Deus* 61, *Som*.1.164, 1.191, 1.226, *Cont*.25, *QG* 4.8.

[3] See A. J. Festugière, *La Révélation d'Hermes Trismegiste* (Paris, 1949), vol.2, pp.545-551; Salvatore R.C. Lilla, *Clement of Alexandria* (Oxford: Oxford University Press, 1971), pp. 148ff.; V. Nikiprowetzky, *Le Commentaire de L'Écriture chez Philon d'Alexandrie* (Leiden: E.J.Brill, 1977), ch.1; A. D. Nock, *Essays on Religion and the Ancient World* (Oxford: Clarendon, 1972) 1.459-68; Anne D. R. Sheppard, *Studies on the 5th and 6th Essays of Proclus' Commentary on the Republic* (Gottingen: Vandenhoeck & Ruprecht, 1980), ch.4. Most recently, Christoph Riedweg, in *Mysterienterminologie*, devotes 45 pages (70-115) to Philo's use of mystery language.

[4] Goodenough explains the inverted union of Abraham and Sarah in *Abr*.100f. in these words: "This is an introduction into Jewish thought of one of the most abstruse and typically pagan of the mystic conceptions which is much elaborated of Isis and in the Orphic hymns. It goes far back in Egyptian speculation, when very early God was represented as hermaphroditic . . ." *Introduction*, p.141. In his earlier work, *By Light, Light*, he had argued for the existence of a Jewish mystery religion: " . . . by Philo's time and long before, Judaism in the Greek-speaking world, especially in Egypt, had been transformed into a Mystery"(p.7).

Philo and Clement, that the aim is "the stressing of the esoteric character of *gnosis*."[5] Nikiprowetzky thinks along the same line, concluding that when Philo is going to present an argument that some people would ridicule, he hedges it in mystery language, and explains that it is intended only for "initiates." But by *mystēs* (initiate) he means simply someone who is prepared to try to understand. Nikiprowetzky notes the use of mystery terms particularly when Philo is introducing the language of human reproduction to speak of the flowering of virtue in the soul, as in *Cher*.42-48.[6]

F. C. Grant notes in *The Letter and the Spirit* that Chrysippus (3rd.c. B.C.E.) makes reference to Stoic theology as "divine rites" (*teletai*). Thus it is possible that Philo's use of that term (*LA* 3.219; *Cher*.43) drew on Stoic practice.[7] Again, perhaps Philo goes back to a source from which that practice also stemmed.

Riedweg believes that Philo uses *teletē* (*Cher*.43) and *mystēria* (*Cher*.48) as metaphors for the hidden meaning of Scripture, not recognizable by everyone. That is, they signify the allegorical method, and are used in the same sense as *mystērion* in Eph.5:32: "This [Gen.2:24] is a great mystery, and I take it to mean Christ and the church" (RSV).[8]

---

[5] *Clement*, p.154, n.2.

[6] *Commentaire*, pp.17ff.

[7] P.131: "There is no special mystery influence in Chrysippus' reference to Stoic theology as 'divine rites' (SVF II, 42, 1008; *teletai* because 'last' to be taught in the curriculum, *teleutaioi*.)"

[8] The reference to Ephesians is on p.88. Two passages which give the essence of Riedweg's discussion on the matter are as follows:
"Zusammenfassend lässt sich somit sagen, dass nach Philons Meinung die Hl. Schrift einen verborgenen, rätselhaften, tieferen Sinn (theologischer, philosophischer oder ethischer Natur) hat, der nicht jedem sofort erkennbar ist. Es gibt in der alexandrinischen Gemeinde Schriftgelehrte, die sich offenbar sozusagen professionell (*ou parergōs* spec.1.8) mit der Schrift auseinandersetzen"(p.87).
"Mysterienterminologie ist nun an unserer Stelle cher.40-50 und anderswo, wie sich noch wiegen wird, ein beliebte Metapher Philons, um eine solche allegorische Schriftinterpretation zu bezeichnen"(p.88).

I agree that Philo uses the mystery language to signify the hidden meaning of Scripture, and also that precedents can be found for such use. Although he makes allusions that at first glance would make one believe he is familiar with the practice of the mysteries, a closer examination shows that these are more likely elements of a literary convention. For example, Philo speaks of lesser and greater mysteries; in the lesser mystery one sees God through his powers (*Abr.*122), but in the greater mystery one sees God by his own light (*Praem.*46, *LA* 3.100ff., *QG* 4.4). Or in the lesser mystery one controls the passions, and in the greater mystery one replaces physical sex with reproduction in the soul. But both elements--the two levels of mystery and the metaphor of reproduction through sexual attraction--would have been familiar to him from Plato's use of them in the *Symposium* and the *Phaedrus*:

> These are the lesser mysteries of love, into which even you, Socrates, may enter; to the greater and more hidden ones which are the crown of these, and to which, if you pursue them in a right spirit, they will lead, I know not whether you will be able to attain (*Symposium* 209e-210a).[9]

> Thus fair and blissful to the beloved is the desire of the inspired lover, and the initiation of which I speak into the mysteries of true love (*Phaedrus*, 253c).[10]

Investigation thus leads back, perhaps through Stoic convention, to Plato: specifically, to his use of mystery language to frame

---

[9] Benjamin Jowett, *The Dialogues of Plato*, vol. 2. London: Sphere Books, 1970, p.223.

[10] Jowett, *Dialogues*, p.270. For information on the two stages of initiation at Eleusis, see H. W. Parke, *Festivals of the Athenians* (London: Thames and Hudson, 1977), p.56.

important doctrine, and to his figure of the impregnation of the soul.[11]

To return to *Cher*.42-48, we find that the impregnation of the soul is the kernel of the passage:

> Man, the male of the human race, approaches woman, the female of the race, for the purpose of intercourse for the procreation of children. But virtues whose offspring are so many and so perfect may not have to do with mortal man (*andros*), yet if they receive not seed of generation from another they will never of themselves conceive. Who then is he that sows in them good things save the Father of all, that is God unbegotten and begetter of all things? He then sows, but the fruit of His sowing, the fruit which is His own, He bestows as a gift. For God begets nothing for Himself, for He is in want of nothing, but all for him who asks to receive (*Cher*.43f., amended translation).

The idea of the impregnation of the soul has been introduced as "sacred instruction", *teletē* (43). In only one other place does Philo use the term in the same sense, and there again he expresses its content in terms of reproduction in the soul.

> Therefore, O ye initiate, open your ears wide and take in holiest teachings (*teletas*). The "laughter" is joy, and "made" is equivalent to "beget," so that what is said is of this kind, the Lord begat Isaac; for He is Himself Father of the perfect nature, sowing and begetting happiness in men's souls (*LA* 3.219).

Looking specifically at the content of the sacred teaching, we find that the marriages of the patriarchs and their wives are con-

---

[11] Festugière considers these passages of Plato to be the major source of Philo's metaphor. He actually accuses Philo of heavy-handedness and "mauvais goût" in his treatment of it. He also cites the sacred marriages of mystery religions, and the Biblical metaphor of marriage between God and Israel as contributing sources. (*Révélation*, pp. 545ff.) He does not discuss the way Philo changes the figure so as to avoid its homosexual aspect, but since I consider it significant for this study, I shall proceed to do so.

trasted with ordinary, physical marriage, for example the marriage in which Adam "knew" Eve (*Cher*.40, with reference to Gen.4:1). The wives appear to have been transformed into "virtues." In order to understand Philo's meaning we need to go back a few lines:

> The persons to whose virtue the lawgiver has testified, such as Abraham, Isaac, Jacob and Moses, and others of the same spirit, are not represented by him as knowing women. For since we hold that woman signifies in a figure sense-perception, and that knowledge comes into being through estrangement from sense and body, it will follow that the lovers of wisdom reject rather than choose sense. And surely this is natural. For the helpmeets of these men are called women, but are in reality virtues (*Cher*.40f.).

We note that Philo is reluctant to retain the name "women" for these individuals; Sarah, Leah, Rebecca and Zipporah have ceased to be women, and are now virtues.[12] In *Cher*.50 they are called virgins as well as virtues:

> For it is meet that God should hold converse with the truly virgin nature, that which is undefiled and free from impure touch; but it is the opposite with us. For the union of human beings that is made for the procreation of children, turns virgins into women. But when God begins to consort with the soul, He makes what before was a woman into a virgin again, for He takes away the degenerate and emasculate passions which unmanned it and plants instead the native growth of unpolluted virtues. Thus He will not talk with Sarah till she has ceased from all that is after the manner of women, and is ranked once more as a pure virgin.

A close examination of Philo's wording in this passage shows that although the virgin is functionally female (as the partner of God),

---

[12] The wording of *Abr*.99 suggests that Philo drew on an already existent tradition of designating the wives of the patriarchs as virtues :"I have also heard some natural philosophers who took the passage [about Abraham and Sarah in Egypt] allegorically, not without good reason. They said that the husband was a figure for the good mind . . . . The wife, they said, was virtue . . . ."

she is qualitatively equivalent to male. She can be unmanned--turned into a woman--*ekthēlunousan*: ". . . He makes what before was a woman into a virgin again, for He takes away the degenerate and emasculate passions which unmanned it . . . ." In this statement virgin and male appear to be equivalent and desirable states, but womanhood to be an inferior state wrought by passion.

Returning to *Cher.*43f., we realize further that no husband (*andros*) fathers the offspring of these virtues. God sows the seed in the virtues, as a gift to the husbands.

Does Philo really believe that the flesh and blood ancestors of the race fathered sons only through this type of divine intervention? Did they really not "know" their wives? No. Moses was responsible for the generation of his own sons. And Abraham fathered a child by Hagar.[13] Isaac did "sport with" Rebecca (*Plant.*169f.) Nor does Philo advocate complete celibacy, for Moses is set out as a model (*Mos.*1.158f.). It appears to be primarily for allegorical purposes that Philo attaches importance to the fact that Scripture does not explicitly say that the patriarchs "knew" their wives.

The case is built up on very faint evidence--in fact, from the argument from silence:

> The persons to whose virtues the lawgiver has testified, such as Abraham, Isaac, Jacob and Moses, and others of the same spirit, are not represented by him as knowing women. (*Cher.*40)

In rendering the predicate of this sentence as they have, the translators have been true to the text. The point is that these men "are

---

[13] "For on his belly he bestowed no more than the necessary tributes which nature has appointed, and as for the pleasures that have their seat below, save for the lawful begetting of children, they passed altogether even out of his memory" (*Mos.*1.28). Moses is still, however, presented as self-restrained. So is Abraham; Philo clarifies what is only suggested in Scripture (Gen.16:6), namely that Abraham "kept" Hagar "only till she became pregnant" (*Abr.*253). We have noted before this that Philo makes use of every opportunity to underscore the self-restraint of his people. The allegorical celibacy of the patriarchs thus harmonizes with the overall tone of his writing.

not represented by him as knowing women," and not that they "are represented by him as not knowing women." Technically, Philo is correct, as a close reading of his statements together with their Scriptural bases will show. I shall quote the passages from *De Cherubim* in order, following each with its corresponding passage in the Septuagint.[14]

> I can give as a warrant for my words one that none can dispute, Moses the holiest of men. For he shows us Sarah conceiving at the time when God visited her in her solitude, but when she brings forth it is not to the Author of her visitation, but to him who seeks to win wisdom, whose name is Abraham. (*Cher*.45)

> And the Lord visited Sarrha, as he said, and the Lord did to Sarrha, as he spoke. And she conceived and bore to Abraam a son in old age . . .(Gen.21:1f.)

> And even clearer is Moses' teaching of Leah, that God opened her womb. Now to open the womb belongs to the husband. Yet when she conceived she brought forth not to God (for He is in Himself all-sufficing for Himself), but to him who endures toil to gain the good, even Jacob. Thus virtue receives the divine seed from the Creator, but brings forth to one of her own lovers, who is preferred over all others who seek her favour. (*Cher*.46)

> And when the Lord God saw that Lea was hated, he opened her womb; but Rachel was barren. And Lea conceived and bore a son to Jacob . . .(Gen.29:31f.)

> Again Isaac the all-wise besought God, and through the power of Him who thus was besought Steadfastness or Rebecca became pregnant. (*Cher*.47)

---

[14] The Septuagint translation is from Bagster's edition (London, 1889?). Bagster spells the proper names differently from Colson.

And Isaac prayed the Lord concerning Rebecca his wife, because she was barren; and the Lord heard him, and his wife Rebecca conceived in her womb. (Gen.25:21)

And without supplication or entreaty did Moses, when he took Zipporah the winged and soaring virtue, find her pregnant through no mortal agency. (*Cher*.47)

And Moses was established with the man, and he gave Sepphora his daughter to Moses to wife. And the woman conceived and bore a son . . . . (Ex.2:21f.)

*Dependence on The Symposium*

We have seen from examining *Cher*.42-48 that the metaphor of reproduction in the soul is central to Philo's allegory. We see too that the wives of the patriarchs are elevated to virginity but absorbed by their husbands.

As I stated above (n.11), Festugière has remarked on Philo's dependence here on passages in the *Phaedrus* and the *Symposium*. Riedweg specifically links the *Cherubim* passage to the *Symposium*.[15] I should like to extend their line of thought by discussing the ways in which Philo has altered the Platonic metaphor.

*Symposium* 206c-212a constitutes the body of Diotima's speech to Socrates which traces the growth of the soul from the love of beautiful bodies to the love of Beauty itself. Diotima speaks of the excitement generated by sexual attraction. Between a man and a woman this excitement is dissipated in the natural course of child-begetting, bearing and rearing. Between two men, however, the excitement is discharged through more spiritual channels, and thereby the growth of the soul begins. Diotima employs here the figure of the pregnancy of the soul, a figure we have seen to be central to

---

[15] "Die Gedankenwelt des platonischen Symposions ist m.E. in der Ausgestaltung unserer Philonstelle durchaus erkennbar . . . ." Riedweg notes also that Philo takes over the metaphor of man giving birth from *Symposium* 209d-e (*Mysterienterminologie*, p.76).

Philo's mystery in *Cher*.42-48 : " . . . all men (*anthrōpoi*) are pregnant . . . both in body and in soul" (Symposium 206c).¹⁶

This is an unusual figure of speech. In an essay in the first edition of his *Platonic Studies*, Gregory Vlastos remarks on its uniqueness: "For this striking image of male pregnancy there is no known precedent in Greek literature." In the second edition he defends the position against opposition raised against it:

> The image is most certainly meant to apply to males; its force would be sadly blunted if it were restricted to females in 206C-D; anyhow, it is quite explicitly applied to males in the sequel (209A-C).¹⁷

In Diotima's speech the soul of man gives birth in a process that is similar, but spiritually superior, to the physical mating of a man with a woman:

> Now those who are teeming in body betake them rather to women, and are amorous on this wise, by getting children . . . . . But pregnancy of soul--for there are persons . . . who in their souls still more than in their bodies conceive . . . [and bring forth] prudence and virtue in general . . . (208e-209a).¹⁸

Philo has expressed the same contrast between physical and spiritual mating in *Cher*.43 (quoted earlier in this chapter).

In Plato, spiritual contact between a man and his young lover is required before the birth in the soul can occur:

> For I hold that by contact with the fair one and by consorting with him he bears and brings forth his long-felt concep-

---

¹⁶ *LCL, Plato*, vol.v, p.201.

¹⁷ Gregory Vlastos, *Platonic Studies*, 2nd edition. Princeton University Press, 1981 (1st edition, 1973 ), p.21 and p.424.
Cf. *Theaetetus* 150b, where Socrates says his art of midwifery is practised on men (*andras*).

¹⁸ *LCL, Plato*, vol.v, p.199.

tion, because in presence or absence he remembers his fair. Equally too with him he shares the nurturing of what is begotten, so that men in this condition enjoy a far fuller community with each other than that which comes with children, and a far surer friendship, since the children of their union are fairer and more deathless (209c).[19]

There is no parallel to this in Philo. Instead, we find the marriage to virtue, signified by Zipporah, Sarah, Leah and Rebecca. The reason for the abrupt change in the image is not hard to find, for we are fortunate in having Philo's own commentary on the matter. That is in *De Vita Contemplativa*, where he contrasts the banquets of the Therapeutae with the famous banquets of Greek literature, those described by Xenophon and Plato. It is obvious from his words that Philo interprets Plato's *Symposium*, which culminates in Diotima's speech, as little more than blatant advocacy of homosexual practice. He entirely misses the point that the sexual energy engendered through the attraction of man for boy is redirected into spiritual growth. Instead, he sees it as promoting an activity expressly forbidden by Moses. Although Philo usually reveres Plato as an authority, in a situation like this, where two systems of morality clash, he parts company with his mentor.[20]

> In Plato's banquet the talk is almost entirely concerned with love, not merely with the love-sickness of men for women, or women for men, passions recognized by the laws of nature, but of men for other males differing from them only in age. For, if we find some clever subtlety dealing apparently with the heavenly Love and Aphrodite, it is brought in to give a touch of humour. The chief part is taken up by the common vulgar love which robs men of the courage which is the virtue most valuable for the life both of peace and war, sets up the disease of effeminacy in their souls and turns into a hybrid of man and woman those who should have been

---

[19] *LCL, Plato*, vol.v, p.201.

[20] For his reverence towards Plato, see *Op*.119, 133, *Aet*.13-17, 25, 33, 52, 141, *Prob*.13.

disciplined in all the practices which make for valour. And having wrought havoc with the years of boyhood and reduced the boy to the grade and condition of a girl besieged by a lover it inflicts damage on the lovers also in three most essential respects, their bodies, their souls and their property. For the mind of the lover is necessarily set towards his darling and its sight is keen for him only, blind to all other interests, private and public; his body wastes away through desire, particularly if his suit is unsuccessful, while his property is diminished by two causes, neglect and expenditure on his beloved. As a side growth we have another greater evil of national importance. Cities are desolated, the best kind of men become scarce, sterility and childlessness ensue through the devices of those who imitate men who have no knowledge of husbandry by sowing not in the deep soil of the lowland but in briny fields and stony and stubborn places, which not only give no possibility for anything to grow but even destroy the seed deposited within them (*Cont.*59-62).

In this passage Philo completely ignores Plato's claim that homosexual attraction can be used as an elevating spiritual force. He dismisses it in a single sentence: *kai gar ei ti peri erōtos kai Aphroditēs ouraniou kekompseusthai dokei, charin asteismou pareilēptai*. Following this is a twenty-line tirade against homosexuality, reaching its climax in threats of the destruction of cities and the sterility of the race.

It is likely that Philo is fascinated by the figure of the pregnancy of the soul, but repulsed by the homosexual content of Diotima's "mystery" teaching. He sets out deliberately to correct it, by producing his own version of the "mystery." Although allusions to it abound throughout the Allegory, it is stated formally in *Cher.*42-48. Philo has taken Plato's image of the pregnancy in the soul, cleansed it of the homosexual component, and added God as the ultimately creative power. For sensuous love he substitutes the relationships of the patriarchs to their wives, but strips them of all but spiritual qualities. God has been given the place of Beauty, and all couplings are male-female, in accordance with the laws of nature.

Although this inclusion in the core of the mystery appears to elevate the great women of scripture, their role is clearly functional. Vlastos concludes in his article on Plato that the failure of Plato's type of love is that it refuses to see the love object as anything other than useful or beautiful. Its value lies not in itself but in its function.[21] Philo appears to have adopted this attitude along with the figure of speech.

With this understanding of the role of the matriarchs in Philo's central allegory, I move now into detailed examination of Philo's treatment of the individual "virgins," Zipporah, Sarah, Leah, Tamar and Hagar. I shall mention also Rachel, who appears at times as a foil to the virgins, and at other times as their equal.

---

[21] *Platonic Studies*, p.31f: "This seems to me the cardinal flaw in Plato's theory. It does not provide for love of whole persons, but only for love of that abstract version of persons which consists of the complex of their best qualities."

# CHAPTER NINE

# BIBLICAL VIRGINS (II): SARAH AND REBECCA

*Introduction*

In *Cher*.42-48 Philo expresses in a most formal and solemn way the sacred teaching regarding the marriages of the patriarchs. The men are allegorized as minds or souls, the women as virtues that belong to those souls. The virtues open the souls to God's fertilizing power, and thus, in a manner similar to human reproduction, bring forth benefits to their husbands. But in these marriages the wives remain virgins, and therefore, according to Philo's understanding of the word, not women at all. For a woman is one who has been defiled and corrupted by a man, but God's consorts suffer no such pollution.

Men and women receive unbalanced treatment in this kind of allegory. We see that the Biblical men, on the one hand, have been allegorized into soul types. Philo intends that a man should identify each of these within himself (*QG* 4.138, 206). The women, on the other hand, have become only constituent parts of their husbands. It is clearly not Philo's intention here that Jewish women should, in parallel fashion to the men, identify the matriarchs within themselves. This is made even more explicit by the fact that, although they are wives of the patriarchs, they are rendered by Philo as perpetual virgins, thus representing an impossible dream for Jewish women, destined by biology and custom to a life of "defilement" and "corruption."

That is Philo's central teaching about the matriarchs. In this chapter and the next I shall round out the picture he presents by looking at his overall treatment of the women allegorically designated as virgins.

When a literary text is treated allegorically, two planes or levels of meaning run concurrently throughout. They are not necessarily of equal importance to the author. For Philo, the literal meaning usually pales in the light of the allegorical. This is the case in his treatment of some of the "virgins" of scripture--Leah, Zipporah, Tamar and Hagar, whose human personalities hardly emerge. But with Sarah and Rebecca it is different. In the Hebrew tradition these two are firmly established as folk-heroines. The well-known Biblical accounts paint them vividly as self-determining women. For example, Sarah gave orders to Abraham, and Rebecca hoodwinked Isaac. Philo cannot completely ignore the humanity of these women, who probably come closest of their kind to being role models for women in his day.[1] It will be informative for our understanding of Philo's perception of women to examine how closely his treatment of this pair tallies with the Biblical accounts.

The sheer amount of material Philo devotes to Sarah and Rebecca in *Questiones in Genesin* suggests that he is fully aware of their popularity as folk-heroines. Sarah appears fairly regularly from *QG* 3.18 to 4.73, and Rebecca from *QG* 4.88 to 4.239. By contrast, Leah is not mentioned in that work at all. Philo ends his commentary on Genesis before the story of Jacob's marriages. As a result, the overall picture of Leah that emerges from Philo's writing is far less colourful than that of the other two.

It is not enough, then, for Philo to treat Rebecca and Sarah as types, or for him to present them solely in allegory. Accordingly, we shall find that his treatment of them is multi-faceted. But we shall also find that when Philo treats of them on the human level, he downplays their initiative and moulds them into submissive helpmates, similar to the acceptable women we discussed in chapter seven.

---

[1] Louis Ginzberg, in the Index to *The Legends of the Jews*, lists 40 entries under "Sarah," and 37 under "Rebekka." Sarah is "the only woman with whom God spoke," and Rebecca is "the counterpart of Sarah."

## Sarah

We can divide Philo's treatment of Sarah into two general sections, the literal and the allegorical. But we must bear in mind that Philo does not maintain neat distinctions. The two threads, instead of running parallel to one another, occasionally become entangled together, as can be seen in this passage from *LA* 3.244:

> Quite a different woman [from Potiphar's wife] claims our compliance, a woman [or wife] such as Sarah is seen to have been, even paramount virtue. The wise Abraham complies with her when she recommends the course to follow.

Here Philo alludes to the well-known story of Sarah's planning and regulating Abraham's encounters with Hagar (Gen.16:1-6), including the fact that the Bible depicts Abraham as following Sarah's advice. But by using the term "paramount virtue," Philo elevates the woman Sarah, temporarily at least, to the allegorical level.

The quotation from *LA* 3.244 illustrates a second matter. We have already seen that Philo believes the proper order of things is overturned when men listen to women's advice.[2] Yet the Bible depicts Abraham doing just that. We shall note a number of devices Philo employs to account for this element in the story.

With these preliminary remarks made, I shall begin Philo's depiction of Sarah by examining the passages where he appears to concentrate on the literal story.

There are two treatises devoted to Abraham, *De Migratione Abrahami* and *De Abrahamo*. The first belongs to the *Allegory* and the second to the *Exposition*. Treatises in the former category follow the Biblical texts closely. *De Migratione Abrahami* covers the first six verses of Genesis 12. But there is a significant omission. Verse 5, the only place where Sarah is mentioned, is omitted: "And Abram took Sarai his wife, and Lot his brother's son, and all their possessions which they had gathered, and the persons that they had gotten

---

[2] ch.6 above, n.7.

in Haran; and they set forth to the land of Canaan." In the whole treatise, Sarah is mentioned in only three sections (*Mig.*126, 140, 142). Philo evinces no intention of presenting her as Abraham's partner in the great migration. In *De Abrahamo* the emphasis again is on Abraham's solitary decision, a point not made in the Biblical account: "But Abraham, the moment he was bidden, departed with a few or even alone . . ." (66).[3] In this treatise, Sarah does not enter the story until section 93, the incident in Egypt (Gen.12:11).

By way of contrast to the earlier omission, in *Abr.*245 Philo alludes to Sarah's having accompanied Abraham throughout his journeys. Here, significantly, the emphasis is on her wifely love, *philandria*. Philo does call Sarah a partner, *koinōnos*, but the context argues against our reading any suggestion of equality into the term:

> She showed her wifely love by numberless proofs, by sharing with him the severance from his kinsfolk, by bearing without hesitation the departure from her homeland, the continual and unceasing wanderings on a foreign soil and privation in famine, and by the campaigns in which she accompanied him. Everywhere and always she was at his side, no place or occasion omitted, his true partner in life and life's events, resolved to share alike the good and ill (*Abr.*245f.; cf. *Spec.*1.138).

In fact, the ensuing statement reveals Philo's real purpose here: to cast the literal Sarah in the role of model helpmeet: "She did not, like some other women, run away from mishaps and lie ready to pounce on pieces of good luck, but accepted her portion of both with all alacrity as the fit and proper test of a wedded wife" (*Abr.*246).

Sarah is presented on the literal plane when she is first mentioned in *De Abrahamo*, in section 93: "He had a wife distinguished greatly for her goodness of soul and beauty of body, in

---

[3] "The Scriptural patriarch who moved with family and flocks is replaced by the Sage who makes a journey of soul not to a new land, but home." Sandmel, *Philo's Place*, p.111.

which she surpassed all the women of her time." Again, in 255, when he is concluding his discussion of Sarah's merits, Philo still speaks of her on the human level. Here he makes the point of ranking Sarah against her husband. Since the direct comparison is without Biblical authority, it appears to be another deliberate attempt by Philo to establish the proper order of things. That is, even a meritorious wife has a husband who is yet more deserving: "We need give no further proofs of the merits of the wife. More numerous are those of the Sage . . . ."

Still on the human, literal level, in *De Abrahamo*, the action for which Sarah merits Philo's highest praise is her offering Hagar to Abraham to bear his child. It is curious that Philo introduces the section (*Abr*.247-254) by calling Sarah *anthrōpos*: "Many a story could I relate in praise of this woman (*tēs anthrōpou*).[4]

Philo alters the story of Sarah's taking the initiative and giving commands to Abraham in the matter of Hagar. The Biblical account clearly attributes the scheme to Sarah. Her motive is to obtain children for herself using her maid to bear the child:

> Now Sarai, Abram's wife, bore him no children. She had an Egyptian maid whose name was Hagar; and Sarai said to Abram, "Behold now, the Lord has prevented me from bearing children; go in to my maid; it may be that I shall obtain children (*teknopoiēsōmai*) by her." And Abram hearkened (*hypēkouse*) to the voice of Sarai (Gen.16:1f., RSV; the Greek verbs are from the *LXX*).

As the story proceeds, Sarah again takes command:

> And God said to Abraham, "Be not displeased because of the lad and because of your slave woman; whatever Sarah says to you, do as she tells you, for through Isaac shall your descendants be named" (Gen.21:12).

---

[4] This is the Loeb translation, which takes no note of the peculiarity of the Greek wording. In *PA* it is translated *der Frau*.
See also ch.4, n.7, above.

These Biblical verses present Philo with a dilemma.[5] The wording of Gen.16:2b is reminiscent of that in Gen.3:18 (the expulsion from Eden), "Because you have listened to the voice of your wife . . . ." (The slight difference is that the verb in Gen.16:2 is *hypēkouse* instead of *ēkousas*, as in 3:18.) In *LA* 3.222-224 that story (of Adam's obeying Eve) inspires a lengthy discussion about such a "violation of the right principle," that is, about the disasters that ensue when a man hearkens to his wife. Therefore, we can expect some subtle changes in Philo's version of the story of Abraham's obeying Sarah.

In the encomium on Sarah in *De Abrahamo*, Philo stresses her wifely forethought and *philandria* (252) and does not mention that she devises her scheme in order to relieve herself of childlessness. He emphasizes rather that the child will enhance Abraham. Further, in this account, he does not refer to Abraham's obedience to Sarah, as recorded in 16:2 and 21:12 of Genesis. In *De Congressu* Philo actually changes the earlier verb of 16:2, *teknopoiēsomai*, rendering it: "Go in, then, to my handmaid . . . that first you may have children by her (*teknopoiēsē*)." The overall effect is to make Sarah more self-effacing than she appears in the Bible. But by this altered behaviour she also conforms more closely to Philo's ideal of a wife.

The story receives fuller treatment in *Legum Allegoriae* 3, and the matter of Abraham's obeying Sarah on both occasions is met directly. Part of Philo's explanation has been quoted earlier but bears repeating. He brings an allegorical interpretation to the story, by referring to Sarah three times as "virtue":

---

[5] Josephus also appears to have been uncomfortable with the Biblical account, for he introduces similar changes. In his retelling of the story in *Antiquities* 1.10, he tempers Sarah's initiative by having her take action "at God's command." This transfers the first move from Sarah to God. Josephus ignores the matter of Abraham's obedience to Sarah in Gen.21:12, saying of it only that Abraham "resigned" Hagar to Sarah's hand.

Josephus, like Philo, believes that it is the role of the wife to obey: "Scripture says, 'A woman is inferior to her husband in all things.' Let her, therefore, be obedient (*hypakoueto*) to him . . ." (*Contra Apionem* 2.24.201).

Quite a different woman claims our compliance, a woman such as Sarah is seen to have been, even paramount virtue. The wise Abraham complies with her when she recommends the course to follow . . . he shall be brought to compliance by an oracle of God bidding him, 'In all that Sarah saith to thee listen to her voice.' Let that which seems good to virtue be law for each one of us; for if we choose to hearken to all that virtue recommends, we shall be happy (*LA* 3.244f.).

One of the ways, then, in which Philo deals with the problem of Abraham's obeying Sarah's commands is this semi-allegorical way in which, since she is virtue, she is a "different woman" (*heterai gynaiki*).

In the treatise *De Congressu Eruditionis Causa*, the literal thread is practically indiscernible, and Philo treats the story of Abraham's compliance with Sarah almost exclusively on the allegorical level.[6] In this elaborate allegory, which we already examined in our study of Hagar, Sarah has become wisdom, which a man takes unto himself after he has passed through the stage of the lower learning, i.e., Hagar. In sections 1 through 70 Philo comments on Gen.16:1f., with no hesitation about the correctness of Abraham's obedience: " . . . he is represented not as hearing, but as hearkening, a word which exactly expresses assent and obedience" (*Cong*.68). Philo can do this because Abraham and Sarah are no longer real people.

Another way in which Philo justifies Sarah's superiority is by emphasizing the meaning of her name, both before and after it is changed (*Cher*.3-10, *Cong*.1-13, *Mut*.61, 77-80, 130). In *Mut*.62 Philo reveals how important he considers names and their changes, by citing supposed divine retribution that befell someone of his acquaintance who had ridiculed their significance. Sarah's original name means "my sovereignty," a specific virtue, and when it changes it becomes generic virtue (*Mut*.78, cf. *Cher*.5). A similar point is made by implication in *Cher*.51, where generic virginity is contrasted with

---

[6] Several times he states that the story is not to be understood literally: *Cong*.12, 54, 180.

specific virginity. The generic form is secure and unchanging, and therefore superior, just as generic virtue or wisdom is superior to the specific: " . . . the oracle makes itself safe by speaking of God as the husband not of a virgin, but of virginity, the idea which is unchangeable and eternal" (*Cher*.51). Sarah is generic sovereignty or virtue.

> Wisdom in the good man is a sovereignty vested in himself alone, and its possessor will not err if he says, "The wisdom in me is my sovereignty." But in the wisdom which is its archetype, the generic wisdom, we cease to have the sovereignty of the particular individual, but sovereignty its very self (*Mut*.79).

We have seen several ways in which Philo deals with Sarah's giving orders to Abraham. He ignores it, combines allegorical and literal interpretation, or completely allegorizes the story. He also stresses the significance of Sarah's name "sovereignty." It is only right for a man to obey his sovereign.

When she is allegorized, Sarah is absorbed into Abraham as a quality of his character. He is the wise man; she is his wisdom (*Cher*.10, *LA* 2.82, *Mut*.264). He is the virtuous man; she is his virtue (*Det*.59, *Post*.62, *LA* 3.217f., *Heres* 258, *Abr*.99).

> Why does He again say in the singular,"Where is Sarah, thy wife, and he answered, In the tent"? . . . To this question he replies, "Behold, virtue is not only in my mind but also in an empty and safe tent, in my body, extending itself and spreading as far as the senses and the other functional parts (of the body). For in accordance with virtue I see and hear and smell and taste and touch, and I make other movements in accordance with wisdom, health, fortitude and justice." (*QG* 4.11).

The effect of the allegory thus is both to elevate and to dissolve her.

Philo uses more than one means to minimize Sarah's womanhood. In chapter eight we concentrated on the theory behind his transforming Sarah and the other matriarchs into virgins. Other passages dealing with Sarah's sexuality speak of her abandoning femininity for masculinity and being distanced even from female parentage:

> "Sarah was quit of her experience of what belongs to women" (Gen.xviii.11); and the passions are by nature *feminine*, and we must practise the quitting of these for the *masculine* traits that mark the noble affections (*Det*.28, emphasis mine).

> . . . Sarah, who is Virtue, "forsakes the ways of women" (Gen. xviii.11), those ways on which we toil who follow after the *unmanly* and really *feminine* life (*Fug*.128, emphasis mine).

> She is declared, too, to be without a mother, and to have inherited her kinship only on the father's side and not on the mother's, and thus *to have no part in female parentage.* (*Ebr*.61, emphasis mine).

> . . . male descent is the sole claim of her, who is the motherless ruling principle of things, begotten of her father alone, even God the Father of all (*Heres* 62).

Sarah occasionally is presented as functionally male. In *Cong*.7 she both sows (*spermatōn*) and engenders. And in *Abr*.100f. we find a long and convoluted explanation of the reversal of sex roles:

> Now in a marriage where the union is brought about by pleasure, the partnership is between body and body, but in the marriage made by wisdom it is between thoughts which seek purification and perfect virtues. Now the two kinds of marriage are directly opposed to each other. For in the bodily marriage the male sows the seed and the female receives it; on the other hand in the matings within the soul, though virtue seemingly ranks as wife, her natural function is to sow good counsels and excellent words and to inculcate tenets truly profitable to life, while thought, though held to take the place of the husband, receives the holy and divine sowings.

Philo goes on to claim that it is a mistake in language that the Greek word for virtue is feminine and the word for mind masculine, on the grounds that the opposite should be true, since Sarah (virtue) impregnates Abraham (mind). Thus Sarah is completely relieved of female characteristics.

To sum up what we have discovered about Philo's treatment of Sarah, we see that when he treats her on the human level, he alters the Biblical account to make her into the ideal, but subservient, wife.[7] When he accepts the vigorously independent Sarah of Scripture, he robs her of both her womanhood and her humanity, through allegory. The person Sarah whom Philo allows to emerge is thus only a shadow of the Biblical Sarah.

*Rebecca*

Rebecca is another folk-heroine who is followed in the Biblical account from her girlhood (in Genesis 24) well into marriage and parenthood (in Genesis 27). I have already mentioned the lengthy treatment Philo gives her in *Questiones in Genesin* 4. Sections 88 to the end are a verse by verse commentary on Genesis 24 to 27. Philo refers to Rebecca in a total of twelve treatises.[8] Extended passages occur in *De Posteritate Caini* and *De Fuga et Inventione*. Like Sarah, Rebecca is presented on the human, as well as on the allegorical level.

*Questiones in Genesin* paints a vivid and literal picture of Rebecca the person. For example, Philo says that Rebecca had two virginities, of body and of soul, and beauty surpassing the mere

---

[7] The same alteration of the stories of Abraham and Sarah is indicated in the wording of 1 Pet.3:1-6: "Likewise you wives be submissive to your husbands, so that some, though they do not obey the word, may be won without a word by the behavior of their wives . . . as Sarah obeyed Abraham, calling him lord."

[8] *LA* 3.88f., *Cher*.8, 40f., 47, *Sac*.4, *Det*.30f., 45, 51, *Post*.62, 77f., 132-153, *Plant*.169f., *Mig*.208-211, *Cong*.34-38, 111-113, 129, *Fug*.23-25, 39-52, 194f., *Som*.1.46, *Virt*.208f., *QG* 4.88-end.

fairness of form that harlots have, for her soul shone through her countenance (*QG* 4.99). She was far more beautiful than the virgins of Philo's day (*QG* 4.143). She hastened to tend to the need of Abraham's servant because "excellent and good people perform their good works without delay" (*QG* 4.124). Furthermore, in *Questiones in Genesin* the virginity motif is frequently left behind:

> Why was Isaac forty years old when he took Rebekah to wife? The fortieth year is the right time for the marriage of the wise man . . . . It is necessary to receive enjoyment in love and affection from a wife and to fulfil the law concerning the rearing of children . . . . For . . . it was not for the sake of irrational sensual pleasure or with eagerness that he had intercourse with his wife but for the sake of begetting legitimate children (*QG* 4.154).

Philo puts both a literal and an allegorical interpretation upon the simple Biblical account of the first meeting of Rebecca and Isaac: " . . . and when she saw Isaac, she alighted from the camel . . ." (Gen.24:64):

> In the literal sense, it was because of modesty and veneration. But as for the deeper meaning, it was because of the humility and submissiveness and perception of virtue (found) in a genuine and sincere lover (*QG* 4.142).

The motives of modesty and veneration on which the literal Rebecca acted are characteristics of Philo's model wife, and are his own addition to Scripture.

In the treatises in the *Allegory*, Philo does not so clearly distinguish between allegory and story. Usually Rebecca is presented allegorically, but sometimes the real woman is there too. This is most evident in another account of her first meeting with Isaac, in *Quod Deterius Potiori Insidiari Soleat*. Isaac has come out into the plain to converse with God. His self-taught wisdom enables him, like Moses and Abraham, to see God. Rebecca comes upon him as he is thus engaged:

> ... and when she saw Isaac, she alighted from the camel and said to the servant, "Who is the man yonder, walking in the field to meet us?" (Gen.24:64f.)

The wording of the Scriptural account indicates that Rebecca saw only one man, Isaac. This means to Philo that she did not see God. But Isaac did. In this account Philo hovers between the literal and the allegorical; Rebecca is a separate individual, but she is also persistence, just as Isaac, the man, is also wisdom:

> ... Rebecca, who is persistence, will presently inquire of the servant as seeing one and receiving an impression of one only, "Who is this man who is coming to meet us?" For the soul that persists in noble courses is indeed capable of apprehending self-taught wisdom, which is represented by the title "Isaac," but is unable as yet to see God the Ruler of wisdom (*Det*.30).

Just as Sarah, though meritorious, is not so meritorious as Abraham, so Rebecca, though spiritually advanced, is not so advanced as Isaac.

Once Rebecca and Isaac are married, Philo is at pains to emphasize their complete harmony, even at the expense of the natural sense of Scripture. Gen.25:28 reads, *ēgapēse de Isaak ton Hēsau . . . Rebekka de ēgapa ton Iakōb* (And Isaac loved Esau . . . but Rebecca loved Jacob). Philo builds on the difference between the meanings of the aorist and imperfect verb forms and ignores the movement of the subject from Isaac to Rebecca. The verse means, then, that the parents' love of Esau was brief, but their love of Jacob was lasting. As parents they were really of one mind:

> For the admission of evil and weakness, if it does sometimes occur, is shortlived and ephemeral, but that of virtue is, in a certain sense, immortal . . . (*QG* 4.166).

Again, in their actions towards their sons, the disharmony is only superficial. Together the parents are working towards a single goal, that the better should rule the worse:

> The wishes and characters of the parents do not fight and contend with one another, as some are accustomed, but without division and separation the couple (are) in harmony, for they are eager to reach one end although they are motivated by different thoughts (*QG* 4.200).

In the treatise *De Virtutibus* (although not in the *QG* treatment of the same text), Philo alters the Scriptural account of Isaac's blessing on his sons in Gen.27:27-29 and 39f., in order to include Rebecca:

> Therefore, for the younger they prayed that he should be blessed above all others, all which prayers God confirmed and would not that any of them should be left unfulfilled. But to the elder in compassion they granted an inferior station to serve his brother, rightly thinking that it is not good for the fool to be his own master (*Virt*.209).

We detect a deliberate effort on Philo's part to pass over the familiar stories of Rebecca's helping Jacob to trick Isaac. Instead he presents the married Rebecca as a person whose thoughts and actions completely harmonize with her husband's.

Allegorically, Isaac and Rebecca together symbolize the soul wedded to goodness, or virtue and its possessor (*Post*.62). Rebecca is an aspect of Isaac's character, usually constancy, steadfastness or patience.[9] As such she adds an element of permanence to her husband's wisdom: she effects a "great work" which "is the divine, holy and consecrated marriage of the soul, the harmony of the self-taught reason. Wherefore he will be unchangeable who is wise by nature without teaching" (*QG* 4.91). Philo sees in her a certain similarity to, or continuity with, Sarah, who is motherless wisdom:

> Isaac and Moses take wives indeed, but they do not take them purely of themselves, but Isaac is said to have taken

---

[9] She is *epimonē* (*Cong*.111, *Cher*.47, *Fug*.45, etc.), *hypomen* (*Det*.30, *Som*.1.46, *Cong*.37, etc.), the "queen and mistress virtue" (*Cong*.37), *hē hypomonētikē psychē* (*LA* 3.88).

one when he entered into his mother's dwelling (Gen.24:67) (*Post*.77).

> . . . since the mother of the self-taught person was motherless wisdom, whose right reason is symbolically called "house," it was changed into a bridal-chamber for him so as to be a unity of betrothal and a partnership of the self-taught kind with ever-virginal Constancy, from the love of whom may it never come about that I cease (*QG* 4.145).

Thus, as well as symbolizing constancy, Rebecca sometimes represents reason or wisdom itself.

For other characteristics, Philo relies on his readers' knowledge of the main events of the Biblical story--how Abraham's servant went to Mesopotamia to choose Rebecca, how she returned with him and met Isaac, how she conceived and bore twins, how she manipulated them so that Jacob would gain the upper hand. Each event shows a quality that Rebecca adds to Isaac's soul. The virgin Rebecca meeting the servant at the well represents pure intention, wisdom and knowledge, coupled with eagerness and ability to teach in accordance with the learner's needs.[10] As mother of Jacob and Esau she is the ability to discriminate between good and evil within oneself:

> The souls then whose pregnancy is accompanied with wisdom, though they labour, do bring their children to the birth, for they distinguish and separate what is in confusion within them, just as Rebecca, receiving in her womb the knowledge of the two nations of the mind, virtue and vice, distinguished the nature of the two and found therein a happy delivery (*Cong*.129; cf. *QG* 4.158, *Sac*.4).

Philo justifies her disguising Jacob as his brother by explaining it in this way:

---

[10] Philo deals at length with Rebecca the good teacher in *Post*.140-150.

And the physician who is skilled in worldly matters does foolish things for a time (but) wisely, and unlasciviously and moderately does lecherous things, and bravely does cowardly things, and righteously does unrighteous things. And sometimes he will speak falsehoods, not being a liar, and he will deceive, not being a deceiver, and he will insult, not being an insulter (*QG* 4.204).

In this type of action Rebecca shows the quality of "judicious patience" (*Fug*.24), or of advocating the middle way "of precaution that nothing unforeseen and irremediable be experienced" (*QG* 4.239).
It is a form of practical wisdom or even expediency. Philo downplays the questionable morality of Rebecca's action; he emphasizes rather that she enriches her husband's soul with her astuteness. The part of the story Philo uses most frequently to illustrate this quality is Rebecca's advice to Jacob to go away and visit Laban until Esau's anger (at her deceitful action) has abated. Over and over he draws the moral that the spiritual man must be able to navigate the waters of the practical life:

Yet sometimes even running away is serviceable, when a man does it not out of hatred for the better, but that he may not be exposed to the designs of the worse. What, then, is the advice of Patience? A most marvellous and valuable one! If ever, she says, thou seest stirred up to savagery in thyself or some other person the passion of wrath and anger, one of the stock bred and reared by our irrational and untamed nature, beware of whetting its fierceness and yet more rousing the beast in it, when its bites may be incurable, but cool down its excessive heat and perfervid temper and quiet it, for should it become tame and manageable it will inflict but little hurt. What, then, is the method of bringing it to a quiet and subdued state? Adapt and transform yourself in outward appearance and follow for the moment whatever it pleases . .
(*Mig*.209; cf. *QG* 4.239, *Fug*.26, 43, 45, 49, *Som*.1.46).

A final but important observation is that allegorically, Philo actually attributes to Rebecca, in her role as co-parent with Isaac, spiritual development equal to her husband's. Rebecca advises Jacob to behave such that "thou mayest obtain the very prize obtained by thy parents: and the prize is the unfaltering and untiring ministry to the only wise Being" (*Fug*.47).

In summarizing Philo's treatment of Rebecca, we find that he treats her as a traditional heroine, as he does Sarah. He changes the Biblical picture, however, so as to make her conform to his own ideal: Rebecca the maiden shows modesty and veneration to her bridegroom, and Rebecca the wife acts in harmony with her husband. She is spiritually mature, but not so advanced as Isaac.

Allegorically, Rebecca, like Sarah, is absorbed into her husband.[11] She adds to his character the virtue constancy which is in keeping with the meaning of her name, as sovereignty was in keeping with Sarah's. On this level she is treated as Isaac's spiritual equal.

*Conclusion*

While maintaining his basic allegory, in which Sarah and Rebecca are the virgin wives who bring forth virtues through God's intervention, Philo takes advantage of their popular images to mold them into the likeness of his ideal wife, obedient and deferential to her husband.

---

[11] Like Sarah, she is reduced to one aspect of a man who is a role-model for Everyman. So Philo can speak of Sarah and Rebecca with reference to himself: "So Sarah, the virtue which rules my soul, was a mother, but not a mother for me . . ." (*Cong*.6); " . . . ever-virginal Constancy [Rebecca], from the love of whom may it never come about that I cease" (*QG* 4.145).

# CHAPTER TEN

# BIBLICAL VIRGINS (III)
# LEAH (RACHEL), DINAH, TAMAR, AND HANNAH

*Introduction*

In the passage from *De Cherubim* studied in detail in chapter eight, four "virgins" are named: Zipporah, Sarah, Rebecca and Leah. These represent the virtues of Moses and the three patriarchs. It is understandable that Philo should group the four men together. But it is somewhat surprising to find the parallel grouping of Zipporah, Sarah, Rebecca and Leah. Zipporah is prominent neither in the Bible nor in the rest of Philo's writing.[1] Rachel, on the other hand, is. Besides that, she is as much a patriarch's wife as the others. The more natural grouping of female figures, then, would be Sarah, Rebecca, Leah and Rachel. They are all folk-heroines as well as matriarchs. But Philo never explicitly makes such a grouping. His stance toward Rachel is ambivalent.

Occasionally, he does seem to rank Rachel with the other three, or at least with Leah, and thus by extension with Sarah and Rebecca. When he recounts the story of Jacob's flight from Laban, in *De Fuga et Inventione*, he presents Rachel and Leah together as the faculties (*dynameis*) of Jacob, virtues torn from their father Laban, the senseless (16), worthless (17), and good-for-nothing (18) man.

---

[1] Apart from this passage in *Cher.*, her name occurs only two other times in Philo, and then only in passing references (*Post.*77f., *Mut.*120).

> And so the faculties of the Practiser lift their voice aloud, proclaiming their grounds for hatred . . . . Virtues are what has been stripped from him, and has become the property of the worthy . . .(*Fug.* 15-18; cf. *Det.*3).

In *Cong.*27, similarly, he says that "the virtue we call Rachel . . . trains us to despise all that should be held of little account . . . ." Here again, by calling Rachel "virtue," Philo seems to elevate her to the status of the other matriarchs.

In another place he alludes to her receiving seed from God; we recall that in the mystery teaching of *Cher.*42-48 Philo equated this with being virgin. The allusion occurs in his explanation of why, after years of barrenness, Rachel was finally able to conceive. Initially Rachel made the mistake of demanding of Jacob: "Give me children" (Gen.30:1). Philo's commentary on this is as follows:

> . . . the Supplanter [Jacob] will find fault with her [Rachel] and say, "Thou hast greatly erred, for I am not in the place of God, who alone hath power to open the wombs of souls, and to sow virtues in them . . ." (*LA* 3.180).

Some time later, Rachel repents and directs her appeal not to Jacob but to God, whereupon, according to Philo, she conceives:[2]

> Rachel . . . made a recantation breathing true holiness, for Rachel's recantation stands written in a prayer dear to God "Let God add to me another son" (*Post.*179).

The occasional passage such as this inclines the reader to believe that Philo thinks of Rachel as "virtue" and "virgin" along with Sarah, Rebecca and Leah. But in his total treatment of Rachel this is only a minor theme.

---

[2] Gen.30:24 says that she called her first-born Joseph, which means "addition." Philo interprets the name as the prayer, "May the Lord add to me another son." Strictly speaking, this would be a prayer for a second son, which was answered by the birth of Benjamin. But Philo's implication is that her prayer to God brought about her first conception.

The major "virgins," then, are only three, Sarah, Rebecca and Leah. In chapter nine we observed certain similarities in Philo's treatment of Sarah and Rebecca. I shall begin this chapter by discussing his treatment of Leah.

### Leah, Contrasted to Rachel

I showed in the last chapter that, largely by virtue of his detailed treatment of their stories in *Questiones in Genesin*, Philo maintains the tradition of Sarah and Rebecca as folk-heroines, albeit with some modifications. In his retelling of their stories they still sparkle with some individuality. Philo ends *Questiones in Genesin*, however, just as Jacob goes off to seek a wife; thus he does not mention Leah there at all. This omission contributes to the overall impression that Philo's Leah is hardly an individual. She appears rather as a type, a static aspect of the soul, or an experience in the life, of man. Nevertheless, Philo has a great deal to say about her.[3]

A word must be said here about Philo's identification with Jacob. We have already noted that the other patriarchs are to be

---

[3] Leah appears in 16 treatises in all. Most of the treatments of her are short or even incidental. Philo capitalizes on two Biblical passages: Gen.29:31, "The Lord seeing that Leah was hated opened her womb, but Rachel was barren," and Deut.21:15-17:

"If a man has two wives, the one loved and the other hated, and both the loved and the hated should have borne him children, and the son of the hated should be first-born; then it shall be that whensoever he shall divide by inheritance his goods to his sons, he shall not be able to give the right of the first-born to the son of the loved one, having overlooked the son of the hated, which is the first-born. But he shall acknowledge the first-born of the hated one to give him double of all things which shall be found by him, because he is the first of his children, and to him belongs the birthright."

Combining the ideas of the two passages, Philo presents Leah as the hated but deserving wife. This fits the Hebrew meaning of her name: "rejected and faint" (*Cher*.41, cf. *Mut*.254). The most extended passage about her, *Sac*.19-44, actually does not mention her by name. But since Philo so regularly identifies Leah with the hated wife, she is clearly in the background of this passage.

In two other places, *Heres* 49f. and *LA* 2.47f., Philo does explicitly relate Deut.21:15-17 to Gen.29:31, so as to identify Leah with the hated wife.

emulated. But Jacob, or Israel, is in a special sense the prototype of a struggling people, and of the individual striving for perfection. He is the one made perfect through practice. He makes mistakes, but keeps trying. Philo's identification of himself and his reader with Jacob is evident in these two passages:

> . . . anyone whose mind is set on enduring to the end the weary contest in which virtue is the prize, who practises continually for that end, and is unflagging in self-discipline, will take to him two lawful wives and as handmaids to them two concubines. And to each of them is given quite a different nature and appearance (*Cong*.24f.).

> God opens the wombs of virtue, sowing in them noble doings, but the womb, after receiving virtue at God's hand, does not bear to God--for He that IS is in need of no one--but bears sons to me Jacob (*LA* 3.181).

Leah, then, is to be seen in relationship to Jacob, who, in turn, is identified with Jewish man in general.

Philo has dispensed with the element of folk-heroine in his presentation of Leah. Two main portrayals of her remain: a) an element of character that the mature man takes unto himself, and b) an ideal wife. The former tends to be an allegorical portrayal, and the latter more literal. But, as is customary with Philo, the two lines of interpretation meet and combine. Leah appears consistently in Philo as a static type, devoid of any dynamics of personality. Rachel is usually presented in the same way, as a foil to Leah.

Indeed it would be difficult to delineate Philo's Leah without presenting Rachel as well. Although, as we have already seen, Rachel is occasionally identified with the other matriarchs, much more frequently she is presented as the antithesis of Leah. In all, four patterns of contrast can be found in Philo's depictions of Rachel and Leah:

a) Leah is Sarah the virgin and Rachel is Eve the woman.
b) Leah is Sarah, wisdom, and Rachel is Hagar, lower education.
c) Leah is the noble woman and Rachel is the harlot.

d) Leah is the hated wife and Rachel is the loved wife.

As I discuss Leah as virgin, wisdom, noble woman and hated wife, respectively, I shall include Philo's contrasting remarks about Rachel. Finally, I shall mention the one glimpse of character development in these pictures, viz., Rachel's repentance.

The first pattern contrasts Rachel the Eve-like woman with Leah the Sarah-like virgin. In the quotation from *LA* 3.180, above, Jacob reprimands the barren woman, Rachel, when she demands children of him. But when Leah the virgin commands him, "Thou shalt come in unto me today" (Gen.30:16), he complies, "for whither indeed should he go in, he who is tending the seeds and saplings of knowledge, save to virtue, the field of his husbandry?" (*Cong.*123). These actions conform to the pattern we have already established, viz., that a man does not obey a woman, because woman is inferior to man, but he does obey virgin virtue, because it is functionally equivalent to a male element within his female soul.

Leah receives divine impregnation, for so Philo interprets Gen.29:31, "The Lord . . . opened her womb:

> But for Leah, estrangement on the human side brings about fellowship with God, and from Him she receives the seed of wisdom, and is in birth-throes, and brings forth beautiful ideas worthy of the Father Who begat them (*Post.*135, cf. *Mut.*132f.,254).

She conforms further to the pattern of virgin virtue in the soul, which we have already observed in Sarah and Rebecca, by being the virtue possessed by Jacob (*Post.*62), beauty of soul (*Sob.*12), and the bearer of divine offspring (*LA* 2.95).

Rachel, in contrast, is comeliness of body (*Sob.*12), and the unreasoning part of the soul that acts through sense (*Cong.*25ff.). These we recognize as characteristics of woman, as opposed to virgin. This perception of Rachel is emphasized in *Ebr.*54-59. It is an allegory on Rachel's menstruation as a sign of moral weakness, and is inspired by the words of Gen.31:35: "I cannot rise before thee, because the custom of women is upon me." Rachel represents custom (menstruation), "the special property of women . . . the rule of the weaker and more effeminate soul." Until her conversion she is unable to bear offspring to God. To a large extent, she plays Eve to Leah's Sarah.

Philo also contrasts Leah and Rachel according to the pattern he has established for Sarah and Hagar. In the treatise *De Congressu Eruditionis Causa*, which for the most part allegorizes Sarah as wisdom and Hagar as *paideia*, he inserts a section (*Cong*.24-33) in which Leah and Rachel play these two roles. The same pattern occurs in *Ebr*.49, the reference to sisters signifying an allusion to Leah and Rachel:

> And therefore to this day the lovers of true nobility do not attend at the door of the elder sister, philosophy, till they have taken knowledge of the younger sisters, grammar and geometry and the whole range of the school culture.

In another passage, where he is illustrating the difference between Isaac, the husband of one, and Abraham and Jacob, who each had several women, Philo says:

> When God rains down from heaven the good of which the self is a teacher and learner both, it is impossible that that self should still live in concubinage with the slavish arts, as though desiring to be the father of bastard thoughts and conclusions (*Cong*.36).

Here Hagar and Rachel, as partners of Abraham and Jacob respectively, represent the "slavish arts." Philo continues in this vein when he presents Laban as the Sophist who wants to put philosophy before *paideia*. That is why he tricks Jacob into marrying Leah (philosophy) before Rachel (*paideia*). When Jacob challenges Laban, the latter urges him to terminate (*sunteleson*), his association with Leah (Gen.29:27). Jacob responds by fulfilling (*aneplērōse*) her (Gen.29:28). The *LXX* uses the two verbs to convey similar meanings, viz., "to be done with" Leah. But Philo distinguishes between them to show the difference between Laban the Sophist and Jacob the wise. Laban urges that Jacob abandon Leah; Jacob responds by

## Biblical Virgins (III): Leah, Dinah, Tamar and Hannah 167

"fulfilling" her, that is, by rounding out his philosophical education by taking on the *paideia* which he should have married first.

The final two points of contrast between Leah and Rachel are those that show the difference between noble woman and harlot and between loved and hated wife. Here the allegorical thread is intertwined with the literal. Philo presents the two sisters in two ways: both as aspects of the soul to be fostered or rejected, and also as individual women to be accepted or spurned. Here, when we find Leah presented as woman, we come close to Philo's prescription for the kind of woman a Jew should marry. We also find between her and Rachel something similar to the distinction discovered in the chapter on Biblical women, between the women admitted to Miriam's choir and those excluded.

For this kind of treatment literary precedents abound. In the Jewish tradition there are already the loved and hated wives of Deut.21:15-17. Isa.3:16-24 describes the wantonness of the daughters of Zion that leads to the downfall of the men (v.25). Chapter 31 of Proverbs portrays the good wife, and chapters 7 to 9 present Wisdom competing with the seductive woman for the young man's attention. In the Greek tradition there is Xenophon's well-known fable of Hercules' meeting with the two women, Virtue and Vice.

I shall examine in some detail Philo's one extended passage about such a pair, *Sac*.20-45.[4] Although dependence on his Biblical sources is obvious, the pattern Philo is following is clearly that of Xenophon's *Memorabilia* of Socrates 2.1. [5]

---

[4] Sections 21-32 were omitted by Mangey, whose edition of Philo preceded the standard one of Cohn and Wendland (1896-1914), but Colson argues for their authenticity (*PLCL*, vol.2, p.93), although admitting that "the treatise is improved by their absence. The picture has a certain vigour, but is not on the whole in Philo's best vein, and the catalogue of vices with which it concludes is surely ridiculous."
    The passage is embarrassingly heavy-handed, and has, perhaps with justification, been neglected by Philonic scholars. Its main topic, the presentation of the two women, is given no attention in Goodenough's *By Light, Light*, Wolfson's *Philo*, or Winston's anthology, *Philo of Alexandria*.

[5] See Bréhier, *Les Idées*, pp.265f.

Philo begins by quoting Deut.21:15-17, the passage about the loved and hated wives. He continues, "each of us is mated with two wives," an allusion to Rachel and Leah. From this introductory material he makes an awkward transition into a paraphrase of Xenophon, for when Pleasure, the first woman, makes her appearance (*Sac*.21), she comes not as a wife but as a stranger. She comes "in the guise of a harlot or courtesan," with a loose gait and rolling eyes, and "assumes a stature which Nature has not given her." These features follow, with some embellishment, Xenophon's description of Vice who approaches with eyes wide open, trying to seem taller than her natural height (*Mem*.22). Philo adds a note of judgement to his description: "a strumpet of the streets, she takes the market-place for her home; devoid of true beauty, she pursues the false" (*Sac*.21). Later we are told that Pleasure resorts to magic and trickery: " . . . for by her talismans and witchcrafts the sorceress was pricking him, and working in him the itch of desire" (*Sac*.26). She is "Pleasure, that lewd dealer in magic and inventor of fables . . . " (*Sac*.28). She has " . . . a false and spurious comeliness, which is mere nets and snares to take you as her prey" (*Sac*.29).[6]

In each account this woman accosts the man with an opening speech that promises a life of ease and freedom (*Sac*.22-25, *Mem*.23-25). After this we are ready to hear Virtue's argument in her own defence. Xenophon describes this woman as modest, engaging and sober, plainly clad and moving with graceful mien (*Mem*.22). Her counterpart in Philo is similar, but again described more elaborately: a freeborn citizen, firm, serene, modest, moral, honest, plainly dressed, with unaffected carriage, and a host of virtues in her train (*Sac*.26f.).[7] This woman's speech, in Philo, begins with a tirade

---

[6] Cf. *Ebr*.49 and *Post*.135, where Philo accuses Rachel of using *philtra*. Philo uses similar accusations against the Midianite women (*Mos*.1.311 "bewitched"; *Spec*.1.56 "love charms"); the charge of using hunting devices (nets and snares) is also made against them (See ch.7, above).

[7] Cf. the description of the good woman in the Neopythagorean document given in translation in Lefkowitz and Fant, *Women's Lives*, pp. 104f.: "As far as adornment of her body is concerned, the same arguments apply. She should be dressed in white, natural, plain. Her clothes should not be transparent or ornate. She

against Vice, culminating in what must surely be the most exaggerated vice list in literature--almost 150 items (*Sac.*32)--one of which is "womanish" (*thēludrias*).[8] When Philo has exhausted his list, he returns to paraphrasing his source, as a comparison of the following passages will show:

> . . . of what is valuable and excellent, the gods grant nothing to mankind without labour and care; and if you wish the gods, therefore, to be propitious to you, you must worship the gods . . . (*Mem.*28).

> Choose any good thing whatsoever, and you will find that it results from and is established through toil. Piety and holiness are good, but we cannot attain to them save through the service of God . . . (*Sac.*37).

Each praises toil, the gift Virtue holds out for mankind. The basic difference between the two is that Philo has changed the references to Greek deities in order to comply with his belief in one God.

Philo's presentation of the two women differs significantly from Xenophon's in tone.[9] Besides giving her outward description, Philo imputes motives to Pleasure. She is presented as deceptive, using unfair tactics like magic. Whereas Xenophon's Virtue addresses Vice (Pleasure) directly in challenge, Philo's Virtue addresses the man, warning him against the traps of the other. The dangerous character of Pleasure or Vice predominates.

---

should not put on silken material, but moderate, white-coloured clothes. In this way she will avoid being over-dressed or luxurious or made-up, and not give other women cause to be uncomfortably envious. She should not wear gold or emeralds at all; these are expensive and arrogant towards other women in the village. She should not apply imported or artificial colouring to her face--with her own natural colouring, by washing only with water, she can ornament herself with modesty."

[8] This is actually a noun, meaning "a womanish person," but Colson translates it as an adjective.
Xenophon's counterpart to this section is much more modest.

[9] See Bréhier's comparison of the two passages in *Les Idées*, pp.265f.

Xenophon's account ends with Hercules at the point of making a choice. Philo, however, rambles on. Finally he states Mind's choice. It "turns away from pleasure and cleaves to virtue, for it apprehends her loveliness, so pure, so simple, so holy to look upon" (*Sac*.45).

A shorter and more artistic presentation of the same theme occurs in *Sob*.23:

> . . . we declare that in the beloved wife we have a figure of pleasure and in the hated wife a figure of prudence. For pleasure's company is beloved beyond measure by the great mass of men, because from the hour of their birth to the utmost limits of old age she produces and sets before them such enticing lures and love-charms; while for prudence, severe and august as she is, they have a strange and profound hatred . . . .

Each of Philo's treatments of the theme is characterized by a pessimistic note; the mass of mankind is destined to choose the worse and to hate the better.

The theme of Leah as the hated wife recurs in *Heres* 45ff. and *LA* 2.47, as well as in *Post*.135, where Leah represents the soul that seeks God and thereby is estranged from humanity. This interpretation conforms to the meaning of her name, "rejected." Whereas in his comparisons of the loved and hated wives we have just been examining, it seems appropriate to interpret Philo's words partly on the human level, here we return to pure allegory. Leah seems here to represent Philo's feelings of ostracism as a pious Jew in a hostile environment. That is, virtue, Leah, stands for its possessor, Jacob, whose spiritual journey Philo relives. In other words, Leah, Jacob and Philo are identified:

> . . . Leah, who is above the passions, cannot tolerate those who are attracted by the spells of the pleasures that accord with Rachel, who is sense-perception; wherefore, finding themselves treated with contempt by her they hate her. But for Leah, *estrangement on the human side brings about fellowship with God*, and from Him she receives the seed of

wisdom, and brings forth beautiful ideas worthy of the Father Who begat them. Then if thou too, O soul, follow Leah's example and turn away from mortal things, thou wilt of necessity turn to the Incorruptible One, Who will cause all the springs of moral beauty to pour their streams upon thee (*Post*.135, emphasis mine).

In *Heres* 45ff. again Leah stands for a whole person. Philo is dividing human beings into three types: the two extremes which contemplate God and creation respectively, and the mixed type, which vacillates between the two. Isaac and Moses are born into the first type, and Abraham rises to reach it. People like Jacob and Philo belong to the intermediate group, but have the hope of short-lived flights into the first: "It is the mixed life, which often drawn on by those of the higher line is possessed and inspired by God, though often pulled back by the worse it reverses its course" (*Heres* 46). In this passage Philo places Leah also in this level, but relegates Rachel to the third: "Now Moses while he gives the crown of undisputed victory to the Godward kind of life, brings the other two into comparison by likening them to two women, one of whom he calls the beloved, and the other the hated" (*Heres* 47). This is high praise for Leah, though it must be observed that it is through identification with her husband Jacob that she attains this honour.[10] It is complemented by the statement in *Plant*.135 that Leah reaches perfection.

Returning to the more earthly level, I believe we have enough evidence to show that Leah and Rachel represent two extremes of womanhood, the freeborn lady and the slavish harlot.

Philo is ambivalent about slavery. Occasionally he can deplore it as an accident of birth, but more frequently he accepts it as part of the chain of being, integral to the overall scheme of things. Slaves are slavish by nature, and, again by nature, rank lower

---

[10] For a full discussion of Philo's three levels of attainment, and the terms he uses in connection with them, see Mendelson, *Education*, ch.3.

than free men and women.[11] Thus "slavish" and "freeborn" become terms of evaluation. In the same way, the noun *astē*, female citizen, becomes a term expressing favourable judgement, related to the adjective *asteia*, "noble," "urbane," rather than being any sort of technical term. Philo's highest praise for a woman--apart from transforming her into a virgin--is to call her a free and noble citizen. If we recall the two women, Virtue and Vice, of *Sac*.20-45, we will remember that Virtue had "all the marks of a free-born citizen" (*Sac*.26), whereas Vice came "in the guise of a harlot or courtesan" (*Sac*.21). In *Mig*.95-99 Philo uses the terms *astai te kai asteiai*, "citizen women and worthy of their citizenship." He intertwines two stories here, as he often does: in this case the stories are those of Leah and of the women who contributed their treasures to the tabernacle. He begins by referring to Leah's words when she has borne Asher: "Happy am I, for the women will call me happy." It is more customary of Philo to speak disparagingly of the women's quarter (cf. *Som*.2.9; *QG* 4.15) which represents the lower, female, life. But in this passage he distinguishes the worthwhile women from the others, and says that it is important to have a good reputation among the better class of women in the women's quarter:

> It is characteristic of a perfect soul to aspire both to be and to be thought to be, and to take pains not only to have a good reputation in the men's quarters, but to receive the praises of the women's as well . . . . These [the women who contribute to the tabernacle], in whose eyes Leah, that is virtue, desires to be honoured are citizen women and worthy

---

[11] Philo's attitude is illustrated by two passages from *De Josepho*: Joseph claims, ". . . I am not a slave, but as highly-born as any, one who claims enrolment among the citizens of that best and greatest state, the world"(69). When he comes out of jail, he is recognized by one of his own kind: "The king, judging him by his appearance to be a man of free and noble birth, for the persons of those whom we see exhibit characteristics which are not visible to all, but only in those in whom the eye of the understanding is quick to discern . . ."(106).
    See also *Spec*.4.14-18 where Philo deplores the selling of noble and freeborn men into slavery, not because slavery is wrong, but because it is wrong *for these people* to be slaves.

of their citizenship (*astai te kai asteiai gynaikes hōs alēthōs*) (*Mig*.96-99).

This is a reminder of the distinction Philo makes when he speaks of Miriam admitting the "best" of the women to her choir. Thus, it appears that when Philo is considering women on the human level, he divides them into two classes, i.e., noble, freeborn women, and slavish harlots. Leah and Rachel represent these two extremes.

We cannot leave the discussion of Leah and Rachel without considering the change that takes place in Rachel. As we observed earlier, after years of barrenness Rachel conceives because she has recognized that it is God who gives her children. Repentance, for Philo, is a very noble virtue, second only to perfection, and a sign of a robust and truly manly soul (*Abr*.26). Yet his treatment of Rachel's repentance does not sustain this conception. Rachel never loses the taint of her earlier life.[12] In *Post*.178f. she is portrayed as grasping repentance, and no longer pursuing pleasure. She is rewarded with the birth of Joseph and Benjamin. Yet Philo does not see her now as a completely changed person. He attributes Joseph's character flaws to his mother. Manifest in him is the "irrational strain of sense-perception, assimilated to what he derives from his mother, the part of him that is of the Rachel type" (*Som*.2.16). Joseph is unable to acknowledge the creative power of God, again like his mother (*LA* 3.180). And the birth of Benjamin is accompanied by Rachel's death:

> And so God's interpreter [Moses] could not but represent the mother of vainglory dying in the very pangs of childbirth. Rachel died, we read, in hard labour (Gen.35:16,19), for the conception and birth of vainglory, the creature of sense, is in reality the death of the soul (*Mut*.96).

---

[12] Cf. *Spec*.1.102, where Philo maintains that the harlot, though repentant, still bears scars. In contrast to that, Philo writes in *Spec*.1.187 that the Day of Atonement is "a time of purification and escape from sins, for which indemnity is granted by the bounties of the gracious God Who has given to repentance the same honour as to innocence from sin."

When Jacob dies, he is buried not with Rachel, but with Leah (*Post*.62).

Philo does not appear to have thought through his position on Rachel. His overall portrayal of her is not satisfactory because he does not carry the theme of repentance to its expected conclusion. Rachel is still dogged by her womanliness, even when she makes short flights into virginity and virtue, and she dies a tragic figure.

## *The Other Virgins*

Sarah, Rebecca and Leah, along with Rachel to a very limited degree, are the virgins who receive major treatment in Philo. There are four others. We have already mentioned Zipporah, about whom Philo says virtually nothing. The remaining three, Dinah, Tamar and Hannah, receive short but significant treatment.

### Dinah

Since her father Jacob is also Israel, Dinah represents the daughters of Israel. Scripture says that there shall not be a harlot of the daughters of Israel (Deut.35:17). Philo builds on the meaning of that verse to deny that Dinah was the victim of the rape recorded in Genesis 34. By doing so he indicates that in his mind the harlot and the victim of rape are equal, in that they are both "defiled." The point of his remarks is that the daughter of Israel remains virgin and undefiled. But this is entirely an allegorical interpretation, in which Dinah represents a particular virtue of the soul, judgement:

> For Justice has indeed existence, Justice the abhorrer of wickedness, the relentless one, the inexorable, the befriender of those who are wronged, bringing failure upon the aims of those who shame virtue, upon whose fall the soul, that had seemed to have been shamed, becomes a virgin. Seemed, I said, because it never was defiled. It is with sufferings which we have not willed, as it is with wrongdoings which we

have not intended. As there is no real doing in the second case, so there is no real suffering in the first (*Mig*.225, cf. *Mut*.194f.).

Dinah does not appear in Philo as a person, and there is no outrage addressed to the fact of her being the victim of rape.

## Tamar

Tamar is mentioned in seven treatises in all, but like Dinah, she is completely allegorized (except for one instance).[13] Her name means palm tree, the sign of victory (*LA* 3.74). The fact that her two husbands have died means that she is "widowed of the passions which corrupt and maltreat the mind" (*Deus* 136). Philo does not discuss the morality of Tamar's or Judah's actions. He stresses that she is not what she appears; that is, although she appears to be a harlot, and therefore representative of Judah's body, she is actually a high-born lady, his mind (*Fug*.153f.).

It is interesting that in the midst of this allegory Philo puts into Judah's mouth a capsule definition of what we have come to recognize as his ideal woman:[14]

> "Is it not my heart-felt prayer that my understanding (*dianoia*) should be a true and high-born lady (*asteian te kai astēn hōs alēthōs*), eminent for chastity and modesty and all other virtues, devoted to one husband and keeping watch with delight over the home of one, and exulting in a sole ruler" (*Fug*.154).

---

[13] Tamar appears in *LA* 3.74, *Deus* 136f., *Cong*.124, *Fug*.149-156, *Mut*.134, *Som*.2.44, and *Virt*.221.

[14] Colson notes in a footnote that "the allegory seems to get a little confused at this point" (*PLCL*, vol.v., p.93).

Tamar did not see the one who fathered her child, because her face was veiled, but Philo implies that it was God (*Mut*.134). Thus he establishes Tamar as another virgin (see *Cher*.50).

The one instance in which Tamar is presented as a woman is in the treatise *De Virtutibus*. Philo has been lauding Abraham as the ideal proselyte (*Virt*.219). Then he adds a section on women proselytes, giving Tamar as the example of a free-born foreign woman and Bilhah and Zilpah as examples of slaves. The Bible omits mention of Tamar's lineage, but Jewish tradition presents her in two different ways: both as daughter of a priest and as a foreign convert.[15] Philo chooses the latter and praises her, saying that

> bred in a home and city which acknowledged a multitude of gods and was full of images and wooden busts and idols in general . . . she kept her own life stainless and was able to win the good report which belongs to the good and to become the original source to which the nobility of all who followed her can be traced (*Virt*.221f.).[16]

Philo may be serving an apologetic aim here, justifying Tamar's place in the royal lineage of Israel, or he may be making allowances for the intermarriage he sees around him, but establishing certain limits for it.[17]

---

[15] *The Jewish Encyclopedia*, s.v. Tamar; Ginzberg, *Legends of the Jews*, vol.2.

[16] Alan Mendelson suggests that Philo is gentle in his treatment of foreign women (Hagar, Bilhah, Zilpah, Zipporah) on pragmatic grounds: " . . . we might conclude that, on a practical level, the alternative to intermarriage was conversion of the alien . . . . Philo's laxness on the subject may be a sign that such unions were not unknown and that the better part of wisdom was to hope for the conversion of the non-Jewish partner." *Philo's Jewish Identity* (unpublished typescript, p.73)

[17] To support the belief that intermarriage did occur see Feldman: "We ought not to be surprised if, with participation on the part of the intelligentsia in such basic Greek cultural institutions as the gymnasium and the theatre, we should find considerable apostasy and intermarriage" ("Orthodoxy," p.227).

## Hannah

Finally, there is Hannah. Though mentioned only in five places in Philo, she is afforded the highest honours.[18] She is named prophetess and mother of a prophet (*Som*.1.254), disciple and successor of Abraham (*Deus* 5), and soul beloved of God (*Deus* 10). She represents the God-possessed soul in *Ebr*.146f., a commentary on *LXX* 1 Kings (1 Samuel) 1:14, where Eli's servant accuses Hannah of being drunk because he cannot recognize the signs of possession. Hannah is even likened to Abraham; just as Abraham showed his devotion to God by offering his son, so Hannah does the same with Samuel, returning the gift to the giver (*Deus* 5, based on Philo's reading of 1 Kings (1 Sam.) 1:28; the *LXX* actually reads *chrēsin*, "loan" in v.28, but Philo may be remembering that v.11 has *doton* "gift").

Philo attests to her virginity: "But when she has become barren . . . she is transformed into a pure virgin" (*Praem*.159). Thus even though he also says of her that "her nature is of a happy and goodly motherhood" (*Deus* 13), he elevates her far above mere womanhood, and her motherhood exists in the soul rather than in the body. It is made even clearer that Philo sees Hannah as a soul type, to be understood purely in allegory, when he introduces the story of Samuel her son in these words:

> Now probably there was an actual man called Samuel; but we conceive of the Samuel of the scripture, not as a living compound of soul and body, but as a mind which rejoices in the service and worship of God and that only (*Ebr*.144).

If Samuel the person is irrelevant to the statements Philo wants to make, how much more so is his mother. Thus in Hannah, the most glorified of the virgins of Scripture, we find a figure least related to actual womanhood.

---

[18] *Deus* 5, 10f., *Ebr*.145-152, *Mut*.143, *Som*.1.254, *Praem*.159f.

*Conclusion*

This chapter and the preceding two have been a presentation of the women of the Bible to whom Philo attributes virginity. This virginity occurs only on the allegorical level. When he is interpreting Scripture literally, Philo presents them as women. But the allegorical material outweighs the literal, both in sheer amount and in the importance Philo places upon it.

It is on the allegorical level that these persons gain Philo's highest praise. Sarah, Rebecca and Leah are their husbands' virtues. Tamar, Dinah and Hannah represent soul types; these three are presented entirely on the allegorical level, except for one instance where Tamar becomes the representative proselyte.

Leah as woman is the good wife, the citizen woman, in contrast to the harlot, Rachel. Rebecca and Sarah are folk-heroines, but their stories are subtly modified so as to make them inferior to their mates, and of one mind with their husbands.

The point of contact between the matriarchs of Scripture and the "good" women whom we studied earlier is the description *asteia te kai astē*. Such a one is a real person, a woman, yet one who has earned Philo's admiration, like the virgin. She takes the place in society that is prescribed for her, and exercises freedom within its constraints. The purpose of her action and her existence is to contribute to the well-being of man. When the matriarchs of Scripture are presented as women, they are made to fit this description. This is further evidence for the soundness of the hypothesis presented in chapter seven, i.e., that acceptable women operate within a framework prescribed by men, and in their actions they defer to men.

Whereas the virgin has little in common with the vast majority of real women, it is likely that when he is assessing the women of his own society Philo will use the Biblical *astē* as the model for good womanhood.

# CHAPTER ELEVEN

# WOMEN OF PHILO'S WORLD

*Introduction*

We have observed that Philo employs sexual distinctions both philosophically and practically. Throughout this study I have defended the position that these two modes of sexual distinction are inextricably intertwined: Philo presupposes that there is a natural difference between the sexes, and that this difference should and does permeate all aspects of being. I have described the pattern by which he views reality as a particular version of the Great Chain of Being-- that pattern which presents the cosmos as a hierarchy in which each inferior member is drawn in *eros* and service to those above, and each superior member accepts the deference of the lower, at the same time supporting them in an attitude of *noblesse oblige*.[1] Philo equates masculine with the qualities that are superior, active and more spiritual, and feminine with their opposites.

Philo's treatment of the women of the Biblical stories reflects this world view. He bends Scripture to fit the pattern, all the while professing loyalty to its unchanging power.[2] We have seen that in presenting the women of Scripture he achieves his ends by liberal

---

[1] See my discussion of the Great Chain in chapter six.

[2] "So whether what he [Moses] told them [the Israelites] came from his own reasoning powers or was learnt from some supernatural source they held it all to come from God and after the lapse of many years, how many I cannot say exactly, but at any rate for more than two thousand, they have not changed a single word of what he wrote but would even endure to die a thousand deaths sooner than accept anything contrary to the laws and customs which he had ordained." *Hyp*.6.9. Cf. *Mos*.2.14.

use of allegory, by omission, by emphasis, and even by alteration of the text.

Under his hand the most admirable of the Biblical women are for the most part allegorized into virgins, and thus freed from the inferiority which womanhood entails. On the occasions when he allows them to emerge as real women, their virtues always pale beside their husbands', and discordant wills are harmonized.

Those persons who are presented as women fall into two groups, depending upon whether they are useful or dangerous to good men. The groups are designated by the terms *astai* and *pornai*, or figuratively identified with those included in or excluded from Miriam's chorus. Good women, *astai*, know and accept their place in the system, whereas bad women, *pornai*, do not.

Having seen how Philo fits the female figures of the Bible into his *Weltanschauung*, we turn now to his perception of the women round about him. Here again, we shall see that the same world-view predominates. Philo views contemporary women from virtually the same perspective.

Sources

Most of the statements that deal directly with women of Philo's day appear in the large section of his work called the *Exposition*. This section presupposes less familiarity with scripture than the other large section, the *Allegory*.[3] It is generally held, therefore, to be directed towards a wider readership--perhaps to disaffected Jews, or even to the Gentile public.[4] For our purposes it does not

---

[3] See ch.3, n.14, for the basic distinction between the *Allegory* and the *Exposition*.

[4] The former position is held by Sandmel. The latter had been proposed earlier by Goodenough. Sandmel, *Philo*, p.47, argues, in reaction to Goodenough, "that there is no evidence that Gentiles (as distinct from Christians) read any Jewish writings, whether the Septuagint or Philo." He continues: "Yet an obliquely related missionary purpose is tenable, especially if we conceive of the presence in Alexandria of Jews nearly on the verge of leaving the Jewish community, as did Philo's

really matter how far afield Philo was directing his work; the important observation is that in the *Exposition* he is thinking of a readership beyond his inner circle, and consequently adopts an apologetic stance. It is clearly his purpose to present the regulations of Scripture as the finest and most reasonable representations of the natural law.

The treatises in which he undertakes this task most explicitly are *De Decalogo* and the four books of *De Specialibus Legibus*. The first of these covers the ten commandments, and the succeeding four examine specific laws, which Philo groups under the heading of one or other of the ten in turn. Philo introduces the enterprise as follows:

> Having related in the preceding treatises the lives of those whom Moses judged to be men of wisdom, who are set before us in the Sacred Books as founders of our nation and in themselves unwritten laws, I shall now proceed in due course to give full descriptions of the written laws. And if some allegorical interpretation should appear to underlie them, I shall not fail to state it. For knowledge loves to learn and advance to full understanding and its way is to seek the hidden meaning rather than the obvious (*Dec*.1).

Part way through the last book of *Special Laws*, having come to the end of his ten categories, Philo changes his approach. In the remainder of the book, as well as in the following two, *De Virtutibus* and *De Praemiis et Poenis*, he presents more laws under a different set of headings, and makes general observations about the law.

Most of the material relating the law to women occurs in the four books of *Special Laws*. Although Philo promised to employ allegory (*Dec*.1, quoted above), he limits its use to his discussion of certain topics. In fact, his treatment of social and civic law is almost

---

nephew. *The Exposition* might well have been addressed to them."
    Regarding the assertion that Jewish works were unknown to pagans, however, see D. A. Russell, *'Longinus' On the Sublime* (Oxford: Clarendon Press, 1964), pp.93ff. Russell says that *On the Sublime* 9.9 makes specific reference to the Genesis story, and that there are noteworthy similarities in thought between Philo and Longinus.

allegory-free, leaving the reader usually with only one level of meaning to grasp.[5] Thus we should be able to find in these treatises a clear and unambiguous picture of Philo's perception of contemporary women.

Another treatise in the *Exposition*, *On the Contemplative Life*, provides a description of an ascetic group, the *Therapeutae*, which has women members.

A third source of material relevant to this study is the treatise *Apology for the Jews*, or *Hypothetica*, which contains Philo's account of the Essenes and their relation to women.

## Tendencies

A question that has exercised some scholarly minds is whether or not in the *Special Laws* Philo is describing actual legal practice. Interesting as it is, this question is not immediately relevant to the topic at hand. Let me explain with an example. In several instances Philo calls for the death penalty, sometimes even "without bringing the offender before jury or council or any kind of magistrate at all" (*Spec*.1.55; cf. 3.51). For the present purpose it is enough to know that Philo considered certain crimes to be such a threat to the Jewish community that the transgressors must be eliminated. Demands for the death penalty primarily reveal something about Philo's thought. Although it would be interesting to know whether anyone followed the suggestions with action, that knowledge would not alter the perception underlying the words. And the present study is concerned with perceptions.

At the same time, we should take into account the possibility that Philo is deliberately, or even subconsciously, creating an effect

---

[5] " . . . allegory is almost entirely absent from the *De Dec.* itself and only appears occasionally in the civil or social laws of the *Spec. Leg.* though many of these have been allegorized at length in the Commentary . . . . On the other hand, when he is dealing with the sacrifices in Book I and the feasts in Book II allegory or rather symbolism is almost universal. Naturally enough. For both sacrifices and feasts have little meaning for him except the spiritual." *PLCL*, vol.7, xiii.

because of the need to write apologetically. We have already noted that in most of the source material we are discussing in this chapter he is writing for a readership that may be skeptical if not hostile, and that therefore it may legitimately be expected that his work will have an apologetic note.

With regard to women, the possibility of two tendencies should be considered.

The first is the desire to present female sexuality with a low profile. This would accord with Philo's proclivity, mentioned elsewhere, to outdo Scripture in portraying the Jews as a sexually restrained people. A similar tendency is evident in certain passages in the New Testament, where the motive for restraining women is openly declared.[6] In each case the writer is aiming to guard the group's reputation in the larger community. Since home-centred women were universally admired by men of ancient culture--pagan, Jew and Christian alike--a group that kept its women bound to the home would gain general respect.

The second tendency is, in a sense, opposite to the first: to present Jewish law as being in tune with the times. In the survey in chapter two we observed that in the gentile society of Alexandria-- Roman, Egyptian or Greek--women had more rights than their forebears had enjoyed a few centuries earlier. Philo could not fail to observe the increased independence of women, whether he "was intimately in touch with all aspects of the teeming life of Alexandria," as Goodenough believed, or travelled only in the more

---

[6] Titus 2:4f.: "[The older women should] train the young women to love their husbands and children, to be sensible, chaste, domestic, kind and submissive to their husbands, *that the word of God may not be discredited*" (RSV, emphasis mine).

1 Tim.5:13f.: "[Young widows] learn to be idlers, gadding about from house to house, and not only idlers but gossips and busybodies, saying what they should not. So I would have younger widows marry, bear children, rule their households, *and give the enemy no occasion to revile us*" (RSV, emphasis mine).

*Philoteknia* and *philandria* were womanly virtues generally praised in pagan culture. See Martin Dibelius and Hans Conzelmann, *The Pastoral Epistles* (Philadelphia: Fortress Press, 1972), p.140 for references to authors, particularly Plutarch, and inscriptions.

privileged circles of society, as seems more likely.[7] Since he believed that the Mosaic law could never be outmoded, he may have genuinely believed that it could acknowledge certain societal trends while still remaining true to itself. His *Weltanschauung*, as we have observed, leads him to be less concerned with absolutes than with relative positions. Lower forms (designated as feminine, passive, inferior) need not be eliminated or crushed, but, rather, controlled. On the interpersonal level, woman need not be degraded or even ostentatiously put in her place. She need simply be subject to male command and male interest.[8] A passage from *De Migratione Abrahami* expresses very clearly how Philo expects the elements in a hierarchy to interact. In this passage Philo uses "earth" and "kindred" to represent body and sense-perception; we are more accustomed to his using "woman" in that sense.

> We have now shewn how Moses uses "earth" to represent the body, "kindred" to represent sense-perception, "thy father's house" to represent speech. The words "Depart out of these" are not equivalent to "Sever thyself from them absolutely," since to issue such a command as that would be to prescribe death. No, the words import "Make thyself a stranger to them in judgement and purpose; let none of them cling to thee; rise superior to them all; they are thy subjects, never treat them as sovereign lords; thou art a king, school thyself once and for all to rule, not to be ruled; evermore be coming to know thyself, as Moses teaches thee in many places, saying "Give heed to thyself"(Ex.xxiv.12), for *in this way shalt thou perceive those to whom it befits thee to shew obedience and those to whom it befits thee to give commands* (7f.; emphasis mine).

---

[7] Goodenough's statement is from *Jurisprudence*, p.2. Later in this chapter I raise the possibility that Philo's observations of women excluded a large class that fell between the two extremes that he termed "ladies" and "harlots."

[8] Once the proper relationship of dominance and submission is established, Philo then speaks as though equality exists: " . . . reflection . . . should lead both husbands and wives to cherish temperance and domesticity and unanimity, and by mutual sympathy shewn in word and deed to make the name of partnership a reality securely founded on truth" (*Spec*.1.138).

It is possible, then, for Philo to perceive the law as condoning, indeed foreshadowing, a situation in which women play an increasingly active role, as long as they remain within the limits of his view of what is right, viz., "for the better to rule always and everywhere, and for the worse to be ruled" (*LA* 1.72).

As we look at Philo's remarks about contemporary women, it is probable that we will find, then, two apologetic tendencies: on the one hand, to present Jewish women as sexually restrained, and, on the other, to show them enjoying freedom comparable to that of their gentile sisters. We can acknowledge the existence of these tendencies without resorting to Goodenough's claim that Philo is actually describing current practice under the guise of interpreting Scripture.[9]

### The Decalogue and the Special Laws

Starting with Philo's introduction to the laws in his treatise *On the Decalogue*, I shall draw the reader's attention to apparent concessions to women's importance, which illustrate the second tendency just mentioned. Twice in this treatise Philo adds to the Septuagint wording an expression that might be construed in this way. It is my conclusion, however, that these two concessions, and others like them, are only superficial. As I explained in introducing this tendency, Philo will not allow any real disturbance of the fundamental subordination of female to male.

---

[9] What I would observe as a "tendency," Goodenough interprets as evidence that Philo was reporting the laws as they had been adapted to Alexandrian Jewish society: ". . . he always has a definite purpose in what he is writing, the purpose of squaring the letter of the Scriptures with the Alexandrine thought of his generation. Usually it is Alexandrine idealism which he is reading back into the Written Word, but often it is Alexandrine ethics, or just plain common sense" (*Jurisprudence*, p.2). "The influence of Egyptian legal equality of womanhood is everywhere apparent in a way a philosopher in his study would not have introduced it, but as social pressure of generations would have made itself felt" (ibid., p.99). See Appendix A.

One instance is simply an additional phrase; Philo comments on the fifth commandment, "Honour thy father and thy mother" (Ex.20:12), that it enjoins "the duty of honouring parents, each separately and both in common" (*Dec.*51). He stresses this commandment and distinguishes it from the others on the ground that it embodies two kinds of virtue: both piety towards God, like the first four, and love towards humanity, like the last five. His reasoning is that parents, through their powers of generation, act in the place of God to their offspring:

> . . . we see that parents by their nature stand on the borderline between the mortal and the immortal side of existence, the mortal because of their kinship with men and other animals through the perishableness of the body; the immortal because the act of generation assimilates them to God, the generator of the All (*Dec.*107).
>
> For parents are the servants of God for the task of begetting children, and he who dishonours the servant dishonours also the Lord (*Dec.*119).

In emphasizing this commandment as he does, Philo is not actually departing from Scripture, but the reasons he offers are drawn from the wider world.[10] I believe, then, that these statements about the importance of parents are demonstrations that Torah complies with what is generally recognized as good. Philo reveals here a tendency to appeal to the family ideals which he shares with concerned gentiles, i.e. an emphasis on general family stability.[11] It would be a

---

[10] Goodenough, *Jurisprudence*, p.67f., building on the work of Heinemann and Treitel, claims that it is "on the grounds of gentile conceptions alone that Philo has justified the commandment to honour one's parents." Although he says that the Torah commonly speaks of parents together, he still attributes Philo's insistence on parental agreement to the influence of Egyptian law, "which tended in Egypt till late Roman times to give the woman coordinate legal rights with the man" (p.74).

[11] Like the perceived female virtues of *philoteknia* and *philandria*, honour of parents was a commonplace virtue. Cf. the work attributed to Perictione, which

mistake to interpret "honouring parents each separately and both in common (*peri goneōn timēs kai idia hekaterou kai amphoterōn koinē*)" as advocating equal power for men and women within the family. The larger context of Philo's writing simply does not bear such an interpretation.

This is demonstrated by the fact that although Philo occasionally raises the mother to equal prestige with the father, his inconsistency on the matter is noteworthy.[12] Philo's philosophical denigration of motherhood was discussed in chapter three, above. In the following passage he begins by making a point about parents together, but concludes with an example about father and son:

> For parents have little thought for their own personal interests and find the consummation of happiness in the high excellence of their children, and to gain this the children will be willing to hearken to their commands and to obey them in everything that is just and profitable; *for the true father will give no instruction to his son that is foreign to virtue* (*Spec*.2.236, emphasis mine).

One will not find anywhere in Philo a similar statement about the teaching of the mother.[13]

---

states that a woman must "honor and reverence" her parents, "for parents are in all respects equivalent to gods and they act in the interest of their grandchildren" (Thesleff, *Pythagorean Texts*, pp.142-145 = Stob. 4.28.10, translated by Flora R. Levin, quoted by Pomeroy, *Egypt*, pp.68-70).

[12] In another commentary on the fifth commandment, *Det*.52ff., male dominance, rather than parental equality, is the theme. "Now honour is shown to the mind when it is cared for .... To sense honour is shown when it is ... reined in by the mind, which has skill to direct the irrational powers within us like a pilot or a charioteer .... If you accord a father's honour to Him who created the world, and a mother's honour to Wisdom, by whose agency the universe was brought to completion, you will yourself be the gainer."

[13] Cf. *Spec*.4.68: "Now the principal cause of such misdeeds is familiarity with falsehood which grows up with the children right from their birth and from the cradle, the work of nurses and mothers and the rest of the company, slaves and free, who belong to the household." See also *Virt*.178; *QG* 1.92.

An even clearer indication of the superficiality of Philo's elevating women to equal consideration with men lies in the manner of his repeated use of the expression "men together with women, *andres homou kai gynaikes.*" In describing God's giving of the decalogue to the people (*ho laos*) Philo adds the expression "men and women alike, *andrōn homou kai gynaikōn*" (*Dec.*32).[14] The expression is not, however, integrated into the context. According to the Septuagint, the commandments were given to the assembled "people" (Ex.19:25) who had prepared themselves for the experience in a number of ways; one was by not going near a woman for three days (Ex.19:15).

The Biblical context shows, then, that this was an assembly of men (or that the women's presence was not acknowledged). Philo changes the account to read as follows:

> The ten words or oracles, in reality laws and statutes, were delivered by the Father of All when the nation, men and women alike, were assembled together (*Dec.*32).

But he does not amend the context, so that ensuing verses clarify that he is still thinking in terms of men only:

> Near by stood the people. They had kept pure from intercourse with women and abstained from all pleasures save those which are necessary for the sustenance of life (*Dec.*45).

> Let us, then, engrave deep in our hearts this as the first and most sacred of commandments, to acknowledge and honour one God Who is above all, and let the idea that gods are many never even reach the ears of the man (*andros*) whose rule of life is to seek for truth in purity and guilelessness (*Dec.*65).

From reading these three passages of *De Decalogo* together, I conclude that there are contradictory influences at work here. Philo

---

[14] This expression occurs in the following places in the *Special Laws*: 1.144; 2.43,146; 3.48,51; 4.218.

acknowledges the participation of women, yet does not carry his thought to any significant conclusion.

Generally speaking, as I suggested above, I suspect that Philo's lip-service to women in the *Exposition* is indicative of a desire to portray Judaism as relevant to the age. That he is not entirely consistent can be seen by comparing two references to the Exodus:

> . . . the festival is a reminder and thank-offering for that great migration from Egypt which was made by more than two millions *of men and women* in obedience to the oracles vouchsafed to them (*Spec*.2.146, emphasis mine).

> The departing emigrants had among them over six thousand men of military age (*hoi men andros echontes hēlikian*), while the rest of the multitude, consisting of old men, women-folk and children, could not easily be counted . . . . [Others followed] reverencing the divine favour shewn to the people (*andrōn*) . . . (*Mos*.1.147).

These are Philo's only two commentaries on Ex.12:37f., which, in the *LXX* text, does not mention women, but names men (*andres*), baggage (*aposkeuē*) and a mixed company (*epimiktos polus*). The second passage, in relegating the women to a lesser position, is closer to the Biblical text; the first appears to be making a deliberate concession to societal expectations.

Philo's reasoning about adultery in *De Decalogo* shows, as we have come to expect, his deep conviction of the irresponsibility of women. The husband is the victim of the crime perpetrated by the other man (*Dec*.129); the adulterer's relation to the adulteress is that of teacher to pupil; the crime corrupts not her body, but her soul, which is taught to feel an aversion to and hatred for her husband (*Dec*.124; cf. *Spec*.4.203, where Philo says that adultery ruins the morals of wives). This line of reasoning conforms to what we have observed about Philo's thought. The burden of sexual morality has to be borne by men. The male adulterer is responsible for the crime, and the female is relegated to the role of junior accomplice.

Philo's reduction of wife to the status of child reaches its extremity when he discusses the need for priests to marry virgins: ". . . by mating with souls entirely innocent and unperverted they [priests] may find it easy to mould the characters and dispositions of their wives, for the minds of virgins are easily influenced and attracted to virtue and very ready to be taught" (*Spec*.1.105).[15]

### Special Examples: Phineas and the Levites.

Close to the beginning of the first book of *Special Laws* Philo sets up Phineas, the Biblical hero whose action thwarted the wholesale apostasy of the young men of Israel, as the model of piety. I believe this story must be considered the backdrop for Philo's subsequent cries for capital punishment against those who threaten the community from within, including those he calls harlots.[16] Phineas is the model of zeal who takes the law into his own hands. Speaking of the crime of apostasy, Philo says,

> And it is well that all who have a zeal for virtue should be permitted to exact the penalties offhand and with no delay, without bringing the offender before jury or council or any kind of magistrate at all, and give full scope to the feelings which possess them, that hatred of evil and love of God which urges them to inflict punishment without mercy on the impious. They should think that the occasion has made them councillors, jurymen, high sheriffs, members of assembly, accusers, witnesses, laws, people, everything in fact, so that

---

[15] Note the similarity to the description of the wife in Xenophon's *Oeconomicus*. Ischomachos says to Socrates: "How . . . could she have known anything when I took her, since she came to me when she was not yet fifteen, and had lived previously under diligent supervision in order that she might see and hear as little as possible and ask the fewest possible questions?" (excerpts quoted on pp. 100f., Lefkowitz and Fant, *Women's Life*).

[16] Philo explicitly calls for the death penalty for the recalcitrant child (*Spec*.2.232), the adulterer (*Spec*.3.11), the man who takes back an adulterous wife, along with the wife (*Spec*.3.31), the male prostitute and his partner (*Spec*.3.38), the harlot (*Spec*.3.51), the poisoner (*Spec*.3.102), the murderer (*Spec*.3.106,108).

without fear or hindrance they may champion religion in full security (*Spec*.1.55).

He goes on to praise the one who shows this admirable courage (*to kalon touto tolmēma*), Phineas, and to describe his action as piety (*Spec*.1.57).

Shortly thereafter, Philo refers to the example of the Levites of Exodus 32, who countered apostasy by slaying their own kin. Although Scripture records that their action came at the instigation of Moses (vv.27f.), Philo says that they acted "at no bidding but their own" (*Spec*.1.79).[17] He lauds them for "championship of piety" and "a truly religious deed."

Philo's call for immediate and independent action (*Spec*.1.55, quoted above, and, by implication, in his recollection of the deeds of the Levites) goes beyond the demands of Scripture. The following verses from Deuteronomy, all dealing with suspected apostasy, imply that there should be some community consensus before the death penalty is inflicted.

> . . . thou shalt surely report concerning him, and thy hands shall be upon him among the first to slay him, and the hands of all the people at the last (Deut.13:9).
>
> . . . then thou shalt enquire and ask, and search diligently (Deut.13:14).
> He shall die on the testimony of two or three witnesses; a man who is put to death shall not be put to death for one witness (Deut.17:6).

---

[17] Philo refers to this incident on several occasions. In *Spec*.3.126, he speaks of the zeal that caused the men to take arms "as if at one signal." Similarly, in the account in *Mos*.2.171, he says that the Levites' zeal causes them to speed "like troops for whom one signal is enough." In *Sac*.130 they rushed "with one accord." In *Fug*.90 they act "under the impulse of righteous anger accompanied by an inspiration from above and a God-sent possession." Only in *Ebr*.66-71 does Philo temper the impulsiveness of their action by mentioning that they acted under Moses' command.
  Phineas and the Levites are similar in that they exemplify the principle that all human bonds must give way in the face of apostasy.

Rather than advocate inquiry and community action against offenders at this point, Philo sets the tone of the *Special Laws* by using Phineas, the man who took the law into his own hands, as the model of piety. A few sections later he brings in the action of the Levites. Furthermore, he appears to allude to this same type of impulsiveness several times subsequently. Twice, in calling for the death penalty, he demands that the culprit not be allowed to live "for a day or even an hour" (*Spec*.3.38,94). When the apostate is discovered,

> we must send round a report of his proposals to all the lovers of piety, who will rush with a speed which brooks no delay to take vengeance on the unholy man, and deem it a religious duty to seek his death (*Spec*.1.316).

He appears to condone homicide done in the interest of the law:

> . . . not every kind of homicide is culpable but only that which entails injustice, and . . . as for the other kinds if it is caused by an ardent yearning for virtue it is laudable . . .(*Spec*.3.128).

It may be a misinterpretation, however, to view these passages as though they advocate lynching. Heinemann points out two instances where Philo insists on the importance of following legal procedure.[18] In *Spec*.3.141 he says that the man accused of killing his slave must be "brought before the court, there to be examined under strict investigators of the truth." In *Mos*.2.214, Philo emphasizes the need for legal procedure by adding psychological detail to the text of Num.15:34: "And they placed him [the man gathering sticks on the Sabbath] in custody, for they did not determine what they should do to him."

> . . . hardly able to control themselves, they were minded to slay him. Reflection, however, caused them to restrain the fierceness of their anger. They did not wish to make it

---

[18] Heinemann, *Bildung*, pp.224ff.

appear that they who were but private citizens took upon themselves the ruler's duty of punishment, and that too without a trial, however clear was the offence in other ways . . .(*Mos*.2.214).

One could add to Heinemann's examples the high value Philo places on order, *taxis*. It is "the most excellent and valuable thing which life possesses" (*Spec*.1.120). Probably, then, the real lesson to be drawn from Philo's cries for blood is that apostasy--or any action that would result in apostasy--is the most heinous of crimes.

The Levites and Phineas both exemplify the right attitude to apostasy. By referring to their example at the beginning of the books of *Special Laws*, Philo establishes a point of focus for the succeeding material. The goals of the community are to promote piety and to prevent apostasy.

The story of Phineas has an added twist, namely, that women can instigate apostasy. The crime of the Israelite men was triggered by lust for women. We have noted how repeatedly Philo expresses worry about lust as the most dangerous and slippery of the vices. The following is just one example:

> . . . prudence and courage are able to construct an enclosing wall against the opposite vices, folly and cowardice, and capture them . . . self-mastery on the contrary is powerless to encircle desire and pleasure; for they are hard to wrestle with and difficult to overthrow . . . . So we must be content to face and fight lust (*epithymia*) as a principle (*LA* 1.86; cf. *Spec*.1.9, where sex is called the most imperious pleasure).

Not surprisingly, he uses the language of magic to describe the lure of sex; it connotes both danger and unfair tactics: pleasures "bewitch" the mind, and sex is the most powerful of the "love-lures" of pleasure (*Spec*.1.9). The Midianite women used such "love-lures" (*philtra*, *Spec*.1.56). Philo employs Ex.22:18 ("Ye shall not save the lives of sorcerers; *pharmakous ou peripoiēsete*") to call for immediate death for those who practise magic. In his interpretation of the text Philo adds the detail about magicians producing love potions and their opposites:

> ... a perversion of art, pursued by charlatan mendicants and parasites and the basest of the women and slave population, who make it their profession to deal in purifications and disenchantments and promise with some sort of charms (*philtrois*) and incantations to turn men's love into deadly enmity and their hatred into profound affection (*Spec*.3.101).

It is interesting that Philo never wavers from his position that sexual allure is wrong, in fact an evil power. In *Spec*.3.9 he warns against an excess of "natural pleasure" even with one's own wife.[19] Whereas Ben Sira, who generally fears and despises women, can at least praise the wife who reserves her charms for her husband (26:13-18), Philo suspects the attractive woman even within marriage. He disapproves of Rachel, who uses *philtra* on Jacob (*Ebr*.50); he advocates as a model wife Leah, the unattractive "hated" wife, who is "rough, ungentle, crabbed and our bitter enemy" (*Sac*.20).

I believe that in his charges against women--which generally imply sexual looseness--Philo shows influence of the Phineas story with its depiction of dangerous female sexuality. Dealing in love charms, a charge he made against the Midianite women, is an activity of "the basest (*phaulotata*) of the women," who are likened to vipers and scorpions (*Spec*.3.101-103). Women who join other religions are "abominable and licentious."[20] Philo has a number of terms to designate a woman he judges to be immoral: *pornē, hetaira, chamaitypē*. He uses them interchangeably, without apparent concern over exactness of meaning (see, e.g., *Jos*.43, where he uses all three), and never defines any of them. They are general terms

---

[19] Cf. *Legat*.39f.: "A wife has great power to paralyse and seduce her husband and particularly if she is a wanton, for her guilty conscience increases her wheedling. The husband, unaware of the corruption of his marriage and household, and thinking that her wheedling is benevolence pure and simple, is deceived and little knows that her artifices are leading him to take his worst enemies to be his dearest friends."

[20] "Associations of abominable and licentious women" bribe their way into the mysteries (*Spec*.1.323); i.e., apostasy on the part of a woman denotes sexual looseness.

employed to express disgust with women who fall outside proper male control.

The child of the harlot figures prominently in Philo's allegory as the polytheist--in other words, one who has no real father, but a number of possible fathers (*Mig*.69; *Dec*.8; *Conf*.144; *Spec*.1.332). This insult is directed against all who do not recognize the one God.

The charge of harlotry is made even to cover the victim of rape. This is seen in Philo's implication (*Mig*.224) that the rape of Dinah would have contravened the law that there be no *pornē* among the daughters of Israel (Deut.23:17). The Greek term in the Septuagint is a translation of the Scriptural *qʻdêsāh*, which means cult prostitute, but Philo either is unaware of the specific meaning, or else deliberately ignores it.[21]

When we examine the terms with which Philo contrasts "harlot," we discover that it becomes a blanket term for the woman who is not one of two things: a lady (*astē*), or a wife. In *Spec*.3.80 Philo rails against men who treat their "gentlewomen" wives as though they were harlots; again, in *Praem*.139, he speaks of a wife being outraged as though she were a harlot. If we can comprehend Philo's ideal "lady" or "wife," then by elimination we may understand what he means by "harlot."

First, then, what is a "lady"? *Astos* means, technically, a citizen of Alexandria.[22] Philo uses it in a nontechnical sense to mean a person in good standing in the Jewish community. The stranger is excluded: "He [Moses] bids them also write and set them forth in front of the door posts of each house and the gates in their

---

[21] In *Spec*.1.103 Philo does mention the possibility of becoming a harlot by "necessity," as opposed to "free and deliberate choice." He does not specify his meaning, but his discussion of the example of Dinah suggests that "necessity" would apply to the rape victim. According to Philo, such a one is not blameless, for even in her case "the scars and prints of old misdeeds (*adikēmatōn*) remain."

[22] In *Hellenistic Civilization and the Jews*, trans. S. Applebaum (New York: Atheneum, 1975), p.315, Tcherikover observes that Philo doesn't use legal terms precisely. He gives Philo's use of *politai* as an example.

walls, so that those who leave or remain at home, citizens (*astoi*) and strangers alike, may read the inscriptions" (*Spec*.4.142). Neither is the slave included among the *astoi*. On the contrary, Philo frequently juxtaposes the term *eleutheros* with *astos*. For example, in *Spec*.3.136 he says: "What has been said applies to freeborn persons of citizen rank (*ep' eleutherois kai astois*); the enactments which follow deal with slaves . . . . "

The feminine form, *astē*, appears to denote the kind of woman who would be the wife or daughter of such a man. In the three occurrences of the feminine form *astē* in the *Special Laws*, Colson recognizes that the word has connotations like those of the word "lady." He translates accordingly: "damsel of gentle birth" (*Spec*.3.66); "gentlewomen" (*Spec*.3.80); "like a free-born lady worthy of the name" (*Spec*.3.136; here Philo adds *eleutheras*). Other uses of both noun and adjective imply that the term depicts a good wife.[23]

Let us turn, then, to Philo's picture of an ideal wife. In his longest continuous passage on wives or women (*gynaikes*), Philo prescribes the following:

> The women are best suited to the indoor life which never strays from the house, within which the middle door is taken by the maidens as their boundary, and the outer door by those who have reached full womanhood . . . . A woman, then, should not be a busybody, meddling with matters outside her household concerns, but should seek a life of seclusion. She should not shew herself off like a vagrant in the streets before the eyes of other men, except when she has to go to the temple (*hieron*), and even then she should take pains to go, not when the market is full, but when most people have gone home, and so like a free-born lady worthy of the name, with everything quiet around her, make her oblations and offer her prayers to avert the evil and to gain

---

[23] In *Mig*.99 Philo praises certain women as *astai te kai asteiai*, which Colson translates as "citizen women and worthy of their citizenship." In *Cong*.63 Philo speaks allegorically of two kinds of learning faculties, *astas kai pallakidas*, "the faculties both of the lawful and the concubine type." In *Cong*.76f. he uses the term simply to mean "lawful wife."

the good . . . . Should she not when she hears bad language stop her ears and run away? (*Spec*.3.171-174).[24]

Clearly, this prescription could be followed only in families wealthy enough to afford household help that would free the wife from running ordinary errands. We are faced then with a problem. Where are the women who contribute to the family economy in a respectable manner?[25] One simply cannot find such a middle category in Philo. His neglect of this group, which must have been sizable, prompts some reflection.

Philo may simply be unaware of the way ordinary people live. In other places he drops hints that he is familiar only with a very pampered, privileged sort of woman. He says that women are naturally weak (*Spec*.4.223) and their life "is naturally peaceful and domestic" (*Spec*.4.225). In *Praem*.146 he speaks of wives as "women who have lived in ease and comfort, the dainty product of the luxury that has grown up with them from their earliest years." Philo appears to perceive only two sorts of women: those of his own wealthy class, and the others who most obviously fail to meet his standards. The depiction of a society where all respectable women can afford to stay home in seclusion hardly fits with Baron's picture of first century Alexandria where "the masses lived in dark, congested and

---

[24] Both Goodenough and Heinemann remark on the similarity of this passage to Neopythagorean material. See ch.1, n.27 and text, above.
   That at least some women, probably of the richest class, did live the life of seclusion he prescribes is seen in *Flac*.89. When the Romans searched the homes of some Jews, the men were indignant "that their women kept in seclusion, never even approaching the outer doors, and their maidens confined to the inner chambers, who for modesty's sake avoided the sight of men, even of their closest relations, were displayed to eyes, not merely unfamiliar, but terrorizing . . . ."

[25] As I indicated in the survey in chapter two, there is very little evidence for or against the participation of Alexandrian Jewish women in the economy. Two Alexandrian papyrological documents from the period of Augustus are contracts for the engagement of wet-nurses (Tcherikover, *Corpus*, p.34). Apart from using this scant primary evidence, one can only look at the situation of contemporary gentile women, which is one of considerable freedom of movement and participation in business, and speculate as to the degree the lives of Jewish women resembled those of their gentile sisters. For a good discussion of the matter see Heinemann, *Bildung*, p.233.

unhealthy quarters," and, as in the rest of the Diaspora, Jews were known for poverty rather than wealth.[26] It may well be, then, that Philo writes from very limited observation. He simply does not see the mass of ordinary women.

Another possibility is that in his depiction of the good woman Philo is straining for an ideal that never existed except in the minds of a few men. Certainly the picture is not derived from the Biblical record of the age of the Patriarchs. Women in that society moved fairly freely and engaged in tasks that took them into the public sphere. Is it drawn from the Greek tradition? There, as we observed in chapter one, women were excluded from public affairs. But Philo had never observed that society. His view of it was derived from the literature, which itself may have presented an idealized picture.[27]

No matter which explanation is closer to Philo's case, clearly he perceives women from a distance, with a strong degree of unreality. Contemporary women appear in his writing as elements in the backdrop of life. The players on the stage are men. Women matter only as they impinge on men's actions, giving help, irritation or resistance to men's causes. This is a view which objectifies, indeed reifies women. Despite his many words about them, Philo fails to perceive them in and of themselves. Heinemann's observation is well put:

> . . . es verdient nur Beachtung, dass sein Rationalismus, sein Glaube an die Unentbehrlichkeit der Philosophie für die

---

[26] *History*, p.265f.

[27] Euripides' *Electra* illustrates the clash between the real and the ideal even in fifth century Athens. Electra has been sent from home and married to a peasant. She is required to work hard to stay alive. As she says, "I carry home on my head water from the brook." Her husband, however, complains in these words when he finds her conversing with strangers: "'tis unseemly for a woman to stand talking to young men." His ideal simply does not correspond to reality.

wahre Lebensführung, ihn nicht einmal das Problem der Frauenbildung hat sehen lassen.[28]

When we read Philo's statements directed against harlots we must bear in mind this lack of correlation between reality and his perception of it. The amount of material on the subject gives more indication of Philo's revulsion against harlotry than of the actual numbers of women practising it.

Philo demands punishment for harlots that goes beyond anything in Scripture.[29] "A pest, a scourge, a plague-spot to the public, let her be stoned to death--she who has corrupted the graces bestowed by nature, instead of making them, as she should, the ornament of noble conduct" (*Spec*.3.51). " . . . with us a courtesan is not even permitted to live, and death is the penalty appointed for women who ply this trade" (*Jos*.43). "And it [the law] banishes not only harlots, but also the children of harlots . . . ." (*Spec*.1.326).

The reason for Philo's alteration of Scripture here can only be surmised. It could be an instance of his attempting to show that the Mosaic law could match any other in its moral stringency. Through the Lex Julia of 18 B.C.E., Augustus forbade the marriage of persons of senatorial families to prostitutes, casting the latter in the category of *probrosi*, "morally reprehensible persons." Although this law did not explicitly punish prostitutes, it officially held them

---

[28] *Bildung*, p.236.

[29] *Encyclopedia Judaica* s.v."sexual offences": "But however much prostitution may be condemned (cf. e.g. Jer.3:1-3) it appears in biblical times to have been widespread (cf. Gen.34:31; 38:15; Judg.11:1; 16:1; Isa. 23:15-16; Prov.7:9-22; et al) and not punishable . . ."
Philo appears to base his statements on Deut.23:2: "one born of a harlot shall not enter into the assembly of the Lord," and on the verse prohibiting cult prostitutes.

in disdain.[30] Philo may, then, be attempting here to match the ethics of the governing class.

Another possible way to account for Philo's insistence on a law that is not made explicit anywhere in Scripture is to realize that in his static view of society there is no need for a harlot to exist. Parents care for their daughters, and keep them virgin till marriage. All girls marry, and their husbands have the right to expect virgin brides (*Spec*.3.81). Scripture calls for the stoning of a bride who is found not to be a virgin (Deut.22:21).[31] Orphan girls are looked after by the chief magistrate (*Spec*.2.25), and the law requires charity for widows (*Spec*.1.310). Since Moses has established a social justice system that is all-inclusive, only a wanton would repudiate her place in the system.[32] She is a rebel and a threat to the community.

Philo's description of the harlot is a caricature:

> But a shameless look and an elevated neck and a continuous movement of the eyebrows and a womanish walk and not blushing at, or being ashamed of, any evil at all is the sign of a lewd soul . . . (*QG* 4.99).

> . . . that stranger to decency and modesty and temperance and the other virtues . . . . She flings herself at the disposal

---

[30] The purpose of these laws was to protect the purity of the higher social classes. See Jane F. Gardner, *Women in Roman Law and Society* (London and Sydney: Croom Helm, 1986), p.32.

Justinian's account of the law, dating from the sixth century, does interpret the law as punishing prostitutes: "The Laws punish the detestable wickedness of women who prostitute their chastity to the lusts of others . . . " (quoted in Lefkowitz and Fant, *Women's Life*, p.183).

[31] Philo does not comment explicitly on this verse, although in *Spec*.3.79ff. he goes into some detail about the case where the bridegroom accuses his bride falsely. It is unfortunate that we cannot be sure of Philo's reasoning here. It is certainly interesting that the *LXX* uses the verb *ekporneusai* of the girl who loses her virginity while still under the care of her father. It might have justified Philo's very broad understanding of harlotry, and also given us the reason why Philo can say that a harlot is not allowed to live.

[32] Philo's claims for the all-inclusive *philanthropia* of the Mosaic law are found in *Virt*.51-174.

of chance comers, and sells her bloom like some ware to be purchased in the market . . . . A pest, a scourge, a plague-spot to the public . . . she who has corrupted the graces bestowed by nature, instead of making them, as she should, the ornament of noble conduct (*Spec.*3.51).

Philo's remarks on the repentance of the reformed harlot again reveal the revulsion he feels against such a woman. Commenting on the requirement that the priest should marry a virgin, Philo volunteers a number of reasons (*Spec.*1.102-107). He cannot marry a repentant harlot because "in the souls of the repentant there remain, in spite of all, the scars and prints of their old misdeeds" (*Spec.*1.103). This contradicts his position elsewhere in the same treatise, viz., that God "has given to repentance the same honour as to innocence from sin" (*Spec.*1.187; cf. *Virt.*175-186, *Praem.*164).[33] We had occasion in chapter ten to note that the scars of her former life also remained with Rachel after she had repented, and caused difficulty for her son Joseph. It appears, then, that, in contrast to other repentant sinners, the repentant woman is never freed of her past.

## Shame and Modesty

Self-control, *sōphrosynē*, is one of the four cardinal Greek virtues which Philo, in his eagerness to unite the best of the two cultures, attributes to the Torah. In the following passage he is describing the synagogue:

So each seventh day there stand wide open in every city thousands of schools of good sense, temperance, courage, justice and the other virtues . . .(*Spec.*2.62).

---

[33] Cf. the view expressed in an extant Neopythagorean text about the adulterous woman: "She should also consider the following: that there is no means of atoning for this sin; no way she can approach the shrines or the altars of the gods as a pure woman, beloved of god . . . ." (quoted in Lefkowitz and Fant, *Women's Life*, pp.104ff.)

Thus he states explicitly that the synagogue, in teaching Torah, imparts the Greek virtues.

The particular quality of *sōphrosynē* is difficult to define. It is the subject of the Platonic dialogue *Charmides*, and its amorphous quality is expressed in an introduction to the dialogue by Benjamin Jowett, as follows:

> We have lost the conception of it. Enough is said about it in Greek literature for us to be able to describe it in some fashion, but we cannot give it a name. It was the spirit behind the two great Delphic sayings, "Know thyself" and "Nothing in excess." Arrogance, insolent self-assertion, was the quality most detested by the Greeks. *Sōphrosynē* was the exact opposite. It meant accepting the bounds which excellence lays down for human nature, restraining impulses to unrestricted freedom, to all excess, obeying the inner laws of harmony and proportion.[34]

It was associated in the Greek mind with *aidōs*, a term sometimes translated "modesty" or "shame," but similarly difficult to capture in words. "*Aidos* is what you feel about your own actions: the honour that compels you and the shame that deters you, the truth or remorse that haunts you."[35] The overlapping in meaning of the two terms is illustrated by a quotation from Thucydides 1.84: "*aidōs sōphrosynēs pleiston metechei*."

These are not Jewish conceptions. They occur in Jewish literature only in later works which evince strong Greek influence (Esther, Wisdom of Solomon, Third Maccabees).

But Philo uses these terms, frequently in his interpretation of Biblical stories. The *Septuagint* terms from which he appears to infer them are *tapeinoun* (to humiliate, or, in the passive sense, to sub-

---

[34] *The Collected Dialogues of Plato*, edited by Edith Hamilton and Huntington Cairns. Bollingen Series 71 (Princeton: Princeton University Press, 1961), p.99.

[35] *Encyclopedia Britannica*, 1960 edition, s.v."Homer."

mit), and its cognates. *Tapeinoun* is used of the Egyptian treatment of the Israelites (Gen.15:13; Ex.1:12), of the Jewish attitude on the day of atonement (Lev.16:29, 23:27,29,32--humbling their souls), or of forced intercourse with a woman (Gen.32:2, Deut.21:14, 22:24, 22:29). Evidence of Philo's association of the terms is the wording of *Fug*.4f:

> Hagar's motive for departing is shame. A sign of this is the fact that an angel, a Divine Word, meets her to advise the right course, and to suggest return to the house of her mistress. The angel addresses her in the encouraging words, "The Lord hath hearkened to thy humiliation" (Gen.16:11), a humiliation prompted neither by fear nor by hatred, the one the feeling of an ignoble, the other of a quarrelsome soul, but by shame, the outward expression of inward modesty.

The *LXX* term translated "humiliation" is *tapeinōsis*; but it, and the words related to it in the Bible story, indicate action, and not feeling. In Gen.16:6 we read that Sarah "afflicted" (*ekakōsen*) Hagar, causing her to flee. In verse nine the angel advises that Hagar should "submit", or humble herself before Sarah. Hagar's affliction and humiliation, according to the Septuagint, are *actions* on the part of Sarah. Hagar's submission will be another *action* on her part. Philo adds a psychological dimension which is not present in the Biblical text. The interesting point for our study is that he attributes to Hagar an awareness that she has been engaged in something for which she ought to feel remorse. He does not clarify Hagar's guilt. It appears to stem from her having usurped the position of her mistress, even though she has been forced to do so by circumstances, i.e., by the plan Abraham and Sarah devise. The passage remains problematic.[36]

Philo also tries to interpret Num.12:14 as conveying the Greek concept of shame. The text occurs in reference to Miriam: "If her father had but spat in her face, should she not feel shame seven days?" Philo quotes it in *LA* 2.66f., in a discussion of shame. The

---

[36] It was noted earlier that the wording of the *LXX* precludes the interpretation that Hagar flaunted her pregnancy before Sarah. See ch.7, n.25, above.

verb, *entrapēsetai*, could be translated to mean either that she will be ashamed or that she will be put to shame. The former fits Philo's interpretation, since it conveys the idea of self-imposed shame. The time limit of "seven days," however, runs counter to that interpretation, and conforms to the interpretation that the person is in a state of reproach imposed externally for a specific length of time.[37] His use of this text, then, is another instance of his attempt to see Greek concepts in the Septuagint.

Further investigation shows that Philo uses the term *aidōs* for awareness of one's position in the greater scheme of things, that scheme we have identified as the Great Chain of Being. It is the feeling of man in the presence of God (*Mut.*201, *Mos.*1.84, *Aet.*20, *Legat.*293), of pupils for teachers (*Spec.*4.140, *Legat.*5), of youth for elders and parents (*Post.*181, *Mut.*217, *Prob.*87, *Jos.*257), of subjects for rulers (*Jos.*107, *Mos.*1.161, *Praem.*97, *Legat.*276,352). It is also the attitude Philo prescribes, quite without Biblical authority, for women.

In Philo's *Weltanschauung*, as we have been observing, women occupy a position quite different from men's. They are inferior, passive, submissive, more easily ruled by the passions. It follows, then, that the terms *aidōs* and *sōphrosynē*, since they denote, among other things, "keeping one's place," will have a different meaning when applied to women than when applied to men.[38]

Indeed, it is interesting that of the four traditional Greek virtues, *sōphrosynē*, with its sister virtue *aidōs*, is the only one Philo explicitly expects of women. This is evident from his description of the harlot: "that stranger to decency (*kosmiotētos*) and modesty (*aidous*) and temperance (*sōphrosynēs*) and the other virtues"

---

[37] The Hebrew original, from the root *klm*, can be translated in either way. The RSV makes the choice I favour, rendering the term "be shamed." In similar vein, the NEB says "remain in disgrace." I am indebted to Chris Kachur for the observations in this paragraph.

[38] Pomeroy (*Egypt*, p.70) indicates that women had accepted *sōphrosynē* as the ideal for them: "*Sophrosyne* was the preeminent virtue of Greek women; it is mentioned more frequently than any other quality on women's tombstones."

(*Spec*.3.51), with which we can compare the virtues taught to boys and men: "good sense (*phronēseōs*), temperance (*sōphrosynēs*), courage (*andreias*), justice (*dikaiosynēs*) and the other virtues . . ." (*Spec*.2.62).

On three occasions Philo adds *aidōs* to the Biblical account.

On their first meeting (when they are still in the state of innocence) Eve greets Adam "*met' aidous*" (*Op*.152). Colson translates the Greek words with the quaint term "shamefastly." This is not the shame of awareness of good and evil (Gen.2:35; cf. *LA* 3.65f.), for it occurs before the temptation. What then is Eve's attitude? The only translation which would make sense in the context would be "appropriately" or "as a woman ought." Eve meets her master, she greets him as a woman ought, i.e. deferentially, they fall in love, this leads to desire for pleasure, and only then does the trouble begin. Because the expression occurs here gratuitously, Philo clearly is making a statement about woman's place.

The second occasion where he adds to Scripture is in his treatment of the trial of the woman accused by her husband of adultery. Where Num.5:18 states simply that "the priest . . . shall uncover the head of the woman," Philo says, "the priest . . . removes her kerchief, in order that she may be judged with her head bared and stripped of the symbol of modesty (*aidous*), regularly worn by women who are wholly innocent" (*Spec*.3.56).[39]

Besides requiring *aidōs* of women, this second passage indicates another point: that modesty, although in Greek thought an inward quality, is not within the woman's control: it is the standard imposed by man on woman and symbolically removed at his will, not hers. Without pressing the point, I suggest a similarity here to the *aidōs* Philo insists on attributing to Hagar, although she has *done* nothing to warrant it.

According to their humble position in the greater scheme of things, the Great Chain, women ought to experience an inward *aidōs*,

---

[39] The third example is the "modesty of veneration" which Philo attributes to Rebecca when she first sees Isaac (*QG* 4.142). This has no Biblical warrant. Unfortunately, we do not have the Greek text.

which will manifest itself in outward *sōphrosynē*. This is a peculiar adaptation of a classical masculine virtue of the Greeks (for they said little in their philosophy about women) in such a way as to justify and perpetuate the subject position of women of another culture. Here are some examples of Philo's application of the term *aidōs*, modesty, to women: the maiden Virtue possesses modesty, and it also follows in her train (*Sac*.26f.); the blushes of the Hebrew midwife indicate her modesty (*Heres* 128); despite her outward appearance, Tamar has inward chastity and modesty (*Cong*.124); the daughters of Zelophedad approached the ruler "in the modesty appropriate to maidens" (*Mos*.2.234); brothers should not insult the modesty of maidens: "maidens must blush, why drive the hue from their cheeks?" (*Spec*.3.25); it "debases the sterling coin of modesty" for women to be present in the gymnasium (*Spec*.3.176); the women of the Therapeutae are separated from the men by a chest-high wall, so that "the modesty becoming to the female sex is preserved" (*Cont*.33); for modesty's sake Jewish maidens avoid the sight of men (*Flac*.89; cf. 3.*Macc*. 1.19).

Related to Philo's understanding of the virtues of self-control and modesty to justify the sequestering of women is his reliance on arguments about what is fitting and suitable: *harmottein, prepein*. Such verbs imply that justification is unnecessary, and serve to preclude discussion. Whereas he devotes an entire treatise, *De Congressu*, to a reasoned account of male education, he says--giving no details--that girls should have "education as befits maidens," before entering a "suitable marriage" (*Spec*.2.125). Men "are suited" to business, government, war and action, whereas women "are suited" to life behind closed doors (*Spec*.3.169). The harlot is at fault for not using her femininity "as befits her" (*Spec*.3.51). Women should wear "fitting" adornments (*Virt*.21). Modesty "befits" women (*Cont*.33). Women do not enter wars or even fights, because of "the fitness of things (*to prepon*), which it was resolved to keep unshaken always and everywhere and considered to be in itself more valuable than victory or liberty or success of any kind" (*Spec*.3.172).

I conclude that Philo's zeal to return to an idealized past reaches its apogee in the demands he makes upon women. Upon the outward male-domination of the Jewish heritage, he would impose an internalized humility which he derives, somewhat circuitously, from the Greek philosophical tradition. Added to that are a view of the unchanging adequacy of the Law as he interpreted it and apparent blindness to the actual position of women outside his own privileged circle.

## The Essenes

> Furthermore they [the Essenes] eschew marriage because they clearly discern it to be the sole or the principal danger to the maintenance of the communal life, as well as because they particularly practise continence. For no Essene takes a wife, because a wife is a selfish creature, excessively jealous and an adept at beguiling the morals of her husband and seducing him by her continued impostures . . . . For he who is either fast bound in the love lures of his wife or under the stress of nature makes his children his first care ceases to be the same to others and unconsciously has become a different man and has passed from freedom into slavery (*Hyp.*11.14-17).

This is Philo's celebrated passage on the Essenes, a Jewish sect of his day. The question that has repeatedly arisen is whether this passage reveals Philo's own assessment of "wives," or, by implied indirect discourse, tells what might (as Colson says in a footnote to the text) "be plausibly argued by the Essenes." I have two reasons for holding that this is Philo's own assessment. The first is that this argument has a number of elements in common with Philo's other remarks about women. The second is that other, quite different reasons can be advanced for the Essenes' observed celibacy.

Philo views jealousy as a female characteristic.[40] Even in attributing it to a man, he calls it "the feminine proclivity to

---

[40] Cf. Aristotle, *History of Animals*, 608a-b, quoted in ch.6, above.

jealousy" (*Spec*.1.108). Jealousy frequently occurs between the wives when the older one is superseded by a newer (*Virt*.115).[41] In *Cong*.180 again he speaks of "women's jealousy." Thus it is in character for him to raise jealousy here as a problem in marriage. Similarly, as we have observed, he frequently implies that women use unfair tactics in attracting men: trapping, ensnaring, employing love potions. The words "ensnares", "cajoles" and "love lures" in the passage just quoted are of this genre. The expression "the fawning talk which she practises" (*Hyp*.11.15) reminds one of Philo's words in *Legat*.39: "A wife has great power to paralyse and seduce her husband . . . ." These are all indications that the reasons he gives for the Essenes' celibacy come from Philo's own speculation, based on his understanding of women.

In *A History of the Mishnaic Law of Women* Neusner cites with approbation Isaksson's reasoning that the Essenes allowed marriage for the purpose of procreation in early manhood, but then turned to a life of celibacy as preparation for the Holy War.[42] Since

---

[41] This is the reason Philo gives for a man's being required to grant full freedom to a captive wife of whom he has grown tired. The full passage is an interpretation of Deut.21:10-14, but the introduction of the idea of jealousy is Philo's own contribution.

[42] Vol.5, p.250. The passage to which Neusner refers is on pp.63-65 of Isaksson, *Marriage*. It reads in part: "[Contrary to explanations in Philo and Josephus], the whole view of sexual questions and marriage which is expressed in these writings has proved to have originated in the Old Testament and especially in the Old Testament laws relating to the holy war . . . . The young man has a right to take a wife and live with her for a period of five years . . . . The husband does not need to divorce his wife when he reaches the age of twenty-five but it is likely that such divorces occurred, sometimes on the plea that the husband wished to avoid all suspicion that he had sexual intercourse with his wife even after the age of twenty-five, when under the laws of the holy war he was no longer allowed to have it . . . the Qumran community's view of marriage must not be interpreted as an isolated detail in its ethical system. Its moral principles on the subject of marriage are indissolubly linked with its eschatology."
Cf. Vermes, *Jesus the Jew* (London, 1973) pp.99f.:" . . . the sect of the Essenes, despite the fact that the Qumran texts do not expressly enjoin the renunciation of marriage . . . appears to have made an institution of celibacy, probably in order to be always in a condition to take part in worship, even if Philo and Josephus prefer to attribute the cause to misogyny."
*Hyp*.11.3 can be interpreted to mean that Philo knew only older Essenes who had been married but had divorced their wives: "Thus no Essene is a mere

that argument undermines the probability that Philo is giving an opinion he himself heard from members of the sect, it adds to the likelihood that the reasons he does give are his own. Thus the passage about the Essenes only confirms perceptions of women to which Philo has given expression elsewhere.

## The Therapeutae

We have already spoken of the women members of the contemplative group Philo claims to have known in Egypt. A discussion of these women will round out our picture of Philo's perception of contemporary women. Philo calls these women virgins:

> The feast is shared by women also, most of them aged virgins, who have kept their chastity not under compulsion, like some of the Greek priestesses, but of their own free will in their ardent yearning for wisdom (*Cont*.68).

It would be surprising, in Jewish society as he depicts it, for a woman to avoid marriage. One wonders who these virgins are and where they came from. How did they manage to reach old age as virgins in Jewish society? Possibly Philo means by the term "virgins" women who are not sexually active, a meaning we have encountered already (cf. *Spec*.1.129). In introducing his account of the men of the order, before he mentions that there are women as well, he states that these men are older people who have left their property to their children, abandoning "their brothers, their children, their wives, their parents" (*Cont*.13,18). Perhaps he intended this description to extend, with adaptations, to the women members of the order as well. In any case, in this passage we have the only place where Philo speaks of

---

child nor even a stripling or newly bearded . . . but full grown and already verging on old age, no longer carried under by the tide of the body nor led by the passions, but enjoying the veritable, the only true freedom."

actual women who are "virgins."[43] Having seen in earlier chapters that on the allegorical level virginity surpasses womanhood, we find in this treatise a comparable depiction of virginity in real life:

> " . . . they have spurned the pleasures of the body and desire no mortal offspring but those immortal children which only the soul that is dear to God can bring to the birth unaided because the Father has sown in her spiritual rays enabling her to behold the verities of wisdom" (*Cont.*68).

His wording demonstrates that in real life, as well as in the Bible, the function of bearing children--women's inevitable function-- is of less value than that of producing mental progeny. It elevates a mode of life which, from all the evidence we have garnered, appears to have been an improbable option for women of Philo's society.

Another observation made earlier in the study of Biblical figures is that Philo tends to postulate equality between certain male and female groups, all the while subtly implying male dominance. This is apparent here too, in his description of the common worship of the Therapeutae, where women participate as listeners, while representatives of the men speak: "Then the senior among them who also has the fullest knowledge of the doctrines which they profess comes forward and with visage and voice alike quiet and composed gives a well-reasoned and wise discourse . . . women too regularly make part of the audience . . ." (*Cont.*31f.). The women are actually behind a partial wall: "This arrangement serves two purposes; the modesty becoming to the female sex is preserved, while the women sitting within ear-shot can easily follow what is said since there is nothing to obstruct the voice of the speaker" (*Cont.*33). Only in their singing does Philo indicate equality; they resemble the choirs at the

---

[43] In *Som.*2.185 Philo says "but the high priest is blameless, perfect, the husband of a virgin who, strange paradox, never becomes a woman, but rather has forsaken that womanhood through the company of her husband." Clearly Philo does not intend this passage to be taken literally (cf. *Spec.*1.101). The passage is significant, however, in showing that Philo's preference of virginity over womanhood was not limited to the allegorical plane.

Red Sea, "the men led by the prophet Moses and the women by the prophetess Miriam" (*Cont*.87).[44]

*Homosexuality*

It would be a mistake to leave the study of Philo's perception of contemporary women without considering the implications of the language he uses to describe homosexual men. In one instance Philo says that the passive partner in the homosexual relationship is "sick with the disease of femaleness" (*Spec*.1.325). In the same description he uses the term *androgynos*, which occurs in similar context in *Spec*.3.38. He uses the same term to depict the priests of Demeter, some of whom "have desired to be completely changed into women and gone on to mutilate their genital organs" (*Spec*.3.38).[45] A similar term, *gynaikomorphos*, is found in *Spec*.2.50, where Philo accuses the active homosexual of forcing his partner to change into woman's form. In *Spec*.3.39 the verb used to denote the pederast's action against his partner is *ekthēlynon*, "turning into a woman"; in the same passage the pederast is accused of "becoming a tutor and instructor" in *anandrias*, "unmanliness." All such application of female terms to men who do not perform sexually as men indicate a negative perception of womanliness.

Homosexuality evokes some of Philo's most scathing condemnations (See, for example, *Spec*.3.38). His equating of homo-

---

[44] In *Women Leaders in the Ancient Synagogue* (Chico,California: Scholars Press, 1982), Bernadette Brooten raises the possibility that Philo's description of the Therapeutrides may be constructed as a reaction to religious leadership roles assumed by some Jewish women in Egypt. She cites inscriptional evidence for such leadership. If she is right, Philo's description can be seen as a concession to the religious aspirations of some women, but also a proscription against overt leadership which may have been practised by some Jewish women in his day in Egypt. See particularly pp.73ff., 88ff., 134.

[45] Cf. Aristotle, *On the Generation of Animals*, 783b-784a, where the eunuch is said to have been changed from the male state to the female state.

sexual males with women needs to be considered at least as background material in assessing his view of women.

*Conclusion*

Because of the apologetic nature of the treatises from which most of the material in this chapter has been drawn, I have considered two possible tendencies that might create discrepancy between Philo's perception and his depiction of women. The first was the tendency to present the Jewish people of his community as sexually restrained. Philo might be expected to exaggerate in this regard for two reasons: one would be to counter general charges of lasciviousness; the other to appeal to general admiration of high moral standards.[46] I found no reason to discount this tendency in Philo. Nevertheless, it would serve only to mitigate the position he takes towards female sexuality. The demands for severe constraints on women and their activity would still remain the dominant note.

The second tendency, that of presenting the law regarding women as if it were in step with the times, proved upon examination to be merely superficial.

There is a correspondence between Philo's perceptions of Biblical and contemporary women. In both cases the good and bad are clearly differentiated and designated by the terms *astai* and *pornai*. Good women contribute to the common good in a male-regulated world. Bad women elude male control. The Biblical virgins have no real counterpart in Philo's world. Only the Therapeutrides bear some resemblance to them in their ability to abandon womanhood and to bear spiritual offspring.

Philo presents unrealistic ideals. For women who remain in the mainstream of society, the life of pampered seclusion could be attained only by the privileged. The other, and higher, ideal, pre-

---

[46] In making these points I drew on the argument and evidence presented by Alan Mendelson in his forthcoming book, *Philo's Jewish Identity*.

sented in the persons of the women Therapeutae, belongs only on the fringes of a society where early marriage and child-bearing is the norm. Philo seems not to consider the exigencies of life for the vast majority. Yet he condemns as deserving death any women who do not meet his standards of proper conduct.

# CHAPTER TWELVE

# SUMMARY AND CONCLUSIONS

*Summary*

In this work I have undertaken to study an area of Philonic thought unexamined heretofore, namely, his perception of women. I have attempted to understand the reasons behind Philo's propensity to make distinctions on the basis of gender. I approached the work as a Philonic scholar, attempting to enter his world of thought as far as that was possible, by reading his work carefully and consulting the recognized secondary sources. I assiduously avoided the temptation to pluck quotations out of context, or to fault Philo for not thinking like a modern person.

The body of the work has been an examination of the material Philo wrote about both Biblical and contemporary women. I prefaced the main part with a considerable amount of background information, which constitutes the first four chapters of the work. I did this in order to set the subject in context, and to establish certain parameters for the work.

After introducing the subject in the first chapter, I used chapter two to set the topic in the context of the two main traditions which converged in Philo: the Jewish and the Greek. The resulting material provides a backdrop against which elements in Philo's treatment of woman can be viewed. Chapter two continues with a search for information about the cultural streams which made up the cosmopolitan society of Alexandria that Philo knew. Although it was beyond the scope of this study to determine whether Philo's perception of women matched reality, I have operated on the belief that we can better understand the statements he does make when we picture the world out of which he wrote.

From my earlier study of Philo I suspected that, regardless of the particular context or content, Philo's male-female distinctions were made according to one basic pattern. At the beginning of this study, then, I formulated the hypothesis that one presupposition underlies all Philo's sexual distinctions, viz., that "male" designates good, strong, and active, and "female" bad, weak, and passive; these are relative, rather than absolute, values. In chapter three I test that hypothesis by surveying the breadth and complexity of Philo's use of sexual distinctions, and, through examples, demonstrating their interrelatedness. This chapter shows that, because the basic presupposition exists, an investigation of Philo's perception of women need not be restricted to material where he speaks of woman *qua* woman. This observation is particularly useful, since it is not characteristic of Philo's writing that topics are clearly delineated, but rather that threads of ideas become entwined, and indeed entangled, with one another. In chapter three, then, I establish that the material relating to Philo's perception of women may be broader in scope than one would first suspect.

In chapter four, on the other hand, I demonstrate that certain parts of the text must be rejected in the search for Philo's perception of women. I examine the language in which Philo couches his observations about the human condition in general. There is no explicit precedent in the scholarly literature for the conclusion that women are not considered in these generalizations. Yet by studying the use of *anthrōpos*, *anēr*, and masculine pronouns and adjectives in Philo and, to a limited extent, in his sources, I demonstrate that the exclusiveness of these terms extends beyond mere grammatical form. When we are seeking to determine Philo's perception of women, it is necessary to set these generalizations aside. Philo's perception of woman is of a being other than "man," whether *anēr* or *anthrōpos*.

With chapter five I begin the actual presentation of Philo's view of women, by examining the context of his two most frequent designations, *gynē* and *parthenos*. I find that womanhood is a state or condition of life marked by three signs, menstruation, marital relations and childbearing, which symbolize evil, defilement and corruption. Virginity is the absence of these signs of womanhood. It is a state of elevation beyond the physical constraints of womanhood and, as well, beyond the moral states they symbolize.

Much of the material about women emerges from Philo's commentaries on the female figures of the Bible. Chapters six to ten deal with these figures, the first two chapters with those he calls "women" and the last three with those he calls "virgins.".

Philo devotes an extensive amount of material to interpreting the Eden story. For this reason I use all of chapter six to study his presentation of Eve. She is the archetypical woman. Philo presents her both as the less worthy components of Everyman--passion and irrationality--and as Everywoman. In both instances she represents danger, even death, when she is uncontrolled or when she usurps the position of authority. She is helpful, even necessary, when she is under firm masculine control.

In chapter six I introduce Philo's concept of justice as a cosmic principle which decrees the rule of the superior and the submission of the inferior. Since he accepts without question the natural superiority of the male and the inferiority of the female, it follows that Philo perceives male supremacy as enjoined by cosmic law. Later tradition has named this vision of reality The Great Chain of Being.

Chapter seven examines Philo's treatment of the other Biblical characters Philo calls "women." In this part of the study, I find that Philo sees these women as two types. In this chapter I discuss Philo's use of the terms *astai* and *pornai* to designate acceptable and unacceptable women. In the presence of the former, man exercises control, even though sometimes that control is imperceptible. In other words, *astai* are women who work within the social framework established by men, and their actions contribute to the welfare of men. *Pornai* represent danger, and in their presence man must choose between fight or flight, depending on his own powers of resistance.

I use chapter eight to introduce Philo's allegorical concept that the great women of Scripture were not really women, but virgins. I present the theory that Philo employed this as part of his adaptation of the larger concept of the sacred marriage. For this he used a literary precedent provided by Plato, maintaining the central concept of reproduction in the soul, but substituting the virgin wives for the boy lovers, and naming God as the true source of creation. In this allegory, the wives lose their identities by becoming the virtues of their husbands.

Because Sarah and Rebecca receive lengthier treatment in Philo than any other women besides Eve, I devote a full chapter, the ninth, to them. There is a second reason. Perhaps because they were so well-known in the tradition as folk-heroines, Philo did not entirely eliminate the literal element from his treatment of these two figures. Thus, as well as studying the allegorical treatment of these women, which elaborates the basic pattern outlined in chapter eight, I also examine Philo's interpretation of the literal stories. I discover that when Philo retells the story of the relations of these women to their husbands, he alters the Biblical account so as to make Sarah and Rebecca dependent, subservient, and totally cooperative.

In chapter ten, Leah is the main character. Like Sarah and Rebecca, she appears in a dual role, as the allegorical virgin and as the good wife. In the latter role she is contrasted with Rachel. In Philo's discussion of these two sisters the terms *astē* and *pornē* reappear. Even more than Rebecca and Sarah, Leah represents Philo's ideal wife. The character of a good woman is expressed in the meaning of her name, "Rejected." A good wife is, like Leah, harsh and unattractive. She is completely devoid of the allure which is invariably condemned in Philo.

In chapter eleven, my study of Philo's perception of contemporary women, I find a repetition of the themes already discovered in his treatment of Biblical women. Philo recognizes only two types of women, the ladies, *astai*, and the harlots, *pornai*. The former live a life of virtual seclusion, devoted to home, husband and children. The latter are those who do not meet this standard. Whether they display themselves in public, practise magic, join other religious groups, or actually engage in sexual misconduct, Philo condemns them all as *pornai*, enemies of the people, deserving extinction.

## Conclusions

This study has been an attempt to search Philo's writing for answers to questions that I am convinced he never asked. For this reason I have refrained from presenting his thoughts on women as though they emerged from a clearly-defined pattern in his mind. Attempts to systematize Philo's thought on any subject run the risk of imposing structure from without. The danger is all the greater when one is treating a subject that was incidental to his main concerns.

Nevertheless, I have concluded that a basic conception of the proper relationship of the sexes forms the substratum to all Philo's remarks pertaining to male-female distinctions. The key term is "control." On this point I diverge in my conclusions from Richard Baer, whose book, *Philo's Use of the Categories Male and Female*, provided much of the foundation on which I built. Baer explored the meaning of Philo's sex distinctions on the philosophical level. He established three principles that proved useful for the present work:
1) that Philo designates the lower, carnal part of the individual as female, and the higher, spiritual part as male;
2) that virgin and male are, on the soteriological level, equivalent;
3) that Philo uses sexual language on the cosmic level to depict interactions between certain forces which are strong, superior and active, and others which are weak, inferior and passive.

Baer concluded that Philo advocated escape of the soul from the concerns of the body. In Philo's philosophical language, this entailed abandonment of the female in favour of the male or the virgin. Baer admitted an apparent conflict between this point of view and the traditional Jewish perception of the physical creation as good.

I disagree with Baer's literal acceptance of Philo's statements about abandoning the body or the female elements. Drawing on *Mig*.7-8 as a key text, I conclude that Philo's calls for quitting the body are rhetorical, and that the theme of his work is control of the lower elements rather than separation or elimination.[1] In this passage Philo says that to command the latter "would be to prescribe death." Clearly, then, he does not mean literally that one should sever oneself from the body or from the female elements of life. Here is a shortened version of that text:

> The words "Depart out of these" are not equivalent to "Sever thyself from them absolutely," since to issue such a command as that would be to prescribe death. No, the words import "Make thyself a stranger to them in judgement and purpose; let none of them cling to thee; rise superior to them all; they are thy subjects, never treat them as sovereign lords; thou art a king; school thyself once and for all to rule, not to be ruled; evermore be coming to know thyself, as Moses teaches thee in many places, saying "Give heed to thyself," for in this way shalt thou perceive those to whom it befits thee to shew obedience and those to whom it befits thee to give commands" (*Mig*.7f.).

After using these words to convey the real intention behind his rhetoric, Philo goes on to make the kind of statement upon which, taken alone, one might accept Baer's conclusion: " . . . escape, man, from the foul prison-house, thy body, with all thy might and main . . ." (*Mig*.9). The meaning of the passage taken as a whole is quite different from that of this part seen in isolation: although Philo speaks of escape, he intends control.

It follows that the conflict Baer observed is more apparent than real. Philo perceives the lower elements as dangerous and potentially evil. The fact that they are so, however, calls for their control rather than their excision. On the individual, social or even

---

[1] I have quoted this entire passage in ch.11, above.

cosmic level, the feminine, when it is harnessed, loses its danger, and enhances the masculine.

Philo presupposed that in the correct order of things (that is, according to the principle of *dikaiosynē*), male must relate to female as superior to inferior, strong to weak, and active to passive. The female must be controlled by the male. This principle applies on the human as well as on the philosophical plane.

The one area of reality to which Philo failed to extend his sexual distinctions was the internal make-up of woman herself. He did not raise the question whether it was possible for woman functioning in traditional society to control her own lower, feminine impulses by her higher masculine self. Instead, he postulated external control.

Even when he had the opportunity to praise the great women of the past Philo handled the Biblical text in such a way as to avoid lauding women's independent action. When he discussed the Biblical matriarchs as women, he subordinated them to their husbands, and when he treated them allegorically he transformed them into virgins (the equivalent of males).

Philo envisioned reality as a hierarchy in which the interaction of the successively higher elements could be expressed in sexual terms. Such a world view was not unnatural for a man steeped in patriarchy. In the case of Philo, it was particularly apt, since he admired not one, but two such systems.

In a patriarchal system the subordination of women is accepted as natural. Although they expressed it differently, both the Jewish and the Greek traditions converged on this point.

Nearly all the sexual distinctions Philo combined in formulating his thought were foreshadowed in one tradition or the other. Throughout my presentation of the topic I have been able to supply precedents for almost every point that Philo raises. This indicates that in the matter of sexual distinctions Philo was not an innovator. Any originality on his part lay in his combination of ingredients already at hand.

I have presented a number of factors which may have influenced the particular configuration of Philo's perception of women.

One of them is that Philo believed that the hope for present society was to return to the standards of a better age derived from his reading and enhanced by his imagination. This was the Golden Age of Greece combined with the period of the patriarchs.

An important factor influencing Philo's perception of women was the admiration he felt for the folk-hero, Phineas. Philo mentioned him several times, always with praise. Phineas had rescued the nation from the threat posed by women. The young Hebrew men were succumbing to the Moabite women and committing idolatry and apostasy, when Phineas turned the tide. Philo saw in Phineas a model champion of the faith against seductive pleasure. Moreover, the story illustrated the deadly power of uncontrolled female sexuality.

Philo's aversion to the functioning of the female body could have developed from factors in each tradition. In the Greek tradition there was the Platonic doctrine that the process of generation and birth, that is, of becoming, entails corruption. In the Jewish tradition I have disclosed a menstrual taboo, and have suggested that this taboo is associated with Philo's expressed aversion to blood, which symbolizes the life of the body.

Philo also could have developed his demands for strict controls on sexual intercourse from both traditions. Even towards forms of intercourse sanctioned by law the Jews had expressed vacillation. From early times they had not clearly distinguished between moral transgression and ritual impurity. Philo associated the taint of adultery with intercourse in marriage, postulating a form of purification not required by Scripture. Whatever revulsion he felt because of his Jewish background could have been intensified by the Platonic denigration of the body and Plato's requirement that intercourse be for procreation only.

For women in particular Philo associated intercourse with defilement. On the allegorical level he showed this by elevating the great women of Scripture to virginity. On the human level it can be seen in his praise of the female Therapeutae. This valuing of virginity over womanhood was to play a major role in the history of Christianity and may have received its impetus from Philo.

Philo's insistence on the sexual purity of his people and the restraint of its women may have had the apologetic aim of presenting Judaism to outsiders in the most moral light possible. It may also have been a reaction to anti-Semitic charges of lasciviousness.

All these factors may have played roles in causing Philo to write about women as he did. Whatever the mixture of factors may have been, their combined influence resulted in Philo's conviction that woman's need is to be controlled by man and her function is to serve his ends.

Philo's restricted view of woman's purpose in life stands out starkly against the new spiritual freedom he offered man, the opportunity to undertake an Odyssey of the spirit. That achievement ought never to be belittled. Yet it underscores the limitations he would place upon woman. He simply did not raise the question of her spiritual growth. Hers was to be a derivative salvation. The spiritual accountability he urged upon men had no counterpart in the women's quarters.

# APPENDIX A

# DO THE *SPECIAL LAWS* REFLECT ACTUAL LEGAL PRACTICE?

The hypothesis Goodenough attempts to prove in his book, *The Jurisprudence of the Jewish Courts in Egypt*, is that "the laws as he [Philo] expounds them are the laws he daily administered in his hated duties."[1] Continuing to argue from the point of view that Philo is describing legal administration as it actually occurred, Goodenough concludes from Philo's frequent calls for the death penalty either that Roman authorities acquiesced in Jewish decisions calling for capital punishment, or that they "winked at Jews' lynching of Jews."[2]

Colson, Baron, Heinemann and Tcherikover are among those who disagree with Goodenough, and they do so mainly on the grounds that Goodenough misunderstands Philo's purpose: " . . . he was not a jurist in the same sense that he was a philosopher."[3] "His interests were so overwhelmingly philosophic and ethical that even in a treatise dealing with 'special laws' he lacked legal clarity and precision."[4] "It would be safe to assume that a scrupulous examination of *De specialibus legibus*, . . . would leave little evidence to

---

[1] P.10.

[2] Ibid., p. 25 et al.

[3] *PLCL*, vol.7, "General Introduction," pp. xiif.

[4] Baron, *History*, p.386, n.45.

suggest that Philo's laws were drawn up according to the laws and regulations of the Jewish tribunals of Alexandria."[5]

---

[5] Tcherikover, *Corpus*, p.32, n.84.

# ABBREVIATIONS AND BIBLIOGRAPHY

*Abbreviations: Philonic Treatises*

Unless otherwise indicated, the text and translation of Philo used is from the Loeb Classical Library edition prepared by G. H. Whitaker, F. H. Colson and R. Marcus (10 vols.: 2 supplementary vols.; London, 1929-53). Numbers in parentheses refer to the Loeb volume in which the particular work appears.

| | |
|---|---|
| *Abr.* | *De Abrahamo* (6) |
| *Aet.* | *De Aeternitate Mundi* (9) |
| *Agr.* | *De Agricultura* (3) |
| *Anim.* | *De Animalibus* |
| *Cher.* | *De Cherubim* (2) |
| *Conf.* | *De Confusione Linguarum* (4) |
| *Cong.* | *De Congressu quaerendae Eruditionis gratia* (4) |
| *Cont.* | *De Vita Contemplativa* (9) |
| *Decal.* | *De Decalogo* (7) |
| *Det.* | *Quod Deterius Potiori insidiari solet* (2) |
| *Deus* | *Quod Deus immutabilis sit* (3) |
| *Ebr.* | *De Ebrietate* (3) |
| *Flac.* | *In Flaccum* (9) |
| *Fug.* | *De Fuga et Inventione* (5) |
| *Gig.* | *De Gigantibus* (2) |
| *Heres* | *Quis Rerum Divinarum Heres sit* (4) |
| *Hyp.* | *Hypothetica* (9) |
| *Jos.* | *De Josepho* (6) |
| *LA* 1-3 | *Legum Allegoriae* 1, 2, 3. (1) |
| *Legat.* | *De Legatio ad Gaium* (10) |

| | |
|---|---|
| *Mig.* | *De Migratione Abrahami* (4) |
| *Mos.*1,2 | *De Vita Mosis* 1,2. (6) |
| *Mut.* | *De Mutatione Nominum* (5) |
| *Op.* | *De Opificio Mundi* (1) |
| *Plant.* | *De Plantatione* (3) |
| *Post.* | *De Posteritate Caini* (2) |
| *Praem.* | *De Praemiis et Poenis* (8) |
| *Prob.* | *Quod Omnis Probus Liber sit* (9) |
| *Provid.* | *De Providentia* (9) |
| *QE* 1,2 | *Questiones et Solutiones in Exodum* 1,2 (Suppl.2) |
| *QG* 1-4 | *Questiones et Solutiones in Genesin* 1, 2, 3, 4 (Suppl. 1) |
| *Sac.* | *De Sacrificiis Abelis et Caini* (2) |
| *Sob.* | *De Sobrietate* (3) |
| *Som.*1,2 | *De Somniis* 1, 2. (5) |
| *Spec.*1-4 | *De Specialibus Legibus* 1, 2, 3, 4. (7, 8) |
| *Virt.* | *De Virtutibus* (8) |

*Other Abbreviations*

Journals and standard works in Philonic scholarship are abbreviated only when they are cited frequently.

| | |
|---|---|
| LCL | *Loeb Classical Library* |
| PLCL | *Philo Loeb Classical Library* |
| OPA | *Les Oeuvres de Philon d'Alexandrie*, ed. Roger Arnaldez, Jean Pouilloux and Claude Mondesert (Paris: Cerf, 1966) |
| PA | *Philo von Alexandria, Die Werke in Deutscher Übersetzung.* (Berlin: Walter de Gruyter, 1962) |
| CWA | *The Complete Works of Aristotle, The Revised Oxford Translation.* ed. Jonathan Barnes (Princeton: Princeton University Press, 1984) |

# Abbreviations and Bibliography

*Philonic Texts, Translations, Commentaries*

Comprehensive Editions, Translations

*Les oeuvres de Philon d'Alexandrie*, I-XXXVI. Edited by R. Arnaldez, C. Mondesert, and J. Pouilloux. Paris, 1961-74.
*Philo*, I-X. Translated by F. H. Colson and G. H. Whitaker. *Supplement*, I-II. Translated by R. Marcus. The Loeb Classical Library. Cambridge, Mass., 1929-1962.
*Philonis Alexandrini opera quae supersunt*, I-VI. Edited by L. Cohn and P. Wendland. *Indices*, VII. Edited by H. Leisegang. Berlin, 1896-1930.
*Philon von Alexandria: Die Werke in deutscher Übersetzung*, I- VII. Edited by L. Cohn, I. Heinemann, M. Adler, and W. Theiler. Berlin, 1909-1964.

Single Treatises: Editions, Translations, Commentaries

Box, Herbert. *Philonis Alexandrini In Flaccum*. London: Oxford University Press, 1939; New York: Arno Press, 1979.
Harl, Marguerite. *Quis Rerum Divinarum Heres Sit*. Les oeuvres de Philon d'Alexandrie #15. Paris: Cerf, 1966.
Smallwood, E. Mary. *Philonis Alexandrini Legatio ad Gaium*. Leiden: E.J.Brill, 1970.
Terian, Abraham. *Philonis Alexandrini De Animalibus*. Chico: Scholars Press, 1981.
Winston, David. *Philo of Alexandria: The Contemplative Life, the Giants, and Selections*. New York: Paulist Press, 1981.
Winston, David, and Dillon, John. *Two Treatises of Philo of Alexandria*. Brown Judaic Studies Series #25. Chico: Scholars Press, 1983.

## General Reference Works

*The Compact Edition of the Oxford English Dictionary.* 1971 edition.
*Encyclopedia Britannica,* 1960 edition. s.v. "Homer."
*Encyclopedia Judaica.* s.v. "Population," "Purity and Impurity, Ritual" "Sexual Offences," "Tamar," "Woman."
Hatch, E. and Redpath, H. *A Concordance to the Septuagint.* Oxford: Clarendon Press, 1897.
*Der Kleine Pauly Lexikon der Antike.* s.v."Allegorische Dichtererklärung."
Liddell and Scott, *A Greek-English Lexicon.* 9th edition with supplement. Oxford: Clarendon Press, 1968.
*Jewish Encyclopedia.* s.v."Allegorical interpretation," "Tamar."
Mayer, Gunter. *Index Philoneus.* Berlin: Walter de Gruyter, 1974.
*Reallexikon für Antike und Christentum.* s.v."Frau," by K. Thraede.
Sleeman, J. H. and Pollet, Gilbert. *Lexicon Plotinianum.* Leiden: E. J. Brill, 1980.
*Thesaurus Graecae Linguae.* Henrico Stephano. Paris, 1831-1856.

## Other Texts, Translations, Commentaries

### Apocrypha and Pseudepigrapha

Charles, R. H., ed. *The Apocrypha and Pseudepigrapha of the Old Testament in English,*I-II. Oxford, 1913.
Charlesworth, James H., ed. *The Old Testament Pseudepigrapha.* 2 vols. New York: Doubleday, 1985.
Metzger, Bruce M., ed. *The Apocrypha.* New York: Oxford University Press, 1965.

### Aristotle

Aristotle. Loeb Classical Library.
Aristotle. *Politics.* The Modern Library. 1943.

*The Complete Works of Aristotle*, I-II. Edited by Jonathan Barnes. Oxford, 1984.

### Euripides

*The Plays of Euripides.* Translated by Edward P. Coleridge. London: Bell, 1904. vol.2.

### Hesiod

*The Poems of Hesiod.* trans. R. M. Frazer. Norman: University of Oklahoma Press, 1983.
*Theogony.* ed. M. L. West. Oxford: Oxford University Press, 1966.
*Works and Days.* ed. M. L. West. Oxford: Oxford University Press, 1978.

### Joseph and Asenath

*Joseph and Asenath.* Translated by E. W. Brooks. New York: Macmillan, 1918.
Philonenko, Marc. *Joseph and Asenath.* Leiden: E. J. Brill, 1968.

### Josephus

*Flavii Josephi Opera.* ed. Benedictus Niese. Berlin: Weidmann, 1955.
*Josephus*, I-IX. Translated by H. St. J. Thackeray, *et al.* The Loeb Classical Library. Cambridge, Mass., 1926-1965.
Rengstorf, K. H., ed. *A Complete Concordance to Flavius Josephus.* Leiden: E. J. Brill, 1973.

### Mishnah

*The Mishnah.* Translated by H. Danby. London: Oxford University Press. 1st ed., 1933. Reprinted from corrected sheets, 1950.

## Plato

*The Collected Dialogues of Plato.* edited by Edith Hamilton and Huntington Cairns. Bollingen Series #71. Princeton: Princeton University Press, 1961.
*The Dialogues of Plato.* translated by Benjamin Jowett. vol.2. London: Sphere Books, 1970.
*Plato: The Laws.* translated by Trevor J. Saunders. Penguin Books, 1970.
Plato. Loeb Classical Library.
*Plato: The Republic.* translated by Desmond Lee. 2nd edition revised. Penguin Books, 1974.

## Plotinus

*The Enneads*, I-VI. translated by A. H. Armstrong. The Loeb Classical Library. Cambridge, Mass., 1966-1984.

## Semonides and Phocylides

Lloyd-Jones, Hugh. *Females of the Species: Semonides on Women.* London: Noyes, 1975.

## Septuagint

*The Septuagint Version of the Old Testament.* London: Bagster, 1889?.
*Septuaginta.* edited Alfred Rahlfs. 2 vols. Stuttgart, 1935.

## Xenophon

*The Anabasis or Expedition of Cyrus and the Memorabilia of Socrates.* trans. by J. S. Watson. London: Bell, 1878.
*Memorabilia.* edited L. Breitenbach. Berlin, 1854.

*Xenophontis Oeconomicus*. 2nd edition. edited H. Holden. London: Macmillan, 1885.

Anthologies

Lefkowitz, Mary R., and Fant, Maureen B. *Women's Life in Greece and Rome*. London: Duckworth, 1982.

*Works Consulted and/or Cited*

Books

Allen, Prudence, Sister. *The Concept of Woman: The Aristotelian Revolution 750 B.C. - A.D. 1250*. Montreal: Eden Press, 1985.
Baer, Richard. *Philo's Use of the Categories Male and Female*. Leiden: Brill, 1970.
Balsdon, J. P. V. D. *Roman Women*. Westport: Greenwood Press, 1962.
Baron, Salo Wittmayer. *A Social and Religious History of the Jews*. Vol.1, *To the Beginning of the Christian Era*. 2nd ed. New York and London: Columbia University Press, 1952.
de Beauvoir, Simone. *The Second Sex*. Translated and edited by H. M. Parshley. Alfred A. Knopf, 1952; Vintage Books, 1974.
Benecke, E. F. M. *Antimachus of Colophon and the Position of Women in Greek Poetry*. Groningen: Bouma's Boekhuis, 1970.
Berger, Peter L. and Lückmann, Thomas. *The Social Construction of Reality*. Anchor Books, 1967.
Blank, David L. *Ancient Philosophy and Grammar*. American Classical Studies 10. Chico, CA: Scholars Press, 1982.
Bréhier, Émile. *Les Idées Philosophiques et Religieuses de Philon d'Alexandrie*. 3rd ed. Paris, 1950.

Brooten, Bernadette. *Women Leaders in the Ancient Synagogue.* Brown Judaic Studies No. 36. California: Scholars Press, 1982.

Bullough, Vern L. *The Subordinate Sex.* Urbana: University of Illinois Press, 1973.

Cameron, Averil and Amelie Kuhrt. *Images of Women in Antiquity.* Detroit: Wayne State university Press, 1983.

Center for Hermeneutical Studies in Hellenistic and Modern Culture. #30 *Philo's Description of Jewish Practices.* Berkeley: The Center, 1977.

Christiansen, Irmgard. *Die Technik der allegorischen Auslegungswissenschaft bei Philon von Alexandrien.* Tubingen: J. C. B. Mohr, 1969.

Collins, John J. *Between Athens and Jerusalem.* New York: Crossroads, 1983.

Danielou, Jean. *Philon d'Alexandrie.* Paris, 1958.

Dillon, John. *The Middle Platonists. A Study of Platonism 80 B.C. to A.D. 220.* London: Duckworth, 1977.

Dodds, E. R. *Pagan and Christian in an Age of Anxiety.* New York and London: W. W. Norton, 1965.

Drummond, J. *Philo Judaeus.* London, 1888.

Eichler, Margrit and Lapointe, Jeanne. *On the Treatment of the Sexes in Research.* Ottawa: SSHRC, 1985.

Engelsman, Joan Chamberlain. *The Feminine Dimension of the Divine.* Philadelphia: Westminster Press, 1979, 95-106.

Epstein, Louis M. *Sex Laws and Customs in Judaism.* New York: KTAV, 1948. New Matter, 1967.

Evans-Pritchard. *The Position of Women in Primitive Societies and Other Essays in Social Anthropology.* New York: 1965, 37-58.

Feldman, Louis H. *Scholarship on Philo and Josephus 1937- 1962.* Studies in Judaica. New York: Yeshiva University, 1963?

Festugière, A. P. *La Révélation d'Hermès Trismégiste.* Paris, 1949. vol. 2.

Foster, Samuel Stephen. *The Alexandrian Situation and Philo's Use of "Dike"*. London and Ann Arbor: University Microfilms International, 1979.

Fraser, P. M. *Ptolemaic Alexandria*. 3 vols. Oxford, 1972.

Fruchtel, Ursula. *Die Kosmologischen Vorstellungen bei Philo von Alexandrien*. Leiden: E.J.Brill, 1968.

Gardner, Jane F. *Women in Roman Law and Society*. London and Sydney: Croom Helm, 1986.

Ginzberg, L. *The Legends of the Jews*. 7 vols. Translated by H. Szold and P. Radin. Philadelphia, 1946-7.

Goodenough, E. R. *By Light, Light*. New Haven: Yale University Press, 1935.

_____. *An Introduction to Philo Judaeus*. New Haven: Yale University Press, 1940. 2nd ed. Oxford: Basil Blackwell, 1962.

_____. *The Jurisprudence of the Jewish Courts in Egypt*. New Haven: Yale University Press, 1929.

_____. *The Politics of Philo Judaeus*. New Haven: Yale University Press, 1938.

Grant, R. M. *The Letter and the Spirit*. London: SPCK, 1957.

Headlam, Walter. *Herodas*. Cambridge: Cambridge University Press, 1966.

Heinemann, Isaak. *Philons Griechische und Jüdische Bildung*. Hildesheim, New York: George Olms, 1973.

Isaksson, Abel. *Marriage and Ministry in the New Temple*. Lund, 1965.

Jaeger, Werner. *Paideia: the Ideals of Greek Culture*. translated from the 2nd German edition by Gilbert Highet. 3 vols. Oxford, 1939-44.

Juster, Jean. *Les Juifs dans l'empire Romain*. New York: Bert Franklin, 1914.

Knox, Wilfred. *Some Hellenistic Elements in Primitive Christinity*. London: Oxford University Press, 1944.

Laporte, Jean. *The Role of Women in Early Christianity.* vol.7. Studies in Women and Religion. New York and Toronto: Edwin Mellen Press, 1982.
Lefkowitz, Mary R. *Heroines and Hysterics.* London: Duckworth, 1981.
Leipoldt, Johannes. *Die Frau in der antiken Welt und im Urchristentum.* Berlin: Union Verlag, 1953.
Lewis, C. S. *A Preface to Paradise Lost.* New York: Oxford University Press, 1970. First published in 1942.
Lewis, Naphtali. *Life in Egypt under Roman Rule.* Oxford: Clarendon Press, 1983.
Lilla, Salvatore R.C. *Clement of Alexandria.* Oxford University Press, 1971.
Loewe, Raphael. *The Position of Women in Judaism.* London, 1966.
Lovejoy, Arthur O. *The Great Chain of Being.* Cambridge: Harvard Universiy Press, 1936.
Marrou, H. I. *A History of Education in Antiquity.* translated by George Lamb. London: Sheed and Ward, 1956.
Mendelson, A. *Philo's Jewish Identity.* unpublished typescript.
_____. *Secular Education in Philo of Alexandria.* New York: KTAV, 1982.
Neufeld, E. *Ancient Hebrew Marriage Laws.* London: Longmans, 1944.
Neusner, Jacob. *A History of the Mishnaic Law of Women* Leiden: E. J. Brill, 1980. vol. 5.
Nikiprowetzky, V. *Le Commentaire de l'Écriture chez Philon d'Alexandrie.* Leiden: E. J. Brill, 1977.
Noordtzij, A. *Leviticus.* translated by R. Togtman. Grand Rapids: Zondervan, 1982.
Noth, Martin. *Numbers.* London: SCM Press, 1968. Trans. J. D. Martin. Published in 1960 in Gottingen.
Parke, H. W. *Festivals of the Athenians.* London: Thames and Hudson, 1977.
Pomeroy, Sarah B. *Goddesses, Whores, Wives and Slaves.* New York: Schocken Books, 1975.

_____.*Women in Hellenistic Egypt.* New York: Schocken Books, 1984.
Porter, A. *Leviticus.* Cambridge, Mass.: Cambridge University Press, 1976.
Rajak, Tessa. *Josephus.* Philadelphia: Fortress Press, 1983.
Riedweg, Christoph. *Mysterienterminologie bei Platon Philon und Klemens von Alexandrien.* #26, Untersuchungen zur antiken Literatur und Geschichte. Berlin and New York: de Gruyter, 1987.
Ross, Sir David. *Plato's Theory of Ideas.* Oxford: Clarendon Press, 1951.
Rostovtzeff, M. I. *The Social and Economic History of the Hellenistic World.* 3 vols. Oxford: Clarendon Press, 1941.
Ruether, Rosemary Radford, ed. *Religion and Sexism.* New York: Simon and Schuster, 1974.
_____. *Sexism and God-Talk.* Boston: Beacon Hill Press, 1983.
_____ and McLaughlin, Eleanor, eds. *Women of Spirit: Female Leadership and the Jewish Christian Traditions.* N e w York: Simon & Schuster, 1979.
Runia, David T. *Philo of Alexandria and The Timaeus of Plato.* Leiden: E. J. Brill, 1986.
Russell, D. A. *'Longinus' On the Sublime.* Oxford: Clarendon, 1964.
Russell, Letty M. *Feminist Interpretation of the Bible.* Philadelphia: Westminster Press, 1985.
Safrai, S. and Stern, M., eds. *The Jewish People in the First Century.* Philadelphia: Fortress Press, 1974.
Sandmel, Samuel. *Judaism and Christian Beginnings.* New York: Oxford University Press, 1978).
_____. *Philo of Alexandria.* New York: Oxford University Press, 1979.
_____. *Philo's Place in Judaism.* Augmented Edition. New York: KTAV, 1971.
Schmidt, R. L. *Stoicorum Grammatica.* Halle, 1839.
Schüssler-Fiorenza, Elisabeth. *In Memory of Her.* New York: Crossroads, 1983.

Segal, Alan. *Rebecca's Children*. Cambridge: Harvard University Press, 1986.
Seltman, Charles. *Women in Antiquity*. New York and London: Thames and Hudson, 1956.
Speiser, E. A. *Genesis*. Garden City: Doubleday, 1964.
Stagg, Evelyn and Frank. *Women in the World of Jesus*. Philadelphia: Westminster Press, 1978.
Stern, Menahem. *Greek and Latin Authors on Jews and Judaism*. Jerusalem: The Israel Academy of Sciences and Humanities, 1974.
Stone, Michael. *Scriptures, Sects and Visions*. Philadelphia: Fortress Press, 1980.
Strack, Hermann L. and Billerbeck, Paul. *Das Evangelium nach Matthäus*. 1922.
Swidler, Leonard. *Women in Judaism*. New York: Scarecrow Press, 1976.
Tcherikover, Victor. *Hellenistic Civilization and the Jews*. Trans. S. Applebaum. New York: Atheneum, 1975.
Tcherikover, Victor, Fuks, Alexander, and Stern, Menahem. *Corpus Papyrorum Judaicarum*. 3 vols. Cambridge: Harvard University Press, 1957-64.
Theissen, Gerd. *Sociology of Early Palestinian Christianity*. Trans. John Bowden. Philadelphia: Fortress Press, 1978.
Trible, Phyllis. *God and the Rhetoric of Sexuality*. Overtures to Biblical Theology #2. Philadelphia: Fortress Press,1978.
_____. *Texts of Terror*. Overtures to Biblical Theology #13. Philadelphia: Fortress Press, 1984.
Trenchard, Warren C. *Ben Sira's View of Women: A Literary Analysis*. Brown Judaic Studies Series #38. Chico: Scholars Press, 1982.
Turner, E. G. *Greek Papyri: An Introduction*. Princeton: Princeton University Press, 1968.
Vermes, G. *Jesus the Jew*. London, 1973.
Vlastos, Gregory. *Platonic Studies*. 2nd ed., with corrections. Princeton: Princeton University Press, 1981.

Volker, W. *Fortschritt und Vollendung bei Philo von Alexandrian.* Leipzig, 1938.
Wenham, G. J. *The Book of Leviticus.* Grand Rapids: Eerdmans, 1979.
Wilkin, R., ed. *Aspects of Wisdom in Judaism and Early Christianity.* Notre Dame: University of Notre Dame Press, 1975.
Winston, David. *Philo of Alexandria: The Contemplative Life, the Giants, and Selections.* New York: Paulist Press, 1981.
Wolfson, Harry A. *Philo.* 2 vols. Cambridge, Mass.: Harvard University Press, 1947.
Yaron, Reuven. *Introduction to the Law of the Aramaic Papyri.* Oxford, 1961.


Articles


Archer, Leonie J. "The Role of Jewish Women in the Religion Ritual and Cult of Graeco-Roman Palestine." In *Images of Women in Antiquity*, pp.273-287. Edited by Averil Cameron and Amelie Kuhrt. Detroit: Wayne State University Press, 1983.
Baumgarten, A. "The Torah as a Public Document in Judaism." *Studies in Religion* (Winter, 1985): 17-24.
Bird, Phyllis. "Image of Women in the Old Testament." In *Religion and Sexism*, Edited by R. R. Ruether. New York: Simon and Schuster, 1974.
Borgen, Peder. "Philo of Alexandria: A critical and synthetical survey of research since World War II." In *Aufstieg und Niedergang der Römischen Welt* II 21.1, pp.98-154. Berlin and New York: de Gruyter, 1984.
Cazeaux, Jacques. "Aspects de l'exégèse Philonienne," *Revue des sciences religieuses* 47 (1973): 262-269.
_____. "Philon d'Alexandrie, exégète." In *Aufstieg und Niedergang der Römischen Welt* II 21.1, pp.156-226. Berlin and New York: de Gruyter, 1984.

Chadwick, Henry. "St. Paul and Philo of Alexandria," *BJRL* 48 (1965-6): 286-307.

Conley, T. "Philo's Use of Topoi." In *Two Treatises of Philo of Alexandria*, pp.171-178. Edited by John Dillon and David Winston. Brown Judaic Studies No. 25. California: Scholars Press, 1983.

Dillon, John. "Philo's Doctrine of Angels." In *Two Treatises of Philo of Alexandria*, pp.197-205. Edited by David Winston and John Dillon. Brown Judaic Studies No. 25. California: Scholars Press, 1983.

Exum, J. Cheryl. "'Mother in Israel': A Familiar Figure Reconsidered." In *Feminist Interpretation of the Bible*, pp.73-85. Edited by Letty M. Russell. Philadelphia: Westminster Press, 1985.

Feldman, Louis H. "The Orthodoxy of the Jews in Hellenistic Egypt." *Jewish Social Studies* 22 (1960): 215-237.

Goodenough, E. R., with Kraabel, A. Thomas. "Paul and the Hellenization of Christianity." In *Religions in Antiquity*, pp.23-68. Edited by Jacob Neusner. Leiden: E. J. Brill, 1968.

Gross, Rita M. "Androcentrism and Androgyny in the Methodology of History of Religions." In *Beyond Androcentrism*, pp.7-22. Edited by Rita Gross. Missoula: Scholars Press, 1977.

Hatch, Edwin. "Psychological Terms in Philo." In *Essays in Biblical Greek*, pp.109-130. Oxford: Clarendon Press, 1889.

Jones, H. S. "Claudius and the Jewish Question at Alexandria." *Journal of Roman Studies* xvi (1926): 17-35.

Kee, H. C. "The Socio-Religious Setting and Aims of 'Joseph and Asenath'." *SBL Seminar Papers* (10) 1976: 182-192.

King, Helen. "Bound to Bleed: Artemis and Greek Women." In *Images of Women in Antiquity*, pp.109-127. Edited by Averil Cameron and Amelie Kuhrt. Detroit: Wayne State University Press, 1983.

Koester, Helmut. "NOMOS PHYSEOS: The Concept of Natural Law in Greek Thought." In *Religions in Antiquity*, pp.521-41. Edited by Jacob Neusner. Leiden: E. J. Brill, 1968.

Kraemer, Ross S. "Women in the Religions of the Greco-Roman World." *Religious Studies Review*. vol.9. no.2. (April, 1983): 127-139.

MacMullen, Ramsay. "Women in Public in the Roman Empire." *Historia* 29 (1980): 208-18.

Mack, Burton L. "Philo Judaeus and Exegetical Traditions in Alexandria." In *Aufstieg und Niedergang der Römischen Welt* II 21.1, pp.227-271. Berlin and New York: de Gruyter, 1984.

Melnick, R. "On the Philonic Conception of the Whole Man." *Journal for the Study of Judaism* 11 (Jl., 1980): 1-32.

Mendelson, Alan. "A Reappraisal of Wolfson's Method," *Studia Philonica* 3 (1974-5): 11-26.

Nikiprowetzky, V. "L'exégèse de Philon d'Alexandrie dans le *De Gigantibus* et le *Quod Deus*." In *Two Treatises of Philo of Alexandria*. Edited by David Winston and John Dillon. Brown Judaic Studies Series 25. Chico: Scholars Press, 1983.

_____."Rebecca, vertu de constance et constance de vertu chez Philon d'Alexandrie." *Semitica* 26 (1976): 109-36.

Ortner, Sherry B. " Is Female to Male as Nature is to Culture?" In *Woman, Culture and Society*, pp.67-87. Edited by Michelle Zimbalist Rosaldo and Louise Lamphere. Stanford, Calif.: Stanford University Press, 1974. pp.67-87.

Pervo, Richard I. "Joseph and Asenath and the Greek Novel." *SBL Seminar Papers* 10 (1976): 171-181.

Philonenko, M. "Essénisme et misogynie (d'après Philon)." *Comptes rendus de l'Académie des Inscriptions et Belles-Lettres* (1982): 339-50.

Pomeroy, Sarah."Infanticide in Hellenistic Greece." In *Images of Women in Antiquity*, pp. 207-22. Edited by Averil

Cameron and Amelie Kuhrt. Detroit: Wayne State University Press, 1983.

⎯⎯⎯⎯. "Women in Roman Egypt: A Preliminary Study Based on Papyri." In *Reflections of Women in Antiquity*, pp.303-322. Edited by Helen P. Foley. London, 1981.

Runia, D. T. "How to Read Philo." *Nederlands Theologisch Tijdschrift* 40 (1986): 185-198.

⎯⎯⎯⎯. "The Structure of Philo's Allegorical Treatises." *Vigiliae Christianae* 48 38 (1984): 209-256.

Sanders, E. P. "The Covenant as a Soteriological Category and the Nature of Salvation in Palestinian and Hellenistic Judaism." In *Jews, Greeks and Christians*, pp.11-44. Edited by Robert Hamerton-Kelly and Robin Scroggs. Leiden: E. J. Brill, 1976.

Schüssler-Fiorenza, Elisabeth. "Feminist Theology as a Critical Theology of Liberation." *Theological Studies* 36 (1975): 605-26.

⎯⎯⎯⎯. "Towards a Liberating and Liberated Theology." *Concilium* 15 (1979):22-32.

Wegner, Judith Romney. "The Image of Women in Philo." *SBL Seminar Papers*. (Chico, California: Scholars Press, 1982): 551-563.

Winston, David. "Philo's Ethical Theory." *Aufstieg und Niedergang der Römischen Welt* II 21.1, pp. 372-416. Berlin and New York: de Gruyter, 1984.

# INDEX

## Biblical Passages

Genesis  66
Gen.1:26  55
Gen.1:27  12, 98
Gen.2  68
Gen.2:7  55, 98
Gen.2:8  68
Gen.2:15  68
Gen.2:16  68
Gen.2:18  68
Gen.2:18-25  99
Gen.2:19  68
Gen.2:20  68
Gen.2:21  68
Gen.2:22  12, 68
Gen.2:23  68
Gen.2:24  13, 68, 106, 134
Gen.2:35  205
Gen.3:1-21  99
Gen.3:6  12
Gen.3:9  54
Gen.3:16  74
Gen.3:16-19  13
Gen.3:17  95, 106
Gen.3:18  150
Gen.3:20  103
Gen.4:1  137
Gen.7:11  88
Gen.12:1-6  147
Gen.12:5  13, 147
Gen.12:11  148
Gen.15:13  203
Gen.16:1f.  149, 151
Gen.16:1-6  147
Gen.16:1b  128
Gen.16:2  13, 150
Gen.16:2b  150

Gen.16:4  129
Gen.16:5  129
Gen.16:6  13, 138, 203
Gen.16:8  14
Gen.16:9  203
Gen.16:11  203
Gen.18:11  72, 153
Gen.19:17  118
Gen.19:26  118, 119
Gen.20:7  68
Gen.21:1f.  139
Gen.21:12  13, 149, 150
Gen.21:17f.  14
Gen.24  13
Gen.24-27  154
Gen.24:21  68
Gen.24:64  155
Gen.24:64f.  156
Gen.24:67  158
Gen.25:21  140
Gen.25:22f.  13
Gen.25:23  14
Gen.25:28  156
Gen.26:11  68
Gen.27:5-40  14
Gen.27:27-29  157
Gen.29:27  166
Gen.29:28  166
Gen.29:31  163, 165
Gen.29:31f.  139
Gen.30:1  162
Gen.30:16  165
Gen.30:24  162
Gen.31:35  54, 75, 165
Gen.32:2  203
Gen.34  174

Gen.34:31 199
Gen.35:16 173
Gen.35:19 173
Gen.38:2 68
Gen.38:15 199
Gen.39f. 157
Gen.42:11 68
Ex.1 123
Ex.1:12 203
Ex.2:21f. 140
Ex.12:37 13
Ex.12:37f. 189
Ex.15 121
Ex.15:1-21 114
Ex.15:20 120, 121
Ex.19:15 188
Ex.19:25 188
Ex.20:12 186
Ex.22:18 193
Ex.24:12 184
Ex.32:2f. 67
Ex.32:27f. 191
Ex.35 123
Ex.35:22f. 124
Ex.38 123
Ex.38:26 124
Lev. 77, 78
Lev.12:6f. 78
Lev.14:10-20 78
Lev.15:15 78
Lev.15:16 68
Lev.15:18 77, 78
Lev.16:29 203
Lev.18:19 84, 88
Lev.18:20 77
Lev.18:29 77
Lev.20:10 68
Lev.20:18 88
Lev.21:9 68
Lev.22:12 68
Lev.22:13 68
Lev.23:27 203
Lev.23:29 203

Lev.23:32 203
Num.5:15 68
Num.5:18 205
Num.8:21 78
Num.12 120
Num.12:14 120, 203
Num.15:34 192
Num.19:12f. 78
Num.19:20 78
Num.22-31 14
Num.25 112
Num.25:1 116
Num.25:7f. 113
Num.25:7-9 116
Num.31:16 14, 114
Num.31:19f. 78
Num.31:23 78
Deut.13:9 191
Deut.13:14 191
Deut.17:6 191
Deut. 20:5-7 68
Deut.20:7 68
Deut.21:10-14 208
Deut.21:14 203
Deut.21:15f. 68
Deut.21:15-17 163, 167, 168
Deut.22:5 47
Deut.22:21 200
Deut.22:24 203
Deut.22:29 203
Deut.22:30 68
Deut.23:2 199
Deut.23:17 195
Deut.26:5-9 6
Deut.26:5-10 13
Deut.35:17 174
Judg.11:1 199
Judg.16:1 199
1 Sam.1 13, 14
1 Sam.1:11 177
1 Sam.1:14 177
1 Sam.1:28 177
Esther 202

Job 42:15b  18
Prov.  15
Prov.2:16  15
Prov.5:3-6  15
Prov.5:20  15
Prov.6:24-26  15
Prov.7  167
Prov.7:9-22  199
Prov.7-9  15
Prov.9  167
Prov.11:22  15
Prov.31  15, 167
Eccles.  15
Eccles.7:26  15
Song of Sol.  15
Isa.3:16-24  167
Isa.23:15-16  199
Isa.25  167
Jer.3:1-3  199
Jer.44  33
Eph.5:32  134
1 Tim.5:13f.  183
Titus 2:4f.  183
1 Pet.3:1-6  154
2 Pet.2:15  114
Jude 11  114
Rev.2:14  114

## Philonic Passages

Abr.  147-149
Abr.1  66
Abr.22f.  74
Abr.26  173
Abr.32  61
Abr.66  148
Abr.74  95
Abr.93  148
Abr.94  63
Abr.97  73
Abr.99  100, 137, 152
Abr.100f.  132, 133, 153

Abr.101f.  46
Abr.122  135
Abr.243  93
Abr.245  148
Abr.245f.  148
Abr.246  148
Abr.247  63, 73
Abr.247-254  125, 149
Abr.251  128
Abr.252  150
Abr.253  138
Abr.255  149

Aet. 27
Aet.13-17  142
Aet.20  204
Aet.25  142
Aet.33  142
Aet.41  51
Aet.52  142
Aet.141  142
Agr.9  61
Agr.24  115
Agr.73  48, 95
Agr.80f.  121
Agr.95-99  99
Agr.95ff.  109
Agr.97  93, 94
Agr.107f.  99
Agr.139  96
Agr.148  68
Cher.  139
Cher.3  125
Cher.3-10  151
Cher.5  151
Cher.6  125
Cher.8  125, 128, 154
Cher.10  152
Cher.40  73, 99, 137, 138
Cher.40f.  137, 154
Cher.40-50  134
Cher.41  73, 163
Cher.42  133
Cher.42-48  49, 102, 132, 134, 136, 140, 141, 143, 145, 161
Cher.43  62, 99, 134, 141
Cher.43f.  136, 138
Cher.45  139
Cher.46  139
Cher.47  139, 140, 154, 157
Cher.48  133, 134
Cher.50  46, 73, 75, 76, 80, 137, 176
Cher.51  151, 152
Cher.53f.  99
Cher.57-65  99

Cher.59  104
Cher.62  104
Conf.1-14  93
Conf.23ff.  88
Conf.41  68
Conf.55ff.  112
Conf.63  49
Conf.95  112
Conf.144  195
Conf.147  68
Conf.190  94
Cong.  125, 150, 151, 166, 206
Cong.1-13  151
Cong.1-70  151
Cong.6  160
Cong.7  72, 153
Cong.12  151
Cong.19  65
Cong.23  73
Cong.24-33  166
Cong.24f.  164
Cong.25ff.  165
Cong.27  162
Cong.34-38  154
Cong.36  166
Cong.37  157
Cong.54  151
Cong.63  196
Cong.68  151
Cong.74-80  1
Cong.76f.  196
Cong.80  2
Cong.111  157
Cong.111-113  154
Cong.123  165
Cong.124  80, 175, 206
Cong.129  154, 158
Cong.139  129
Cong.151ff.  129
Cong.171  99
Cong.180  94, 151, 208
Cont.  57, 142, 182
Cont.13  209

Cont.18   209
Cont.25   15, 133
Cont.31f.   210
Cont.33   206, 210
Cont.57-63   102
Cont.59-62   143
Cont.68   73, 209, 210
Cont.80   62
Cont.87   211
Decal.   181, 185
Decal.1   181
Decal.8   195
Decal.32   62, 188
Decal.45   188
Decal.51   186, 52
Decal.65   65, 188
Decal.107   186, 52
Decal.119   186, 52
Decal.124   189
Decal.129   189
Det.   155
Det.3   162
Det.28   46, 72, 153
Det.30   156, 157
Det.30f.   154
Det.45   154
Det.51   154
Det.52ff.   187
Det.54   49
Det.59   152
Det.115   49
Det.139   61
Det.147   49
Deus 5   177
Deus 10   177
Deus 10f.   177
Deus 13   52, 177
Deus 16-18   85
Deus 26   79
Deus 59   93
Deus 61   133
Deus 78   79
Deus 119   82

Deus 136   73, 175
Deus 136f.   175
Ebr.49   166, 168
Ebr.50   194
Ebr.54   54
Ebr.54-59   46, 165
Ebr.55   75
Ebr.61   48, 83, 153
Ebr.66-71   191
Ebr.73-75   117
Ebr.73ff.   112
Ebr.74   118
Ebr.144   177
Ebr.145-152   177
Ebr.146f.   177
Ebr.164   118
Ebr.177   30
Flac.43   2
Flac.89   197, 206
Fug.   154
Fug.1   125
Fug.4f   203
Fug.5   129
Fug.5f.   125
Fug.23-25   154
Fug.24   159
Fug.26   159
Fug.39-52   154
Fug.43   159
Fug.45   157, 159
Fug.47   160
Fug.49   159
Fug.50   81
Fug.51   45, 50, 51
Fug.71f.   61
Fug.82   66
Fug.90   191
Fug.119-131   117
Fug.121f.   119
Fug.128   119, 153
Fug.149-156   175
Fug.153f.   175
Fug.154   175

Fug.177-201  87
Fug.188-194  88
Fug.194f.  154
Fug.202f.  125
Fug.211f.  125
Gig.60-63  120
Gig.65  99
Heres 15-18  162
Heres 45ff.  170, 171
Heres 47-49  68
Heres 49f.  163
Heres 52  103
Heres 52f.  99
Heres 57  63
Heres 61  72
Heres 62  83, 153
Heres 69  6
Heres 128  206
Heres 138f  58, 96
Heres 164  62, 99
Heres 214  3
Heres 216  83
Heres 231  61
Heres 258  68, 152
Heres 274  64
Hyp.  182
Hyp.6.9  12, 179
Hyp.7.3  51, 81
Hyp.11.3  208
Hyp.11.14  52, 82
Hyp.11.14-17  207
Hyp.11.15  208
Jos.37-80  111
Jos.40  112
Jos.41  112
Jos.43  24, 76, 194, 199
Jos.49  112
Jos.66  112
Jos.69  172
Jos.80  112
Jos.106  172
Jos.107  204
Jos.127  69

Jos.257  204
Jos.264  65
LA  99
LA 1.7  82
LA 1.61  113
LA 1.70-72  95
LA 1.72  185
LA 1.76  120
LA 1.86  193
LA 1.105-108  103
LA 2  99
LA 2.1  68
LA 2.7  106
LA 2.7f.  104
LA 2.17  106
LA 2.19  92
LA 2.38  97
LA 2.47  170
LA 2.47f.  163
LA 2.48  68
LA 2.49  49, 68
LA 2.49f.  106
LA 2.51  106
LA 2.57  133
LA 2.66f.  111, 120, 203
LA 2.74  109
LA 2.79ff.  109
LA 2.82  152
LA 2.95  165
LA 2.97  47, 48
LA 2.385  51
LA 3  99, 150
LA 3.3  123, 133
LA 3.7  113
LA 3.11  47
LA 3.27  133
LA.3.49f.  54
LA 3.50  61, 96, 118
LA 3.65f.  205
LA 3.67  104
LA 3.74  175
LA 3.84  95
LA 3.88  157

Index 249

LA 3.88f. 154
LA 3.100ff. 135
LA 3.103 121
LA 3.145 128
LA 3.180 162, 165, 173
LA 3.181 164
LA 3.202 47
LA 3.213 119
LA 3.217f. 152
LA 3.219 133, 134, 136
LA 3.222 106
LA 3.222-224 150
LA 3.222-245 95
LA 3.225 112
LA 3.236-241 111
LA 3.237 112
LA 3.239 112
LA 3.241 112
LA 3.242 112, 113
LA 3.243 112, 123
LA 3.244 125, 147
LA 3.244f. 151
Legat. 2
Legat.5 204
Legat.39 208
Legat.39f. 194
Legat.208 62
Legat.276 204
Legat.293 204
Legat.319 62, 97
Legat.352 204
Mig. 147, 184
Mig.7f. 184, 220
Mig.9 220
Mig.19 112
Mig.31 81
Mig.33-35 49
Mig.69 195
Mig.95-99 172
Mig.96-99 173
Mig.97 124
Mig.97-105 123
Mig.98 124

Mig.99 196
Mig.102 124
Mig.104 125
Mig.104f. 104
Mig.120 65
Mig.126 148
Mig.140 148
Mig.142 148
Mig.185f. 50
Mig.208-211 154
Mig.209 159
Mig.214f. 123
Mig.224 195
Mig.225 175
Mos.1 114
Mos.1.3 66
Mos.1.23 117
Mos.1.28 74, 138
Mos.1.84 204
Mos.1.106ff. 112
Mos.1.134 62
Mos.1.147 66, 189
Mos.1.158f. 74, 138
Mos.1.161 204
Mos.1.180 122
Mos.1.263 117
Mos.1.295ff. 115
Mos.1.299 52
Mos.1.300 115
Mos.1.303f. 116
Mos.1.305 116
Mos.1.311 115, 168
Mos.2.14 12, 179
Mos.2.171 191
Mos.2.210 48, 83
Mos.2.214 192, 193
Mos.2.234 206
Mos.2.256 122
Mut.61 151
Mut.62 151
Mut.77-80 151
Mut.78 151
Mut.79 152

| | |
|---|---|
| Mut.96 173 | Post.77f. 154, 161 |
| Mut.119 61 | Post.78f. 73 |
| Mut.120 161 | Post.124-126 99 |
| Mut.130 151 | Post.130 125 |
| Mut.132f. 165 | Post.132 125 |
| Mut.134 175, 176 | Post.132-153 154 |
| Mut.143 177 | Post.133 80 |
| Mut.149 65 | Post.134 75, 81 |
| Mut.152 93 | Post.135 165, 168, 170, 171 |
| Mut.172 115 | Post.137 125 |
| Mut.194f. 175 | Post.140-150 158 |
| Mut.201 204 | Post.170 99 |
| Mut.217 204 | Post.175f. 118 |
| Mut.254 163, 165 | Post.178f. 173 |
| Mut.255 125 | Post.179 162 |
| Mut.264 152 | Post.180f. 85 |
| Op. 55 | Post.181 204 |
| Op.2 93 | Post.183 117 |
| Op.3 65 | Praem. 181 |
| Op.38 49 | Praem.46 135 |
| Op.43 49 | Praem.97 204 |
| Op.76 99 | Praem.112f. 65 |
| Op.103-105 69 | Praem.139 195 |
| Op.119 142 | Praem.146 197 |
| Op.132 87 | Praem.159 73, 177 |
| Op.133 142 | Praem.159f 71, 177 |
| Op.148 45 | Praem.164 201 |
| Op.150 45 | Prob.13 113, 142 |
| Op.151 104 | Prob.87 204 |
| Op.151-179 99 | Prob.117 61 |
| Op.152 109, 205 | Prob.140 62 |
| Op.156 96, 118 | Provid.2.115 3 |
| Op.157 94 | QE 53 |
| Op.165 47, 50, 104, 107 | QG 53, 58, 125, 126, 163 |
| Op.165-167 54 | QG 1:20 45 |
| Op.166 115 | QG 1.23-53 99 |
| Plant.120 93 | QG 1.25 97 |
| Plant.135 171 | QG 1.26 104 |
| Plant.169f. 138, 154 | QG 1.27 97, 107 |
| Post. 154 | QG 1.28 76 |
| Post.33 99 | QG 1.29 107 |
| Post.62 152, 154, 157, 165, 174 | QG 1.33 97 |
| Post.77 158 | QG 1.37 103 |

QG 1.43  97
QG 1.45  104
QG 1.46  61, 97
QG 1.49  74
QG 1.92  83, 187
QG 3  27
QG 3.18-4.73  146
QG 3.47  87
QG 4.4  135
QG 4.8  133
QG 4.11  152
QG 4.15  47, 74, 101, 172
QG 4.18  45
QG 4.38  47
QG 4.52  118
QG 4.55  118
QG 4.88-4.239  146
QG 4.88-end  154
QG 4.91  157
QG 4.95  71, 73, 77
QG 4.99  155, 200
QG 4.124  155
QG 4.137  74
QG 4.138  145
QG 4.142  155, 205
QG 4.143  155
QG 4.145  158, 160
QG 4.148  128
QG 4.153  48
QG 4.154  74, 108, 155
QG 4.158  158
QG 4.160  48, 52
QG 4.166  156
QG 4.189  61
QG 4.200  157
QG 4.204  159
QG 4.206  6, 145
QG 4.239  159
Sac.1  99
Sac.4  154, 158
Sac.5-8  6
Sac.19-44  68, 163
Sac.20  49, 194

Sac.20-45  167, 172
Sac.21  115, 168, 172
Sac.21-32  167
Sac.21-45  15, 102
Sac.22-25  168
Sac.26  168, 172
Sac.26f.  168, 206
Sac.28  168
Sac.29  168
Sac.32  46, 47, 169
Sac.37  47, 169
Sac.43  125
Sac.45  170
Sac.60  133
Sac.98  49
Sac.103  48
Sac.126  65
Sac.130  191
Sob.8  125, 128
Sob.12  165
Sob.21-25  68
Sob.23  170
Som.1.46  154, 157, 159
Som.1.122-126  64
Som.1.164  133
Som.1.172  93
Som.1.191  133
Som.1.226  133
Som.1.240  125
Som.1.254  177
Som.2.9  64, 172
Som.2.16  173
Som.2.44  175
Som.2.106  112
Som.2.153f.  95
Som.2.184  81
Som.2.185  210
Spec.1  116, 190
Spec.1-4  181, 182, 192, 193, 196
Spec.1.8  134
Spec.1.9  108, 193
Spec.1.55  116, 182, 191

Spec.1.55ff. 112
Spec.1.56 93, 115, 168, 193
Spec.1.57 191
Spec.1.79 191
Spec.1.101 210
Spec.1.102 173
Spec.1.102-107 201
Spec.1.103 195, 201
Spec.1.105 190
Spec.1.108 208
Spec.1.120 193
Spec.1.129 209
Spec.1.138 31, 148, 184
Spec.1.144 62, 188
Spec.1.187 173, 201
Spec.1.200f 48
Spec.1.201 51
Spec.1.275f. 70
Spec.1.310 200
Spec.1.316 192
Spec.1.323 194
Spec.1.325 46, 211
Spec.1.326 199
Spec.1.332 195
Spec.2.25 200
Spec.2.43 62, 188
Spec.2.50 46, 211
Spec.2.54f. 46, 67, 72, 77
Spec.2.56 48
Spec.2.62 201, 205
Spec.2.125 74, 117, 206
Spec.2.133-139 68
Spec.2.146 62, 188, 189
Spec.2.225 82
Spec.2.232 190
Spec.2.236 187
Spec.3.1-6 2
Spec.3.11 190
Spec.3.25 206
Spec.3.31 190
Spec.3.32 85
Spec.3.35 40
Spec.3.38 190, 192, 211

Spec.3.39 46, 211
Spec.3.48 62, 188
Spec.3.51 62, 182, 188, 190, 199, 201, 205, 206
Spec.3.56 205
Spec.3.63 80
Spec.3.66 196
Spec.3.67 37
Spec.3.69 39
Spec.3.79ff. 58, 200
Spec.3.80 195, 196
Spec.3.81 200
Spec.3.94 192
Spec.3.101 194
Spec.3.101-103 194
Spec.3.102 190
Spec.3.106 190
Spec.3.108 190
Spec.3.126 191
Spec.3.128 192
Spec.3.136 196
Spec.3.141 192
Spec.3.169 206
Spec.3.171 52
Spec.3.171-174 197
Spec.3.172 206
Spec.3.176 206
Spec.3.178 99
Spec.3.178-180 51
Spec.4 181
Spec.4.14-18 172
Spec.4.68 82, 187
Spec.4.123 72
Spec.4.140 204
Spec.4.142 62, 196
Spec.4.178 76
Spec.4.180f. 4
Spec.4.203 189
Spec.4.218 62, 188
Spec.4.223 197
Spec.4.225 197
Virt. 176, 181
Virt.8 65

Virt.13   95
Virt.18   47
Virt.21   206
Virt.28   68
Virt.34ff.   112, 116
Virt.36   69
Virt.38   95
Virt.51-174   200
Virt.115   208
Virt.130   82
Virt.175-186   201
Virt.178   187
Virt.199   99
Virt.208f.   154
Virt.209   157
Virt.219   176
Virt.220-225   111
Virt.221   175
Virt.221f.   176

## General Index

Aaron   67, 120, 121
Abraham   13, 73, 108, 129, 131-133, 137-139, 146-152, 154-156, 166, 171, 177, 203
Adam   50, 54, 94-96, 103, 104, 106-109, 150, 205
Adultery   79, 115, 222
Agrippa II   40
Alexandria   1, 32, 34-36, 38, 40, 41, 183, 197
Alexandrian Judaism   8, 79
Alexandrian women   36
Allegory   3, 47, 53, 57, 73, 74, 82, 87, 88, 93-95, 99, 101, 112, 116, 117, 128, 131, 132, 134, 138, 140, 144-146, 150-152, 154, 155, 157, 160, 164, 165, 170, 174, 175, 177, 178, 180-182, 195, 210, 218, 221, 222
Allegory of the Law   53, 143, 147, 155, 180
Allen, Prudence   11, 25, 28, 29, 58, 86
Andersen, F. I.   17
Andromache   22
Anthropology   55, 98, 99
Antisemitism   33
Aphrodite   31
Apocrypha and Pseudepigrapha
   Ben Sira   16, 17, 103, 194
   Fourth Ezra   4
   Joseph and Asenath   19
   Life of Adam and Eve (Apocalypse of Moses)   17, 103
   Second Enoch   17
   Testament of Job   18
   Third Maccabees   19, 202, 206
   Third Sibylline Oracle   17
   Wisdom of Solomon   18, 202
Apollonius   30
Apostasy   116, 190, 191, 193, 194,

222
Aretē 56
Aristotle 23, 25, 27, 29, 84, 86, 98, 100, 105, 207, 211
  Generation of Animals 28, 86, 97, 98, 100
  History of Animals 84, 98
  Metaphysics 23, 28
  Politics 28, 29
  Rhetoric 44
Armstrong, A. H. 48, 105
Asenath 19
Athena 83
Athenian women 35, 36, 39
Athens 35, 37
Aucher, J. B. 3, 4
Augustus 2, 32, 39, 197, 199
Baer, Richard 18, 55-58, 72, 91, 98, 99, 109, 132, 219, 220
Bagster 139
Balaam 14, 114
Balak 14
Balsdon, J. P. V. D. 38, 39, 107
Barnes, Jonathan 28
Baron, S. W. 2, 8, 33, 197, 225
Becoming male 18, 56, 132
Becoming one 55
Becoming virgin 56, 132
Benecke, E. F. M. 21, 30
Benjamin 162, 173
Berger, Peter L. 44
Bilhah 111, 176
Bird, Phyllis 67
Blank, David L. 45
Bréhier, Émile 1, 53, 167, 169
Brooten, B. 211
Bullough, Vern 11, 12, 16, 23, 24, 86
Burchard, C. 19
Bury, R. G. 101
Callicratidas 100
Cameron, A. 75
Cazeaux, Jacques 87

Charlesworth, James H. 17-19
Child exposure 37, 39
Christianity 223
Christians 9
Chrysippus 134
Church 9
Clement of Alexandria 133
Cleopatra 35
Cohn 4, 53, 167
Collins, John J. 18
Colson, F. H. 3, 60, 61, 121, 126, 139, 167, 169, 175, 196, 205, 207, 225
Conley, T. 79
Conzelmann, Hans 183
Dan 109
Defilement 77-81, 89, 145, 217, 222
Diaspora 3, 80, 198
Dibelius, Martin 183
Dillon, John 20, 49, 79, 100
Dinah 174, 175, 178, 195
Diodorus Siculus 2, 38
Diotima 27, 140-142
Egypt 5, 13, 16, 31-34, 36-38, 66, 89, 112, 148, 209
Egyptian law 36, 186
Egyptian women 33, 37, 183
Eichler, Margrit 59
Elephantine 16, 33
Empedocles 86
Encyclical studies 126, 127
Engelsman, Joan Chambers 56, 58
Enoch 108
Esau 14, 156, 158
Essenes 78, 81, 82, 182, 207-209
Etymology 43, 46, 47
Euripides 198
Eusebius 78
Evans-Pritchard, E. E. 101
Eve 16, 50, 53, 54, 62, 73, 91, 92, 94-96, 99, 103, 104, 107-109, 118, 129-131, 150, 164, 166, 205, 217

Index                                        255

Exposition of the Law  53, 116, 147, 180, 182, 189
Exum, J. Cheryl  14
Fant, Maureen B.  11, 23-25, 31, 39, 76, 85, 97, 168, 190, 200, 201
Feldman, Louis H.  1, 4, 32, 33, 176
Festugière, A. J.  133
Foreign women  111
Frazer, R. M.  21
Gaius  2
Gardner, Jane. F.  200
Gender of words  43-45
Ginzberg, L.  128, 146, 176
Goodenough, E. R.  5, 24, 34, 52, 80, 100, 133, 167, 180, 183-186, 197, 225
Grant, F. C.  134
Grant, R. M.  6, 93
Great Chain of Being  105, 171, 179, 204, 205, 217
Greek law  36
Greek women  183
Gross, Rita  9
Hades  31
Hagar  13, 14, 91, 94, 125-131, 138, 144, 146, 149, 151, 164, 166, 176, 203, 205
Hannah  13, 14, 73, 174, 177, 178
Harl, Marguerite  5, 6, 9, 89
Harlot  190, 195, 199, 200, 201, 204, 206
Hatch, E.  67
Headlam, Walter  31
Heinemann, Isaak  24, 34, 52, 74, 186, 192, 197, 198, 225
Helen  22
Hellenistic law  33
Heraclitus  3
Hercules  102, 167, 170
Herodas  31, 34
Hesiod  21, 22
Hilarion  37
Hippocrates  69, 76, 86

Holden, H.  25
Homer  22, 93
Homosexuality  211
Idolatry  115
Inclusive language  59
Isaac  6, 13, 73, 74, 137-139, 146, 155-157, 159, 160, 166, 171, 205
Isaksson, Abel  76, 82, 208
Ischomachos  24, 190
Ishmael  13, 128
Isocrates  126
Israel  12-14, 164, 174, 176
Israelites  14, 95, 179, 203
Jacob  14, 73, 108, 123, 137-139, 156-159, 161-166, 170, 171, 174, 194
Jaeger, Werner  126
Jeremiah  33
Jerusalem  40
Jewish Law  4, 33, 37
Jewish population of Alexandria  2
Jewish women  32, 34, 185, 197
Job  18
Johnson, M. D.  17
Joseph  19, 111, 112, 162, 173, 201
Josephus  82, 208
    Antiquities  78, 114, 150
    Contra Apionem  78, 150
    Jewish War  78
Journey of the soul  5-7, 89, 223
Jowett, Benjamin  135, 202
Judah  175
Julia Augusta  61
Juster, Jean  2
Justice  95, 105, 174, 217
Justinian  39
Kachur, Chris  204
King, Helen  75, 77
Knox, Wilfred  100
Kraemer, Ross S.  9
Krauss  33
Kuhrt, A.  75

Laban  13, 161, 166
Lamech  73
Lapointe, Jeanne  59
Laporte, Jean  44, 54
Leah  13, 14, 73, 131, 137, 139, 142, 144, 146, 161, 163-168, 170-174, 178, 194, 218
Lee, Desmond  26
Lefkowitz, Mary R.  11, 23-25, 31, 39, 76, 85, 86, 97, 168, 190, 200, 201
Leipoldt, Johannes  11, 16, 23, 33
Levin, Flora R.  24
Levites  191-193
Lewis, C. S.  105
Lewis, Naphtali  2, 32
Lex Julia  39, 199
Lilla, Salvatore R. C.  133
Lloyd-Jones, Hugh  21, 22
Loewe, Raphael  108
Logos  49, 56
Longinus  180
Lot  118
Lot's wife  91, 117-119, 129-131
Lovejoy, Arthur  105
Lückmann, Thomas  44
Machon  34
Mack, Burton  100
Malachi  33
Malina, Bruce J.  103
Man  59-71, 95-100, 103-105, 107, 108, 119, 131, 145, 205
Mangey  167
Marcus, R.  3, 76, 126
Marrou, H. I.  126
Massebieau  53
Melnick, R.  56, 58
Menander  30
Mendelson, Alan  6, 8, 93, 108, 117, 126, 127, 171, 176, 212
Meno  25
Menstrual taboo  222
Menstruation  46, 72, 73, 75, 76, 84, 86-88, 165, 217
Midianite women  95, 111-117, 121-123, 129, 131, 168, 193, 194
Midianites  93
Midwives  123, 130, 131
Miriam  91, 113, 114, 117, 119-122, 129-131, 167, 173, 203
Miscellaneous Writings  53
Mishnah
    Niddah  97
Misogyny  56, 58, 91, 208
Moabite women  14, 222
Moses  3, 6, 12, 66, 73, 74, 93, 109, 111, 113, 119, 120, 122, 130, 137-140, 142, 155, 157, 161, 171, 179, 195, 200
Motherhood  82, 83, 177, 187
Mysteries  133, 135, 194
Mystery language  133-135
Mysticism  5, 6
Myth  92-94
Nag Hammadi  133
Nature  49
Neopythagorean tradition  168, 201
Neufeld, E.  76
Neusner, Jacob  91, 208
New Comedy  30
Niese  78
Nikiprowetzky, V.  133, 134
Noah  108
Nock, A. D.  133
Noordtzij, A.  77, 78
Noth, Martin  120
Onan  85
Organism, male and female components  50, 53
Ortner, Sherry B.  101
Paideia  116, 117, 131, 166, 167
Palestine  16
Pandora  21
Parke, H. W.  135
Passion  112, 138

Index                                               257

Patriarchal Society  12
Paul  26
Paulus  39
Pearson, A. C.  30
Penelope  22
Pentateuch  12-14, 16, 40, 67
Perception  7, 8
Perictione  186
Philip of Macedon  36
Phineas  111, 112, 116, 117, 130,
   190-194, 222
Phintys  52
Phocylides  22
Plato  20, 24-26, 66, 82, 85, 86, 102,
   103, 105, 126, 127, 133, 135,
   142, 144, 222
   Cratylus  44
   Laws  25-27, 85, 86
   Meno  25
   Phaedrus  48, 113, 114, 135,
      140
   Republic  25, 126, 127
   Symposium  27, 102, 135,
      140-142
   Theaetetus  27, 66, 141
   Timaeus  25, 61, 86, 101, 102,
      109
Pleasure  95, 103, 104, 106, 109,
   112, 114, 115, 117, 119,
   168-170, 193, 205, 222
Pliny  97
Plotinus  48, 103, 105, 133
Pomeroy, Sarah  11, 13, 23, 24, 30,
   34-39, 76, 186, 204
Porphyry  105
Porter, J. A.  77, 78
Posidippus  37
Potiphar's wife  91, 111-113, 117,
   119, 129, 131
Prometheus  21
Prophets  12, 15
Prostitution  31, 34
Psalms  15

Ptolemaic Egypt, women in  36
Ptolemais  37
Ptolemies  32
Pythagoras  23, 44
Pythagorean tradition  23, 24, 29, 48,
   52, 100
Qumran  208
Rachel  13, 73, 75, 139, 161-168,
   171, 173, 174, 194, 201, 218
Rajak, Tessa  40
Rebecca  13, 73, 80, 132, 137-139,
   142, 146, 154-161, 163, 165,
   174, 178, 205, 218
Redpath, H.  67
Rengstorf  78
Repentance  119, 173, 174, 201
Riedweg, Christoph  93, 133, 134,
   140
Roman Empire  38
Roman Republic  38, 107
Roman women  38, 39, 183
Ross, Sir David  127
Ruether, R. R.  67, 91
Runia, D. T.  101
Russell, D. A.  180
Russell, Letty M.  14
Salvation  4, 55, 56, 132
Samuel  177
Sanders, E. P.  4, 5
Sandmel, Samuel  1, 4, 5, 7-9, 53,
   76, 77, 107, 108, 148, 180
Sarah  13, 48, 63, 72, 73, 75, 77,
   81, 83, 94, 95, 128, 131-133,
   137, 139, 142, 144, 146-154,
   156, 157, 160, 161, 163-166,
   174, 178, 203, 218
Saunders, Trevor J.  26, 85
Schmidt, R. L.  45
Seductive women  111
Segal, Alan  79
Semonides  21
Septuagint  12, 13, 47, 67, 75, 99,
   103, 115, 116, 129, 139, 166,

177, 185, 188, 189, 202-204
Sexual reproduction 49, 50
Shame 120, 129, 202-205
Sheppard, A. D. R. 133
Slavery 171
Smallwood, E. Mary 2
Socrates 24, 25, 27, 44, 135, 140, 141, 190
Solon 69
Sophia 56
Soranus 85
Spittler, R. P. 18
Stagg, Evelyn and Frank 58
Stobaeus 52, 100
Stoics 44, 48, 52, 93
Swidler, Leonard 58, 91
Synagogue Judaism 76
Taboo 78, 84, 88, 89
Tamar 73, 111, 144, 146, 174-176, 178, 206
Tcherikover, Victor 33, 34, 195, 197, 225
Terian, Abraham 1, 3, 4
Thackeray 78
Theano 23
Theiler, Willy 20
Theocritus 30
Therapeutae 15, 18, 32, 57, 102, 142, 182, 206, 209, 210, 213, 223
Therapeutrides 73, 211, 212
Thesleff, Holger 24
Thucydides 202
Tiberius Julius Alexander 40
Torah 77
Trenchard, Warren C. 17
Vermes, G. 208
Vice 167-169, 172
Virginity 19, 20, 57, 71-73, 75, 80, 81, 131, 140, 151, 154, 155, 177, 178, 200, 210, 217, 222
Virtue 83, 137, 138, 142, 145, 150, 152, 153, 157, 160, 161, 162, 165, 167-170, 168, 172, 174, 178, 186, 201, 204, 206, 218
Vlastos, G. 141, 144
Wegner, Judith Romney 57
Wendland 4, 167
Wenham, G. J. 77
Whitaker, G. H. 3, 60, 61
Winston, David 1, 4, 5, 20, 53, 79, 167
Wisdom 15, 16, 18, 49, 51, 56, 62, 131, 151, 152, 157, 158, 164, 166, 167
Wolfson, H. A. 1, 8, 88, 167
Woman 74, 95-97, 99, 100, 103-105, 107, 108, 119, 129, 131, 145, 165, 167, 178, 184, 194, 196, 197, 201, 205, 216, 221, 223
Womanhood 71-75, 77, 81, 88, 89, 91, 108, 109, 112, 123, 129-131, 138, 152, 154, 171, 177, 178, 180, 210, 212, 216, 217, 223
Women's Studies in Religion 9
Writings 12
Xenophon 20, 24, 25, 102, 107, 142, 167, 168, 170, 190
  Memorabilia 167-169
  Oeconomicus 25
Zeus 21, 22, 83
Zilpah 111, 176
Zipporah 73, 137, 140, 142, 144, 146, 161, 174, 176

Brown Judaic Studies

| | | |
|---|---|---|
| 140001 | *Approaches to Ancient Judaism I* | William S. Green |
| 140002 | *The Traditions of Eleazar Ben Azariah* | Tzvee Zahavy |
| 140003 | *Persons and Institutions in Early Rabbinic Judaism* | William S. Green |
| 140004 | *Claude Goldsmid Montefiore on the Ancient Rabbis* | Joshua B. Stein |
| 140005 | *The Ecumenical Perspective and the Modernization of Jewish Religion* | S. Daniel Breslauer |
| 140006 | *The Sabbath-Law of Rabbi Meir* | Robert Goldenberg |
| 140007 | *Rabbi Tarfon* | Joel Gereboff |
| 140008 | *Rabban Gamaliel II* | Shamai Kanter |
| 140009 | *Approaches to Ancient Judaism II* | William S. Green |
| 140010 | *Method and Meaning in Ancient Judaism* | Jacob Neusner |
| 140011 | *Approaches to Ancient Judaism III* | William S. Green |
| 140012 | *Turning Point: Zionism and Reform Judaism* | Howard R. Greenstein |
| 140013 | *Buber on God and the Perfect Man* | Pamela Vermes |
| 140014 | *Scholastic Rabbinism* | Anthony J. Saldarini |
| 140015 | *Method and Meaning in Ancient Judaism II* | Jacob Neusner |
| 140016 | *Method and Meaning in Ancient Judaism III* | Jacob Neusner |
| 140017 | *Post Mishnaic Judaism in Transition* | Baruch M. Bokser |
| 140018 | *A History of the Mishnaic Law of Agriculture: Tractate Maaser Sheni* | Peter J. Haas |
| 140019 | *Mishnah's Theology of Tithing* | Martin S. Jaffee |
| 140020 | *The Priestly Gift in Mishnah: A Study of Tractate Terumot* | Alan. J. Peck |
| 140021 | *History of Judaism: The Next Ten Years* | Baruch M. Bokser |
| 140022 | *Ancient Synagogues* | Joseph Gutmann |
| 140023 | *Warrant for Genocide* | Norman Cohn |
| 140024 | *The Creation of the World According to Gersonides* | Jacob J. Staub |
| 140025 | *Two Treatises of Philo of Alexandria: A Commentary on De Gigantibus and Quod Deus Sit Immutabilis* | David Winston/John Dillon |
| 140026 | *A History of the Mishnaic Law of Agriculture: Kilayim* | Irving Mandelbaum |
| 140027 | *Approaches to Ancient Judaism IV* | William S. Green |
| 140028 | *Judaism in the American Humanities* | Jacob Neusner |
| 140029 | *Handbook of Synagogue Architecture* | Marilyn Chiat |
| 140030 | *The Book of Mirrors* | Daniel C. Matt |
| 140031 | *Ideas in Fiction: The Works of Hayim Hazaz* | Warren Bargad |
| 140032 | *Approaches to Ancient Judaism V* | William S. Green |
| 140033 | *Sectarian Law in the Dead Sea Scrolls: Courts, Testimony and the Penal Code* | Lawrence H. Schiffman |
| 140034 | *A History of the United Jewish Appeal: 1939-1982* | Marc L. Raphael |
| 140035 | *The Academic Study of Judaism* | Jacob Neusner |
| 140036 | *Woman Leaders in the Ancient Synagogue* | Bernadette Brooten |
| 140037 | *Formative Judaism: Religious, Historical, and Literary Studies* | Jacob Neusner |
| 140038 | *Ben Sira's View of Women: A Literary Analysis* | Warren C. Trenchard |
| 140039 | *Barukh Kurzweil and Modern Hebrew Literature* | James S. Diamond |

| | | |
|---|---|---|
| 140040 | *Israeli Childhood Stories of the Sixties: Yizhar, Aloni, Shahar, Kahana-Carmon* | Gideon Telpaz |
| 140041 | *Formative Judaism II: Religious, Historical, and Literary Studies* | Jacob Neusner |
| 140042 | *Judaism in the American Humanities II: Jewish Learning and the New Humanities* | Jacob Neusner |
| 140043 | *Support for the Poor in the Mishnaic Law of Agriculture: Tractate Peah* | Roger Brooks |
| 140044 | *The Sanctity of the Seventh Year: A Study of Mishnah Tractate Shebiit* | Louis E. Newman |
| 140045 | *Character and Context: Studies in the Fiction of Abramovitsh, Brenner, and Agnon* | Jeffrey Fleck |
| 140046 | *Formative Judaism III: Religious, Historical, and Literary Studies* | Jacob Neusner |
| 140047 | *Pharaoh's Counsellors: Job, Jethro, and Balaam in Rabbinic and Patristic Tradition* | Judith Baskin |
| 140048 | *The Scrolls and Christian Origins: Studies in the Jewish Background of the New Testament* | Matthew Black |
| 140049 | *Approaches to Modern Judaism I* | Marc Lee Raphael |
| 140050 | *Mysterious Encounters at Mamre and Jabbok* | William T. Miller |
| 140051 | *The Mishnah Before 70* | Jacob Neusner |
| 140052 | *Sparda by the Bitter Sea: Imperial Interaction in Western Anatolia* | Jack Martin Balcer |
| 140053 | *Hermann Cohen: The Challenge of a Religion of Reason* | William Kluback |
| 140054 | *Approaches to Judaism in Medieval Times I* | David R. Blumenthal |
| 140055 | *In the Margins of the Yerushalmi: Glosses on the English Translation* | Jacob Neusner |
| 140056 | *Approaches to Modern Judaism II* | Marc Lee Raphael |
| 140057 | *Approaches to Judaism in Medieval Times II* | David R. Blumenthal |
| 140058 | *Midrash as Literature: The Primacy of Documentary Discourse* | JacobNeusner |
| 140059 | *The Commerce of the Sacred: Mediation of the Divine Among Jews in the Graeco-Roman Diaspora* | Jack N. Lightstone |
| 140060 | *Major Trends in Formative Judaism I: Society and Symbol in Political Crisis* | Jacob Neusner |
| 140061 | *Major Trends in Formative Judaism II: Texts, Contents, and Contexts* | Jacob Neusner |
| 140062 | *A History of the Jews in Babylonia I: The Parthian Period* | Jacob Neusner |
| 140063 | *The Talmud of Babylonia: An American Translation. XXXII: Tractate Arakhin* | Jacob Neusner |
| 140064 | *Ancient Judaism: Debates and Disputes* | Jacob Neusner |
| 140065 | *Prayers Alleged to Be Jewish: An Examination of the Constitutiones Apostolorum* | David Fiensy |
| 140066 | *The Legal Methodology of Hai Gaon* | Tsvi Groner |
| 140067 | *From Mishnah to Scripture: The Problem of the Unattributed Saying* | Jacob Neusner |
| 140068 | *Halakhah in a Theological Dimension* | David Novak |

| | | |
|---|---|---|
| 140069 | From Philo to Origen: Middle Platonism in Transition | Robert M. Berchman |
| 140070 | In Search of Talmudic Biography: The Problem of the Attributed Saying | Jacob Neusner |
| 140071 | The Death of the Old and the Birth of the New: The Framework of the Book of Numbers and the Pentateuch | Dennis T. Olson |
| 140072 | The Talmud of Babylonia: An American Translation. XVII: Tractate Sotah | Jacob Neusner |
| 140073 | Understanding Seeking Faith: Essays on the Case of Judaism. Volume Two: Literature, Religion and the Social Study of Judiasm | JacobNeusner |
| 140074 | The Talmud of Babylonia: An American Translation. VI: Tractate Sukkah | Jacob Neusner |
| 140075 | Fear Not Warrior: A Study of 'al tira' Pericopes in the Hebrew Scriptures | Edgar W. Conrad |
| 140076 | Formative Judaism IV: Religious, Historical, and Literary Studies | Jacob Neusner |
| 140077 | Biblical Patterns in Modern Literature | David H. Hirsch/ Nehama Aschkenasy |
| 140078 | The Talmud of Babylonia: An American Translation I: Tractate Berakhot | Jacob Neusner |
| 140079 | Mishnah's Division of Agriculture: A History and Theology of Seder Zeraim | Alan J. Avery-Peck |
| 140080 | From Tradition to Imitation: The Plan and Program of Pesiqta Rabbati and Pesiqta deRab Kahana | Jacob Neusner |
| 140081 | The Talmud of Babylonia: An American Translation. XXIIIA: Tractate Sanhedrin, Chapters 1-3 | Jacob Neusner |
| 140082 | Jewish Presence in T. S. Eliot and Franz Kafka | Melvin Wilk |
| 140083 | School, Court, Public Administration: Judaism and its Institutions in Talmudic Babylonia | Jacob Neusner |
| 140084 | The Talmud of Babylonia: An American Translation. XXIIIB: Tractate Sanhedrin, Chapters 4-8 | Jacob Neusner |
| 140085 | The Bavli and Its Sources: The Question of Tradition in the Case of Tractate Sukkah | Jacob Neusner |
| 140086 | From Description to Conviction: Essays on the History and Theology of Judaism | Jacob Neusner |
| 140087 | The Talmud of Babylonia: An American Translation. XXIIIC: Tractate Sanhedrin, Chapters 9-11 | Jacob Neusner |
| 140088 | Mishnaic Law of Blessings and Prayers: Tractate Berakhot | Tzvee Zahavy |
| 140089 | The Peripatetic Saying: The Problem of the Thrice-Told Tale in Talmudic Literature | Jacob Neusner |
| 140090 | The Talmud of Babylonia: An American Translation. XXVI: Tractate Horayot | Martin S. Jaffee |
| 140091 | Formative Judaism V: Religious, Historical, and Literary Studies | Jacob Neusner |
| 140092 | Essays on Biblical Method and Translation | Edward Greenstein |
| 140093 | The Integrity of Leviticus Rabbah | Jacob Neusner |
| 140094 | Behind the Essenes: History and Ideology of the Dead Sea Scrolls | Philip R. Davies |

| | | |
|---|---|---|
| 140095 | *Approaches to Judaism in Medieval Times, Volume III* | David R. Blumenthal |
| 140096 | *The Memorized Torah: The Mnemonic System of the Mishnah* | Jacob Neusner |
| 140097 | *Knowledge and Illumination* | Hossein Ziai |
| 140098 | *Sifre to Deuteronomy: An Analytical Translation. Volume One: Pisqaot One through One Hundred Forty-Three. Debarim, Waethanan, Eqeb* | Jacob Neusner |
| 140099 | *Major Trends in Formative Judaism III: The Three Stages in the Formation of Judaism* | Jacob Neusner |
| 140101 | *Sifre to Deuteronomy: An Analytical Translation. Volume Two: Pisqaot One Hundred Forty-Four through Three Hundred Fifty-Seven. Shofetim, Ki Tese, Ki Tabo, Nesabim, Ha'azinu, Zot Habberakhah* | Jacob Neusner |
| 140102 | *Sifra: The Rabbinic Commentary on Leviticus* | Jacob Neusner/ Roger Brooks |
| 140103 | *The Human Will in Judaism* | Howard Eilberg-Schwartz |
| 140104 | *Genesis Rabbah: Volume 1. Genesis 1:1 to 8:14* | Jacob Neusner |
| 140105 | *Genesis Rabbah: Volume 2. Genesis 8:15 to 28:9* | Jacob Neusner |
| 140106 | *Genesis Rabbah: Volume 3. Genesis 28:10 to 50:26* | Jacob Neusner |
| 140107 | *First Principles of Systemic Analysis* | Jacob Neusner |
| 140108 | *Genesis and Judaism* | Jacob Neusner |
| 140109 | *The Talmud of Babylonia: An American Translation. XXXV: Tractates Meilah and Tamid* | Peter J. Haas |
| 140110 | *Studies in Islamic and Judaic Traditions* | William Brinner/Stephen Ricks |
| 140111 | *Comparative Midrash: The Plan and Program of Genesis Rabbah and Leviticus Rabbah* | Jacob Neusner |
| 140112 | *The Tosefta: Its Structure and its Sources* | Jacob Neusner |
| 140113 | *Reading and Believing* | Jacob Neusner |
| 140114 | *The Fathers According to Rabbi Nathan* | Jacob Neusner |
| 140115 | *Etymology in Early Jewish Interpretation: The Hebrew Names in Philo* | Lester L. Grabbe |
| 140116 | *Understanding Seeking Faith: Essays on the Case of Judaism. Volume One: Debates on Method, Reports of Results* | Jacob Neusner |
| 140117 | *The Talmud of Babylonia. An American Translation. VII: Tractate Besah* | Alan J. Avery-Peck |
| 140118 | *Sifre to Numbers: An American Translation and Explanation, Volume One: Sifre to Numbers 1-58* | Jacob Neusner |
| 140119 | *Sifre to Numbers: An American Translation and Explanation, Volume Two: Sifre to Numbers 59-115* | Jacob Neusner |
| 140120 | *Cohen and Troeltsch: Ethical Monotheistic Religion and Theory of Culture* | Wendell S. Dietrich |
| 140121 | *Goodenough on the History of Religion and on Judaism* | Jacob Neusner/ Ernest Frerichs |
| 140122 | *Pesiqta deRab Kahana I: Pisqaot One through Fourteen* | Jacob Neusner |
| 140123 | *Pesiqta deRab Kahana II: Pisqaot Fifteen through Twenty-Eight and Introduction to Pesiqta deRab Kahana* | Jacob Neusner |
| 140124 | *Sifre to Deuteronomy: Introduction* | Jacob Neusner |

| | | |
|---|---|---|
| 140126 | *A Conceptual Commentary on Midrash Leviticus Rabbah: Value Concepts in Jewish Thought* | Max Kadushin |
| 140127 | *The Other Judaisms of Late Antiquity* | Alan F. Segal |
| 140128 | *Josephus as a Historical Source in Patristic Literature through Eusebius* | Michael Hardwick |
| 140129 | *Judaism: The Evidence of the Mishnah* | Jacob Neusner |
| 140131 | *Philo, John and Paul: New Perspectives on Judaism and Early Christianity* | Peder Borgen |
| 140132 | *Babylonian Witchcraft Literature* | Tzvi Abusch |
| 140133 | *The Making of the Mind of Judaism: The Formative Age* | Jacob Neusner |
| 140135 | *Why No Gospels in Talmudic Judaism?* | Jacob Neusner |
| 140136 | *Torah: From Scroll to Symbol Part III: Doctrine* | Jacob Neusner |
| 140137 | *The Systemic Analysis of Judaism* | Jacob Neusner |
| 140138 | *Sifra: An Analytical Translation Vol. 1* | Jacob Neusner |
| 140139 | *Sifra: An Analytical Translation Vol. 2* | Jacob Neusner |
| 140140 | *Sifra: An Analytical Translation Vol. 3* | Jacob Neusner |
| 140141 | *Midrash in Context: Exegesis in Formative Judaism* | Jacob Neusner |
| 140143 | *Oxen, Women or Citizens? Slaves in the System of Mishnah* | Paul V. Flesher |
| 140144 | *The Book of the Pomegranate* | Elliot R. Wolfson |
| 140145 | *Wrong Ways and Right Ways in the Study of Formative Judaism* | Jacob Neusner |
| 140146 | *Sifra in Perspective: The Documentary Comparison of the Midrashim of Ancient Judaism* | Jacob Neusner |
| 140148 | *Mekhilta According to Rabbi Ishmael: An Analytical Translation Volume I* | Jacob Neusner |
| 140149 | *The Doctrine of the Divine Name: An Introduction to Classical Kabbalistic Theology* | Stephen G. Wald |
| 140150 | *Water into Wine and the Beheading of John the Baptist* | Roger Aus |
| 140151 | *The Formation of the Jewish Intellect* | Jacob Neusner |
| 140152 | *Mekhilta According to Rabbi Ishmael: An Introduction to Judaism's First Scriptural Encyclopaedia* | Jacob Neusner |
| 140153 | *Understanding Seeking Faith. Volume Three* | Jacob Neusner |
| 140154 | *Mekhilta According to Rabbi Ishmael: An Analytical Translation Volume Two* | Jacob Neusner |
| 140155 | *Goyim: Gentiles and Israelites in Mishnah-Tosefta* | Gary P. Porton |
| 140156 | *A Religion of Pots and Pans?* | Jacob Neusner |
| 140157 | *Claude Montefiore and Christianity* | Maurice Gerald Bowler |
| 140158 | *The Philosopical Mishnah Volume III* | Jacob Neusner |
| 140159 | *From Ancient Israel to Modern Judaism Volume 1: Intellect in Quest of Understanding* | Neusner/Frerichs/Sarna |
| 140160 | *The Social Study of Judaism Volume I* | Jacob Neusner |
| 140161 | *Philo's Jewish Identity* | Alan Mendelson |
| 140162 | *The Social Study of Judaism Volume II* | Jacob Neusner |
| 140163 | *The Philosophical Mishnah Volume I : The Initial Probe* | Jacob Neusner |
| 140164 | *The Philosophical Mishnah Volume II : The Tractates Agenda: From Abodah Zarah Through Moed Qatan* | Jacob Neusner |

| | | |
|---|---|---|
| 140166 | Women's Earliest Records | Barbara S. Lesko |
| 140167 | The Legacy of Hermann Cohen | William Kluback |
| 140168 | Method and Meaning in Ancient Judaism | Jacob Neusner |
| 140169 | The Role of the Messenger and Message in the Ancient Near East | John T. Greene |
| 140171 | Abraham Heschel's Idea of Revelation | Lawrence Perlman |
| 140172 | The Philosophical Mishnah Volume IV: The Repertoire | Jacob Neusner |
| 140173 | From Ancient Israel to Modern Judaism Volume 2: Intellect in Quest of Understanding | Neusner/Frerichs/Sarna |
| 140174 | From Ancient Israel to Modern Judaism Volume 3: Intellect in Quest of Understanding | Neusner/Frerichs/Sarna |
| 140175 | From Ancient Israel to Modern Judaism Volume 4: Intellect in Quest of Understanding | Neusner/Frerichs/Sarna |
| 140176 | Translating the Classics of Judaism: In Theory and In Practice | Jacob Neusner |
| 140177 | Profiles of a Rabbi: Synoptic Opportunities in Reading About Jesus | Bruce Chilton |
| 140178 | Studies in Islamic and Judaic Traditions II | William Brinner/Stephen Ricks |
| 140179 | Medium and Message in Judaism: First Series | Jacob Neusner |
| 140180 | Making the Classics of Judaism: The Three Stages of Literary Formation | Jacob Neusner |
| 140181 | The Law of Jealousy: Anthropology of Sotah | Adriana Destro |
| 140182 | Esther Rabbah I: An Analytical Translation | Jacob Neusner |
| 140183 | Ruth Rabbah: An Analytical Translation | Jacob Neusner |
| 140184 | Formative Judaism: Religious, Historical and Literary Studies | Jacob Neusner |
| 140185 | The Studia Philonica Annual | David T. Runia |
| 140186 | The Setting of the Sermon on the Mount | W.D. Davies |
| 140187 | The Midrash Compilations of the Sixth and Seventh Centuries Volume One | Jacob Neusner |
| 140188 | The Midrash Compilations of the Sixth and Seventh Centuries Volume Two | Jacob Neusner |
| 140189 | The Midrash Compilations of the Sixth and Seventh Centuries Volume Three | Jacob Neusner |
| 140190 | The Midrash Compilations of the Sixth and Seventh Centuries Volume Four | Jacob Neusner |
| 140191 | The Religious World of Contemporary Judaism: Observations and Convictions | Jacob Neusner |
| 140192 | Approaches to Ancient Judaism: Volume VI | Jacob Neusner/ Ernest S. Frerichs |
| 140193 | Lamentations Rabbah: An Analytical Translation | Jacob Neusner |
| 140194 | Early Christian Texts on Jews and Judaism | Robert S. MacLennan |
| 140196 | Torah and the Chronicler's History Work | Judson R. Shaver |
| 140197 | Song of Songs Rabbah: An Analytical Translation Volume One | Jacob Neusner |
| 140198 | Song of Songs Rabbah: An Analytical Translation Volume Two | Jacob Neusner |
| 140199 | From Literature to Theology in Formative Judaism | Jacob Neusner |
| 140202 | Maimonides on Perfection | Menachem Kellner |

| | | |
|---|---|---|
| 140203 | *The Martyr's Conviction* | Eugene Weiner/Anita Weiner |
| 140204 | *Judaism, Christianity, and Zoroastrianism in Talmudic Babylonia* | Jacob Neusner |
| 140205 | *Tzedakah: Can Jewish Philanthropy Buy Jewish Survival?* | Jacob Neusner |
| 140206 | *New Perspectives on Ancient Judaism: Volume 1* | Neusner/Borgen Frerichs/Horsley |
| 140207 | *Scriptures of the Oral Torah* | Jacob Neusner |
| 140208 | *Christian Faith and the Bible of Judaism* | Jacob Neusner |
| 140209 | *Philo's Perception of Women* | Dorothy Sly |

Brown Studies on Jews and Their Societies

| | | |
|---|---|---|
| 145001 | *American Jewish Fertility* | Calvin Goldscheider |
| 145003 | *The American Jewish Community* | Calvin Goldscheider |
| 145004 | *The Naturalized Jews of the Grand Duchy of Posen in 1834 and 1835* | Edward David Luft |
| 145005 | *Suburban Communities: The Jewishness of American Reform Jews* | Gerald L. Showstack |
| 145007 | *Ethnic Survival in America* | David Schoem |

Brown Studies in Religion

| | | |
|---|---|---|
| 147001 | *Religious Writings and Religious Systems Volume 1* | Jacob Neusner, et al |
| 147002 | *Religious Writings and Religious Systems Volume 2* | Jacob Neusner, et al |
| 147003 | *Religion and the Social Sciences* | Robert Segal |

www.ingramcontent.com/pod-product-compliance
Lightning Source LLC
Chambersburg PA
CBHW020122240426
43673CB00038B/558